Women's Bodies in Psychoanalysis

Rosemary M. Balsam

D1710245

With a Foreword by Nancy Chodorow and
Adrienne Harris

Routledge
Taylor & Francis Group

NEW YORK AND LONDON

First published 2012 by Routledge
27 Church Road, Hove, East Sussex BN3 2FA

Simultaneously published in the USA and Canada
by Routledge

711 Third Avenue, New York NY 10017

Routledge is an imprint of the Taylor & Francis Group, an informa business

British Library Cataloguing in Publication Data
A catalogue record for this book is available from the British Library

Library of Congress Cataloging-in-Publication Data
Balsam, Rosemary Marshall.Women's bodies in psychoanalysis /
Rosemary Balsam.
    p. cm.
Includes bibliographical references.
ISBN 978-0-415-39029-31. Women and psychoanalysis. 2. Human body.
3. Body image in women. 4. Women–Psychology. 5. Women–Physiology.
6. Psychophysiology. I. Title.
BF175.B24 2012
155.3´33–dc23   2011046370

ISBN: 978-0-415-39029-3 (hbk)
ISBN: 978-0-415-39030-9 (pbk)

Typeset in Times
by Cenveo Publisher Services
Paperback cover design by Andrew Ward

MIX
Paper from
responsible sources
FSC
www.fsc.org   FSC® C004839   Printed and bound in Great Britain by the MPG Books Group

To Annette, forever 30, joyful with her babies
And to Catherine and the twins
And to Maggie and her children
And to our loving family "matriarchy"

Contents

Acknowledgements

There are many people I would like to thank in my "village," because it takes a village to write a book, to paraphrase Hillary Clinton. My village is composed of my community and many years of learning, teaching, and "hanging out" with friends at the Western New England Institute for Psychoanalysis in New Haven, and the Yale University Student Health Services, that have contributed most to the formulation of my ideas as well as my background. I owe a great debt to my patients who shared themselves with me; and to my wonderful and understanding parents and family in Belfast and London who helped me not be guilty about living over here. My mother is a pillar of "the matriarchy," my adorable family gang, to whom I dedicate this book.

My family in Northern Ireland, London, and America, and close friends are always with me in my mind when I'm writing, and most immediately my dear husband Paul, whom I have to restrain myself from using as an editor all the time, because he is not only a good writer but a fabulous and generous guy. He puts up with my vagaries in every way, and my superfluity of commas. He is my beloved companion. We laugh a lot together and appreciate Violet among many, many other things. Catherine and Ed and their wee ones are abidingly close to my heart. My soulmates, Dorothy Crawford, Harriette Ennis, and Elizabeth Rindskopf Parker, are crucial to my well-being and work. Also vital are Art and Barbara Levine, and Kathy Dalsimer, who is also a poetic reader and a loving support. Friends that I single out and who I can't imagine being without are Joan Wexler, Lorraine Siggins, and my fellow analysts on the W.N.E. Education Committee. I will forever miss Iza and Victor Erlich. Our "brother" Dick Munich and "the sister" Adrienne (also a rich source of feminist ideas) are so supportive to all our enterprises, and loving and fun. Nancy Chodorow, my dear CAPS mate, and Adrienne Harris have been beyond terrific. "Wee group" is an ongoing joy, a sustenance and a source for exchange of clinical ideas. Important readers of pieces of my manuscript at different times were Dianne Elise, Ted Tayler, the late Greta Slobin, and the late John Hicks whose opinions I cherish. Analytic friends in Northern Ireland have given encouragement—the late Tom Freeman, and the Lord Alderdice (a.k.a. John), whose help in bringing political peace to my island certainly helped free up my mind to dwell on other things such as the fate of women. Eve Golden has edited my book closely, and is a pleasure to work with. Kate Hawes and Kirsten Buchanan have been most helpful on behalf of Routledge. My supportive in-laws, Evy and Jules, deserve many thanks, as does my sunny and wonderful housekeeper, Hermine.

For invaluably encouraging my writing and thinking, I want to mention Roy Schafer, Hans Loewald, the late Jay Katz, Arnie Richards when he was chief editor of the *Journal of the American Psychoanalytic Association*, the late Al Solnit of *The Psychoanalytic Study of the Child*, Harry Smith when he was the chief editor of *The Psychoanalytic Quarterly*, and Joe Lichtenberg of *Psychoanalytic Inquiry*. I have greatly enjoyed and benefited from my editorial work alongside them, and, most importantly, Steve Levy of the *Journal of the American Psychoanalytic Association*.

I am blessed with great colleagues in APsaA—Nancy, Anne, Ann, Dick, Jon, Alex, Eds, Ellen, Janice, Shelley, Judy, Judy and Judy, Paul, Ted, Dans, Deanna, Muff, Carolyn, Ernst, Lenny, Gabriella, Henry, Leon, Leon, Jay, Ted, Suzanne, Peters, Steve, Helen, Bonnie, Linda, Glen, Margaret Ann, Jane, Phyllis, Bobs, Malkah, Robert, Jocelyn, Betsy, Karen, Erics, Oscar, Kim, Elisabeth, Christine, Elizabeth, Sybil, Barbaras, Warren, Ana-Maria, Lynn, Fred, Cordelia, Arlene, Salman, Larry, Chrissy, Jim, Don, Brenda, Barry, Davids, Jeanine, Janet, Cal, Manny, Bob, Jenny, and many more. Discussions with them all have furthered my thinking, my deep enjoyment of our field, and sustenance as a clinician.

Permissions acknowledgements

I extend many thanks for these invitations and publication permissions.

Chapter 1 is based on the 31st Melitta Sperling Lecture (2005) to the Psychoanalytic Association of New York. Chapter 2 is based on my article "Women Showing Off: Notes on Female Exhibitionism" (Balsam, 2008); Chapter 3 is based on my article "The Vanished Pregnant Body in Female Developmental theory" (Balsam, 2003); and Chapter 4 is based on my article "The Pregnant Mother and the Body Image of the Daughter" (Balsam, 1996).

Chapters 5 and 6 are based on a "Major Lecture" written for the 45th IPA Congress in Berlin, 2007, titled "Remembering the Female Body." Chapter 7 is based on the article "Integrating Male and Female Elements in a Woman's Gender Identity" (Balsam, 2001).

The final, definitive versions of these papers were published in the *Journal of the American Psychoanalytic Association* (SAGE Publications; all rights reserved).

Chapter 8 is based on my chapter "Sisters and their disappointing brothers" in *Brothers and Sisters: Developmental, Dynamic, and Technical Aspects of the Sibling Relationship* (Balsam, 1999). Chapter 9 is based partially on my chapter "Loving and Hating Mothers and Daughters: Thoughts on the Role of Their Physicality" in *What Do Mothers Want?* (Balsam, 2005), and partially on "Sons of passionate Mothering" a talk on a panel "What do women want?" in Symposium

2010: Love, Sex, and Passion: The Anatomy of Desire, in Mt Sinai Medical School, New York City. Chapter 10 is based on my article "Fathers and the Bodily Care of their Infant Daughters" (Balsam, 2008).

Illustrations

Figure 3.1a (left): "Vagina as penis" from Andreas Vesalius, *Fabrica* (1543), and Figure 3.1b (right): "The vagina and uterus" from Vidus Vidius, *De Anatome corporis humani* (1611).

(1543) "De Humani Corporis Fabrica Libri Septem", and "De Humani Corporis Fabrica Librorum Epitome"

Figure 3.2: The female torso, in the form of a piece of broken classical art from which Figure 3.1 was taken.

Figure 3.3: Normal birth position, facing the mother's rear, for both boys and girls. From *La Commare* (Venice, 1601) by Girolamo Mercurio.

(Figures 3.1a, 3.1b, and 3.2 are reproduced from reproductions in Making *Sex: Body and Gender from the Greeks to Freud* by Thomas Laqueur, Harvard University Press, Cambridge, Massachusetts, and London, England, 1990. Figure 3.3 is reproduced from *How to Do It: Guides to Good Living for Renaissance Italians* by Rudolph Bell, University of Chicago Press, Chicago and London, 1999.)

I also wish to thank Lori Bronars from the Kline Science Library, Yale University, for her help in identifying the originals of Figures 3.1a, 3.1b, and 3.2.

Foreword

Nancy J. Chodorow and Adrienne Harris

Rosemary Balsam is uniquely positioned to write the definitive psychoanalytic book on women and their bodies. A leading psychoanalytic writer on women, this deeply clinical observer has, over the past 20 years, in pathbreaking article after article, transformed our ability to see how women live their bodies psychologically and how men and women, boys and girls, and analytic thinkers and practitioners, experience women's bodies. She has documented the difference that such investigations make to our theory of femininity and to the analytic treatment of women. Women and femininity have been central to the psychoanalytic project from the very beginning; however, it is Balsam's singular contribution to focus us explicitly, extensively, and deeply on the body, on materiality, and on the particular meanings to the self and others of female embodiment.

Beginning from Freud's claim, that the ego is first and foremost a bodily ego, expanding this claim with the implicit acknowledgement that the object is also first and foremost a bodily object, this astute thinker has defined the clinical and theoretical territory when ego and bodily ego, object and bodily object, belong to women. She has, quite simply, transformed our perspective on the female body. Reading Balsam, no clinician, theorist, or academic writer on gender will again see femaleness and maleness, femininity and masculinity, in the same way.

Balsam's work combines scholarship, clinical acumen and detailed observation, to give us a groundbreaking revisioning of what women and their bodies are, for women or girls living in their own bodies or observing the bodies of other women or girls, for men and boys who observe or experience these bodies, for clinicians and theorists since Freud and indeed throughout history, for all who have tried to understand these bodies. We are all too familiar with the fear and accompanying degradation of women, the concern with bigness and expansiveness, the anxious unsettledness in cultural and psychoanalytic reactions to female flesh. By contrast, it has been a hallmark of writing about male oedipal development to think of the pleasures of bigness, the delight (and fear) in the boy's links to power and expansiveness. Balsam asks us to question how these processes get reversed when it comes to the maternal body. Where terror and its defensive derivatives of contempt often predominate in our writings, Balsam has made the rehabilitation and psychic deconstruction of these images and constructions of femininity, fecundity, and expansiveness her particular focus. She simultaneously undertakes critique and resignification.

No psychoanalytic writer gives us a more alive sense of the people in the consulting room. Balsam's book teems with palpable, visceral, immediate documentation, as well as with argument, showing that analysts who do not recognize this pervasive embodiment miss much that is going on in their patients' psychic lives and in their own clinical work. She provides detailed observations of how patients experience their own body and the body of the analyst and of how the analyst can (and must) use this knowledge. Being constantly aware of psychic and physical embodiment leads the analyst to see, hear, and feel what is happening in the room and in the patient's mind in a different, deeper, and fuller, way.

Balsam's psychology of femininity accomplishes several things. She returns us to Freud's deeply rooted grounding in the psychosexual body. As we noticed earlier, no one who has read and internalized Balsam can any longer point glibly, as if this was a truism or shibboleth, to Freud's comment that the ego is first and foremost a bodily ego. Balsam's vivid case presentations remind us that, at every moment in the room, there is always a physically and psychically embodied patient in relation to a physically and psychically embodied analyst, not only a mind in relation to another mind. Similarly, from birth, each stage of anyone's development involves a psychophysical presence in relation to others.

Since Freud told us that anatomy is destiny, and that anatomy was, explicitly, the presence or absence of the penis, it has been hard for analysts to conceptualize gender and sexuality apart from this particular sexual difference. Correspondingly, many contributors to the psychoanalytic literature on women have been leery of making women's bodies, or any anatomical destiny, front and central. Instead, writers on the psychology of women have paid attention to mind, gender identity and identifications, and gender development, and when attending to the female body, they have focused more on sexuality and desire, contrasting the genital experience of women with that of men.

In this context, Balsam's consistent, ever-deepening clinical, developmental, and theoretical focus reminds and reaffirms for all of us that the reproductive body and the full range of bodily sexuality—biologically, developmentally, culturally, and world historically—are a forceful, ubiquitous presence in psychic life. How, she wonders—and we wonder after reading her—have we missed this psychic experience that shapes and creates—literally—our very being? In stressing the power of pregnancy, fecundity, and generativity as awesome and dramatic in its impact on children and all others, Balsam restores the female body to a site of power and meaning. Not idealizing femininity but grounding it in materiality, she expands our clinical listening to women patients and indeed to any patient.

Balsam thus returns to and extends, both explicitly and implicitly, the tradition begun by Freud's *Three Essays on a Theory of Sexuality*, a tradition that addresses directly the psychology of bodily sexuality, in its transformations and its impact on psychic life and the clinical encounter. Through these roots, she represents the leading edge of classical psychoanalysis, always in dialogue with Freud and his heirs. At the same time, Balsam is in dialogue with the postmodern literature that addresses psychoanalysis, the body, sexuality, and gender: she does not write in an intellectual or theoretical vacuum about matters that have received much attention in the academy, but allows this academic literature, and dialogue with academic discourse, to inform her clinical observations and theoretical conclusions. Balsam's published and presented work over the years has transformed understanding for both of us and has led each of us in new directions in our own writing and in our ways of listening to patients.

Women's Bodies in Psychoanalysis brings together a remarkable, steadily developed, generative, and original approach to women's bodies in psychoanalytic theory and in psychoanalytic treatment, pointing to the embodiment of all analysts and all patients as the foundation that underlies and informs the analytic process at all times. It is a gift to everyone interested in psychoanalysis and women to have the work of this vivid, engaging writer available here.

Introduction

Seamus Heaney, the Irish poet, was born and bred in the same corner of the earth as I, and his description of how he creates his art captures for me the essence of the psychoanalytic enterprise: "The early-in-life experience has been central to me all right. But I'd say you aren't so much trying to describe it as trying to locate it. The amount of sensory material stored up or stored down in the brain's and the body's systems is inestimable. It's like a culture at the bottom of a jar, although it doesn't grow ... Or help anything else to grow unless you find a way to reach it and touch it. But once you do, it's like putting your hand into a nest and finding something beginning to hatch out in your head" (interview with Dennis O'Driscoll, 2008: p. 58).

Psychoanalysis too is a situation of trying to "reach it," to "touch it," to find that nest where "something" is "beginning to hatch" in one's head. The theory behind our discipline addresses not so much the struggle to describe, as the struggle to *locate* the psychic processes connected to the life force in the participating individuals.

Freud famously noted that poets "discovered the unconscious"[1] before him, and certainly, in his poetry, Heaney knows more than we do about the intense and deep relations between the physical and mental, between body and mind, between animal and earth, between our biology and the rest of our existence, past and present. In his biographical interview, he accents the active effort it takes to locate and touch, within one's own brain and body, the culture of early experience, out of which everything else grows. The "culture at the bottom of the jar"—the agar plate of early bodily and sensory experience—is as hard to reach and touch in psychoanalysis as it is in poetry. What meaning do we assign to early and later body registrations? How much weight do we give them? In the debate between what is "inside" and what is "outside," where is the body located? Is bodily awareness the route to affective awareness in psychoanalysis, or is it an escape—a distraction from anxiety that encourages motor discharge and action and so dilutes verbal communication and undermines our exploratory efforts? How do we talk about bodies? How do we think about our analysands' bodies? How do we contemplate our own bodily presence in the office? How can we think more about our own bodies in relation to our patients? And those messages from past bodily experience that the mind holds in its "jar"—how do we render them to another person to increase their comprehensibility? How does the latency or adolescent body register in the adult body? Moreover, how do family bodies of different sexes, sizes, and competencies become a part of one's inner physical landscape?

The biological body has fallen from grace since Freud's era, and this seems to me to be a problem. Psychoanalysis (appropriately) creates in its theories and texts images of "virtual" bodies, kinds of three-dimensional avatars of people's physical representations viewed through the mind's eye. (My analogy refers to computer games.) This "virtual body" was once more monolithic, but has changed over time and with the evolution of the embedded cultures of the varieties of psychoanalyses over more than a century. However, in the texts of some contemporary theories that are preoccupied with "here and now" interaction, or, say, with an unrelenting search for deep archaic fantasy, or in theories of mind that downplay the individual's history or the unconscious, connections between the biological body and its mentalized representative psychic "virtual body" are often lost. Arguments that purposely undermine scientific aspects of psychoanalysis belong in the postmodern tradition, following Foucault. Claims of objectivity on the part of an analyst have become anathema in many quarters. In their enthusiasm, some postmodern challenges to psychoanalysis fail to distinguish between nineteenth-century positivist science in which Freud was rooted, and the highly interactive principles of neurobiology as we understand them today. With all the interesting attempts to deconstruct science—and even though there have been many advances that have emerged from this fruitful challenge, including the ability to contemplate women with less bias, such as in Evelyn Fox-Keller's 1986/1996 analysis of the story behind the language of science—the biological body usually has been laid aside. Some even claim that it is irrelevant to the truly mental workings of the psyche.

Yet, must we not find a way to acknowledge that each of us humans *does* have a biological housing that has relatively stable and recognizable features? It is not as if we don't know it. All of us have bodies; we can see them, recognize their outlines; touch them, smell them even. We can tell our own bodies apart from other people, at the same time that we know that we are more alike than different. We all eat, extracting in a complicated fashion from the world around us the life-giving elements that we need, and eliminating the waste of that process. We have skin, nerves, blood vessels, and muscle and organ sensations; we walk, talk, see, and hear. We feel pleasure, anger, fear, and pain. We cry. We live cooperatively or we war, or are isolated. All born of females—a fact central to this book—whether we like it or not, we are identified by our genitals as male or female in almost every culture on the globe. We mature as sexual beings. We choose mates; most of us procreate and take care of our young. Once young ourselves, we grow older. Our organs fail; we die. The next generation takes over and mourns loss. All of this raw physicality, with its average-expectable patterning as we live and observe it over the span of our lives, exists somewhere within us. It contributes richly to our private thinking, and serves as a backdrop to all of our interactive dealings with others.

The vast majority of analysts concede that Freud was wrong in his physical conception of women's development. Nevertheless, about much else he was often right. Freud may have been wrong about the particulars of female development, but he understood that bodily experience matters to us, and he offered a brilliant opening gambit upon which analysts have been building ever since. Even if phallocentric, he was bracing in his ability to take female sexuality very seriously. In the second wave of feminism in this country in the 1960s and 1970s, though severely taken to task for his concept of penis envy, he was praised for separating off sexuality from procreation. This separation, then novel in its emphasis, was a liberation, because the political challenge then was to try to free women's identities from the narrow singular expectations of child-rearing to embrace challenges of professional lives and equality in the workplace with men. Childbearing, child-rearing, and holding together family ties were held responsible for women's lack of individually social and sexual development compared to men. However, this political era has now evolved in complicated ways. Without threatening the ongoing push for equality in the work place, I believe that one can ask new questions about this separation between theories of sex and procreation in females that was then, after all, a necessary challenge to the Freudian notion of libido being "masculine." It was necessary then to underline that women too were highly sexual. Baby-making needed to be set aside. Is this still a helpful theoretical separation? I think not. It is time to re-examine how closely these threads are in fact interwoven in female gender considerations, sexuality, and how females choose to live and whom they love, whether married or single, whether gay, heterosexual, or queer. One does not need to invoke any element of a biologically essentialist argument regarding any female's psyche. That logic was challenged and found to be fallacious. So how can we take into account *all* elements of the female biological body qua female, as I would like to propose, and still account for the mind's full kaleidoscopic gender identity of male and female psychic elements that are apparent in our everyday work with women patients on the couch and in the office? This book will address these issues.

How rarely do past or contemporary case reports of women even briefly refer to experiences of childbirths, for example, unless written up as a special focus? Yet, these are common but momentous physical events that most women experience even in life-changing ways, for better or worse. More attention is given to a female's medical history, her choice of lovers, or an account of all the places she lived or her separation anxieties. Young girls are bodily and psychically aware of their future both as sexual and procreative beings. Males deal with their sexuality in a way that is often more separated from procreation. Denying the knowledge of her possession of a procreative body from her earliest body experiences on, I think does a disservice to the full appreciation of her sexuality, for example. My aspiration will be to point out pragmatically what may already be obvious, and at the same time to join the other psychoanalytic writers who have appreciated the frustrations of trying to theorize the body as such, and how the body that lives in the mind. Kleinians who read this introduction will tell themselves that they long ago profoundly knew that women bore children in addition to being sexual. My remarks must only apply to others. What am I talking about? Am I unaware of Klein's focus of all children's aggression toward the imagined hordes of babies in the mother's womb? I am aware, but I contend that though Klein and the neo-Kleinians do acknowledge women as female much more than Freud's follow-ers and many ego psychologists do, Klein was quite uninterested in the rich texture of females' individual and detailed responses to their body experiences as well as the many shifts in their developments over the life span.

I am taking off from the point where Freud (and other theoreticians) have inscribed themselves controversially—on the place of biologically sexed bodies in psychoanalysis. My focus will be on the female body alone, and will therefore be narrower than ideal. I will use that exploration to try to clarify some of the vexed issues that have haunted psychoanalysis through the years. First, my contention is that though women as characters are not ignored in analysis past and present, the female body itself is neglected. I will discuss the history of the theory of the female body and develop clinical demonstrations of its compelling physicality—of the sexed and biological body-ness—that cannot in my opinion be ignored, and its impact on the individual. In this way, I hope to show the over-drawn separations between body and mind that happen when theory is formed, both in the past and also in contemporary psychoanalytic thinking, and I contend that when the biological body is ignored following Foucault, we in fact recapitu-late the flawed Cartesian separation of body and mind that we intended to correct for. I will claim that we cannot sustain any cogent theory of mind or one that is useful for all stages of the life cycle, without establishing the location of the body in our theories of mind, and without paying constant attention to the temporal history and biological evolution of the individual bodies of our patients. Body referents are thus ever-present in our patients' free associations if we do not ignore them.

The female capacity to become pregnant and give birth is so crucial to our biological origins and so salient in the life experience of both women and men that the functional female body needs to be as central to any useful psychoanalytic theory as the male body traditionally has been—as central as other such major theoretical preoccupations as, say, object relations, affect, attachment style, or the self. Yet, the female body, and the act of childbirth that is the physical climax of its existence, have been breathtakingly marginalized and downplayed among clin-ical and psychoanalytic thinkers. By our own theory of repression, this group collusion, and the resulting neglect, are markers not of insignificance, but of a vital import that we have yet to understand. The female body, and our physical, affective, and mental experiences of it, are the culture medium that Seamus Heaney is talking about, the nest in which something is waiting to hatch as soon as it can be brought into consciousness.

The plan of this book reflects my take on how this female-sexed body emerges in psychoanalytic theory, and some of the implications of this emergence. I begin in Chapter 1 with the tradition of female silence and its clinical reflection in silence on the couch. In Chapter 2, I examine what happens when women *do* talk (or alternatively, are analytically "heard" when an analyst thinks about and attends to the many body references). Chapter 3 makes the case I alluded to earlier—that psychoanalysis is not immune to the age-old habit of ignoring the ubiquitous conscious and unconscious human preoccupations with pregnancy. Chapter 4 demonstrates some mentalized details about the procreative body as they are seen clinically in females. Chapters 5 and 6 take up the highly neglected topic of childbirth directly. Chapters 7, 8, and 9 examine how thinking about the sexed and procreative body is included in gender identity; I hope to rebut the common criticism that heterosexuality *must be* the inevitable outcome of an analyst's careful attention to physical experience, and that a psychoanalysis that seriously takes procreation into account along with sexuality must result only in conventional gender moldings.

The last chapter offers a summary of the way trends in theory over the years have addressed issues about the female body, and some thoughts about the future. I am not aspiring here to any monolithic theory of gender. On the contrary, I argue that a psychoanalysis that is more inclusive of the biological body and its development, and that takes the individual's procreative capacity into account, ultimately permits the patient a richer and more highly individual self-portrait (which may include male, female, and mixed-gender elements). Our job is to help patients appreciate for themselves how these elements work and don't work together in the composite picture of each person's own aims. Individualization, adult agency, and choice are precious contributions to living with relative comfort in the world. In this concern, I believe that I am fully in agreement with a similar objective of post-postmodern academic feminists (Wexler, personal communication, 2010), even though I feel that, on the whole, they misunderstand the body. Further examining gender influence and identity in Chapters 7, 8, and 9, I enlarge the field to include more texture about the internalization of the sexed and gendered original objects of attachment, and hence my division of material into topics relevant to sisters and brothers, mothers and daughters, and mothers and sons. In this latter chapter, I also show that males who are primary nurturing fathers, pull, as with females, on their identifications with their own primary nurturer even while their own male-sexed body is influencing their impact on their offspring. This observation has led me to some new ideas on why men may enhance separation processes in their children.

My goal here, as I have said, is not to create new theory per se. For my part, I wish to make a passionate plea that we listen more carefully to the patient herself because I believe that patients' free associations are far from having been adequately mined. New theory frequently pronounces that the old Freudian theory is dead, rather than examining it for what is missing. As precious as the contributions of our own theorizing minds can be, it may be that we are too caught up with them. If we are to hear difficult or repressed materials that we as a group have long overlooked, we must, at least for now, learn to attend elsewhere. Such an effort could lead to a positive re-evaluation of neutrality and abstinence, measured not in destructive silence or cold distance toward our patients, but in moderating the way we privilege the use of the analyst's self-orientation in the treatment process. In recent years, the pendulum has swung far in this direction. However, in any patient's world and mind, there is more unconscious content than can be narrowed into the intense confines of a dyadic transference (Chodorow, 2010). An "old-fashioned" promotion of free association, and free-floating attention can, I believe, really help us to hear from our patients surprising details of the kind we need to keep improving existing theories. I agree with the levelheaded logic of Dale Boesky (2008), who urges that we foster techniques that promote free association, and compare not only different theories, but also clinical samples offered by different practitioners within the *same* theoretical frame, with a view to possible corrections that would result in even more progress in our field. Resorting too easily to the pressure of being original, coming up with yet more theories and new "paradigm shifts," may be flights from the still untapped depths of already established theories that were elaborated from Freud, as well as his existent work that may still be fruitfully mined. Authors, clinicians, and psychoanalytic publishers and organizers may all exhibit the "anxiety of influence" that Harold Bloom in 1973 identified in his theory of the evolution of poetry.[2] In the democratic and free-market atmosphere of contemporary United States, including the discipline of psychoanalysis, there is, I believe, much pressure to be "creative" and always "new" if we are to compete and attract business. To a degree, this can be constructive, but too often such social, economic, and dynamic pressure may result in slickness in the interests of creating more popular "user-friendly" theories that excitedly appeal by superficial claims to debunk and destroy the older theory. In a rush toward post-postmodernity in composing "new" psychoanalytic theory, there are risks in repeating the past—in this case, as usual, overlooking female patients' observations and reactions about their own body experiences that may be hiding in full sight in their free associations.

Notes

1 "The poets and philosophers before me discovered the unconscious; what I discovered was the scientific method by which the unconscious can be studied." On Freud's seventieth birthday (1926); quotation from Lionel Trilling's (1950) *The Liberal Imagination: Essays on Literature and Society* (p. 33).

2 Harold Bloom (1973) *The Anxiety of Influence: A Theory of Poetry*, Oxford University Press. Bloom's idea is that since the Renaissance, "strong" poets have to defy creative authority to assert themselves. Essentially, the master poets have to be overthrown and destroyed if the children are to grow to full stature.

Chapter 1

A language of silence?

How are gender and bodies related? This question is neither as straightforward, nor the answer as clear, as it seemed at the turn of the last century. Gyler (2010) says that "the central questions about the role of the body and mind in the construction of subjectivity remain unsolved" (p. 35), and comments that Birkstead-Breen (1993, 1996) was wise in her assertion that "there is no one-to-one relationship between mind and body. Neither can the body be ignored (that is, anatomy both counts and does not count)" (p. 35). My own understanding is that gender is mostly flexible and subjective, while the sexed biological body is Janus-faced—a relatively stable and predictable entity in terms of development, and capable of being perceived objectively even as it is simultaneously perceived subjectively by the inner eye. To integrate gender and the body is therefore a very complex task, requiring reconciliations between inner and outer, objective and subjective, and 'reality' and psychic reality. The silence of women as they come across in case reports and on the published page about their bodies has not made this easier.

Can we still recognize the lingering fashions of the past, dressed as we are in modern clothes? In this chapter, I will highlight the long and old collusions over women's silence—between women and their surroundings, and between female analysands and their analysts about their functional female bodies. The more explicit ideas about sex and the body are in the public domain, we might imagine, the more at ease a patient will be in her (or his) associations in front of an analyst. Consider the Internet explosion of medical facts, erotica, and other sexually focused material. There are forums and chat rooms and easy access to pictures about everything, from explications of puberty and vaginal herpes for teenagers, to advice on how to have orgasms or get pregnant, to encyclopedias of sex positions (gay and straight), to pornography, perversions, and necrophilia. Even amid this recent public cacophony, silences persist, silences that are abidingly linked to ideals about "femininity," and that show up specifically under the microscope of analytic practice. I will illustrate some of these shortly.

There are interesting differences in the ways female patients have presented bodily complaints to doctors and analysts over the past 150 years, for example, from hysterical paralyses, to "frigidity" mid-century, to the explosion of anorexia and "too fatness" currently. Those misunderstandings are clues to what needs clarification. The mutual communications between analyst and analysand eventually become manifest in the psychoanalytic theories we use as the building blocks of the analyst's working understanding. Analysts are affected by the theories of gender and sex that are current in other academic and medical disciplines—postmodern feminist and queer theories, neuro-biological theory, as examples—and also by the different theories about sex and gender that have arisen among psychoanalysts themselves—the relationalists and intersubjectivists, the ego psychologists, the Kleinians, the Bionians, the attachment theorists, and the French theorists, to mention only some. Confusion about how "sex" and "gender" are defined obfuscates the discussion further: sometimes the two are used interchangeably, and sometimes not. The subtlety of apparent female silence is a limiting factor in our understanding. It is obvious in clinical work that women's silences are deeply influenced by their interactions with their mothers, as well as by the more familiar silencings by men of their wives and daughters that have been identified as manifestations of a phallocentric society.

The silence in psychoanalysis about the female body—whether it is the patient's or the analyst's, and whether it manifests itself in a theory, in treatment, in a *fin de siècle* hysteria, or in a contemporary clinical presentation—suggests that this is yet another venue in which the internal and external aspects of bodily experience have not yet been integrated. Despite our clinical sophistication, it is difficult to sustain a mental integration of body and mind. How humanly eager we all are—analysand and analyst alike—to seek the transient but seductive comfort of dwelling with less anxiety in the mental spaces of splits, schisms, and rifts, where physical explanations and mental ones are kept in separate compartments. Arlow (1961) described an intricate three-dimensional domino effect in the development of psychoanalytic theory: "The theory of [clinical] technique cannot be discussed independently of the theory of neurosis. One of the unique features of the history of psychoanalysis is the fact that a therapeutic device was fashioned which served simultaneously as an investigative tool—a tool which investigated not only the illness it was supposed to cure but the very therapeutic-investigative process itself" (p. 45). The patient's expression of her neurosis stimulates the analyst to create a theory, which is then used to investigate both the neurosis and the tool (psychoanalysis) that is doing the investigation. Each step in an analysis is a mutual interlocking of the patient's symptomatology, her capacity to express herself verbally, and the listening of the analyst who is creating the theory. As one aspect of the patient's capacity to express herself, her silences inform not only the relationship between herself, her neurosis, her analyst, but also the analyst's theory.

Twenty-first century example of tragic silence

Suppression of the full-bodied female voice is being vigorously contested, at least in the Western world. Not so, unfortunately, in other parts of the globe, where the situation for women is closer to the one in medieval and early modern Europe. I will use an example here that shows how deep the prohibition against female expressivity can go. I want to quote briefly from a 2005 account in the bulletin of London's Royal College of Psychiatry, written by mental health workers in Iran[1]: The authors are describing 20-year-old Maryam, who is "sitting in a dark room working on a small carpet. Her face is partially covered by a scarf. When the scarf is removed, the reddish purple leathery scars of a burn are revealed on her face and scalp" (p. 5). When questioned about the scars, the authors tell us, women like Maryam are silent, or they claim that a kerosene lamp turned over. The authors believe that these (mostly) young married women set themselves on fire feeling that they have no other choice, and considering death preferable to a life of domestic violence and suffering. The psychosocial roots of these self-immolations, which lead either to a "slow painful death or horrific disfigurement" (p. 5), are manifest, and include being trapped, economic dependence, premature marriage, and the taboo of divorce. For these young women, lighting a fire to burn their own flesh is the preferred alternative to breaking their verbal silence. In this drama, women like Maryam enact for their perceived torturers the intolerable physical and psychological wounds that have been inflicted on them. They seek power and impact not in the spoken word, but in scenarios played out tragically in their domestic lives. A body mime is transacted in lieu of direct speech. Such silence in the face of animal or human pain is eerie. It is the result of over-whelming duress, in which the senior women of the culture collude.

The sound of silence

Western tradition too has been admonishing women to silence for centuries. One historical illustration is the magnificent collection of sixteenth-century manu-scripts that a Swiss collector donated in 1999 to the Beinecke Rare Book and Manuscript Library at Yale University. The resulting exhibition, about European women's involvement in the printed word at that time, was entitled *My Gracious Silence*. It refers to Coriolanus's appellation for his wife, Virgilia, who has merely 25 lines in the play, and 15 of them are spoken when no men are present. In her catalogue essay (1999), the historian Merry Weisner-Hanks draws a connection between silence and virtue in women: "Because Eve tempted Adam by using words, women's speech becomes linked with sin and disobedience, and female silence is thus interpreted as a divine command" (p. ix). She goes on to say that "Italian, English and German, Protestant, Jewish and Catholic men all agreed that the ideal woman was ... 'chaste, silent and obedient'" (p. vii). Such admonitions to silence and grace were, of course, imposed by men in their own self-interest, to solidify male dominance. However, over the centuries, they inevitably became internalized and are currently valued by women as a style of "femininity," a way of identifying with one's mother. The ideal of female silence thus could persist unchanged through the Middle Ages (Klapisch-Zuber, 1992) and early modern period (Davis and Farge, 1993), including the period of this exhibition, despite the dramatic changes in so many other aspects of European culture. The manuscripts at Yale are short texts. They are religious (as were the works of men of the era). These sixteenth-century women wrote mostly prayers and poems—published often with apologies about their boldness or anonymously, or with pseudonyms. In them, a thickly textured alliance of obedience, silence, and concealment of the body hides in the guise of domestic deference. As a male patient let slip (embarrassed ultimately to reveal to me his unconscious patriarchal support and enjoyment of such female domestic deference), "When I'm away from home what I long for is the sight of my wife silently floating about the kitchen in a long velvet skirt, bending over the oven and taking a pie out...[sigh]... just for me!" We can note here the nonspeaking female, her physically abject rear position, her body covered to the ankles, about to serve and feed "her" male who appetitively awaits the service that is his due. One could imagine such a woman in the sixteenth-century, shyly hiding her secret scribblings from her squire, who valued her metaphorical "pie" much more! Many of the feminist writers of the "second wave" exposed this internalization of retiring behavior as a reaction to the male aggressor, an expression of a dependent wish to please for social survival's sake (Davis, 1989). Cultural value systems such as this can turn ideals into a kind of personal "character armor" (Reich, 1933), behind which authentic connections to the embodied self retreat. The environment of male domination in a phallocentric society makes it psychologically important for *women themselves* to be internally silent, consolidating superego prohibitions against public or interpersonal discourse about their bodies. Female-to-female family dynamics are another strong conditioning factor. The feminist sociologist and anthropologist Nancy Chodorow, in her early book *The Reproduction of Mothering* (1978), spoke accurately and astutely about how the powerful projections, reprojections, and internalizations of value systems between mothers and daughters foster the ongoing expectation of young women to become mothers themselves. She therefore called on women to push men to do half of the domestic labor with children as a possible remedy for the young girls' proclivity to internalize exclusively *female* childcare and mothering expectations (Chodorow, 1978). Chodorow, now also a practicing psychoanalyst, has agreed with her younger self's profound psychological analysis, but has reassessed the social remedy as a bit utopian (Chodorow, 2003). While the feminist movement has helped shape the young men of this century into more domestically skillful people than were their fathers, the powerful and archaically anchored mother-to-daughter same-sex, same-body-based internalizations are less easily open to change by external urgent social appeal.

Another feminist critic, Toril Moi, looked back to Simone de Beauvoir's *The Second Sex* (1949) to echo her and contemplate the body as "situation." In her 1999 essay "What is a Woman?" Moi observes the feminist literature with some exasperation, noting that "the effort to rescue the word 'woman' from its so-called inherent essentialism, for instance by claiming that one uses it 'strategically' or that one really thinks of it as an 'umbrella term' or … that one always mentally add quotation marks to the word in order to place it under deconstructive erasure, are misguided because they are unnecessary" (p. 8). She picks up on an overdone effort to try to liberate women's minds at the expense of ignoring their bodies.

Some women may exercise verbal silence about their bodies but favor body expressiveness. For example, in therapy, a woman may never verbally refer to the fact that most of her legs are showing below her very short skirt, or her feelings about that in relation to the therapist, but she may repeatedly cross and uncross her legs in studied poses that are clearly designed for the watcher's delectation, or she may repeatedly pull her miniscule skirt down as if to hide her legs. As in the title to this chapter, such silence is noted as a "language"—i.e., a nonverbal body language. The lack of verbal language may have hindered efforts to theorize this silent mime phenomenon, which might in turn have aggravated the nefarious slippage into male comparisons that note what is *lacking* rather than what is *present* in women. For example, a woman may appear to a male analyst to be envious of him should she, say, one day complain about the lack of parking for his office. He possesses a parking space; she does not. She could be interpreted as being in a state of "have-not," and knowledge of classical theory may lead the analyst to build this interpretation. He may freely associate to penis envy, and become convinced that this is the root of her anger. A woman may even comply with his interpretation to her, and thus he reasonably feels that he is correct in his assumption. A male-body-oriented interpretation of a female dilemma is recorded as successful in his notes. However, should this female patient elaborate verbally further—she might speak about how she fell and hurt her ankle earlier, but that it pained her to talk to him about her walk from her parking place. She'd rather suppress this experience because it would draw his attention to her body, to her ankle, a prideful sensuous part of her anatomy when not injured. Her mother had always told her that no man ever wanted to hear about her body pains and aches, say. In fact, she should not openly draw his attention to her body as admirable either, but she should await the man's compliments. In this session, she was therefore in silent compliance with her mother's view of men's fear of women's physical complaints. She would prefer silently to "support" the male doctor in his own assumptions about her and thus keep her own gracious silence! Thus, this clinical interaction could evoke quite different interpretive trajectories according to whether the male analyst inadvertently supported the patient's silence, as in the first version, or if he were suspicious enough of her silence to help her elaborate. To the extent that women do not talk about their bodies, they encourage the misperception of women's bodily experience as "lack" rather than presence, and the fact of the silence removes the detail of the subject matter from theory-making attentions. The silence is passed on from mother to daughter and so becomes an intergenerational tradition, manifesting in treatment as tendencies to "acting in"—a mime containing hidden assumptions about the analyst's response—in lieu of direct interaction and using more words in the office. I suspect that women's little-understood and little-verbalized (perhaps, in many instances, even little-mentalized) experiences in giving birth may underlie some aspects of this defense against direct communication (see Chapters 5, 6).

Charcot and Freud

Of the 5,000 patients in the so-called City of Sorrows, the Salpêtrière Hospital in Paris, the girl known as "Augustine," was Charcot's favorite patient. She was just over 15, a photographer's model and the most famous hysteric of the Salpêtrière. In *The Invention of Hysteria* (1982/2005), Georges Didi-Huberman, a Lacanian French art historian, traces the encounter among photography, memory, and psychiatry in the late nineteenth century, richly illustrating his text from the hospital's vast archive of photographs from the 1870s and 1880s.

The patient Augustine's hysterical fits, her "language," her silent body drama recorded for posterity in the many photographic exposures of her exotic postures, were, according to Didi-Huberman, intensely interpreted by the crowd of mostly male spectators in the hospital ward as 'Attitudes Passionelles' (p. 115). In photograph after photograph, her face coyly eyes the camera lens (or perhaps the camera *man* draped in his black cloth), her hands pressed together at her breasts half-draped in white flowing cotton, her eyes cast to heaven. The care with which her scenarios were staged with lights and props, and the staff's preparation of her for the photo shoots rivaled that of a silent movie star. Now, it is true that Augustine actually did speak, because a Dr. Bourneville took careful notes of what she said: "she talked repetitively of a rape scene," he wrote, but the medical men were more interested in her physical postures.

Charcot's clinical behavior with his patients is what caught Didi-Huberman's attention. The gaze of the doctors was on the visual manifestations of her physicality. Hoffman (2009) in her essay "Archival Bodies" comments in depth about the objectification of the female body in this photographic era of diagnostics prior to the Freudian shift toward the subject's narrative. Augustine was an exemplar of this era's female silent "language-tableau" (Didi-Huberman p. 24). Her narrative drew much less medial attention, presumably because her silent body drama invited others to interpret the story of her impact.

The recent discovery of an 1892 unpublished diagram of Charcot's, however, seems to presage Freud's first topographical theory of the unconscious and its ability to repress ideas from consciousness. This shows that Charcot, therefore, in the background was actively evolving theories on the role of trauma or lost memory and the idée fixe in hysteria (Bouchara et al., 2010), even though in the foreground, clinically, he seemed a charismatic showman more fascinated with the neurology of the women's silent posturing behaviors than in coaxing them to talk about repressed traumatic life events. That would come later with Freud.

In his 1893 obituary, Freud rightfully called Charcot "an artist," "a *visuel*" (p. 12). Not unlike his patients, he was dramatic and used few words. Didi-Huberman says that during an examination, he spoke only to the patient who was completely naked before him, to ask that she turn this way or that or to make her speak in order to study the quality of her voice. He would then think deeply, and ask for another patient and another and another to compare his neurological musings in silence. He would abruptly leave as soon as the clock struck noon, leaving a few instructions to the assistants. In public clinical performance, by contrast, his verbal showmanship of all the spectacular manifestations of hypnosis and hysteria was legendary. Charcot carefully and literally watched over these women who became his stage marionettes. The female patient was always a silent participant in this drama of manifest caretaking. In addition to his more psychological theory, Charcot was searching for an elusive "ever-shifting kind of neurophysiological lesion in the cortex." Didi-Huberman aptly calls these demonstrations "tableaux" (p. 24). Charcot felt that a photograph could more truly reveal what the history of an illness concealed. *Medical objectification seemed to aid and abet these women's silent secrets.*

What Freud had seen there at the Saltpetriere Hospital led to the birth of his talking cure. Given the propensities for females to be silenced, this was indeed a promising and ingenious treatment for silent and embattled women.

Contemporary patients

Ms AB, a 55-year-old analysand, was a widow with no children. This vignette shows an intense mother/analyst transference in which I am invited to collude both in an affective pseudo-sweetness and in holding my tongue.

When the story of her severe perimenopausal symptoms, constant vaginal bleeding, and cramps finally emerged in the analysis, I asked AB how she had managed to keep so silent about it for so long. "You know me by now," she said, offering this response coaxingly, seductively, and softly, with the accent on "*YOU* know!" Yes, she asks me to agree. I know. I'm so special; I know everything without any plebian need to ask, and that means that she does not have to tell. If I were to ask, I'd be betraying a comfortable sense of intimacy and womanly cama- raderie. It is very important to her to keep this fantasy undisturbed, and she fears that to complain in a straightforward way, or to look to me directly for sympathy would be to shatter it. "It's very hard for me even to remember to think about my body. It's all tucked away somewhere inside my mind—I'm sure it's not that I don't notice—but, *YOU* know [the plea to me again] I never speak about these kind of things to anybody. You know me and religion…" She goes on in what is both an implicit illumination of the transference and an allusion to her glorified mother (as in the Bible quotation regarding the Virgin, "Mary kept all these things, and pondered them in her heart.")

AB's role model was indeed Mary the mother of Jesus. In this identification, she felt unassailable, imagining the Holy Mother, full of grace. (My own fleeting thought as she associated in her session was the addition of the end of the Hail Mary "and blessed is the fruit of thy womb." Nevertheless, AB preferred to keep wombs out of it: even the womb of a dead and safe Saint was risky. "No flesh and blood here, please!" she seemed to say.) Mary had been the role model for her mother too, who had taught her little girl by example and by deed *not* to translate complicated or negative feelings into words, especially words about her sexed and gendered body. A good woman merely "ponders these things in her heart."

One day when AB was 12, finding blood in her underpants, she came running home from school early. She had been well warned that "her time" was coming—as her mother had put it, with a special emphasis on "your TIME," "your 'time' when you'll be able to have babies." However, looking back, AB could see that her young self had been in a panic. She panted out to her mother "It's TIME—I saw IT!"—as if IT were a dreaded banshee. Her mother ran to get fresh underpants and a pad, which she stuffed between her daughter's legs and fastened with safety pins. AB was to go to bed for the rest of the day and soon she'd "feel better," And on no account was she to mention this to her father or brothers.

This transaction between mother and daughter had all the trappings of a physical illness. Nevertheless, no clear words were given to the event of her newly menstruating body; on the contrary, her mother transmitted the strong message that she was not to speak further about it—and certainly not to outsiders—to men. Through multiple transactions such as this one, AB grew up to feel that the gold standard of femininity was silence regarding body anxiety or pleasure, and that regressive mutual enactments of baby-to-mother *caretaking* were what good feminine women were supposed to do. Beneath that conviction lay a muddle of confusion and few emotionally useful words with which to express it. AB had tightly woven into her character something approaching a vow of silence about the body's functions, especially its sexual aspirations, its disappointments, and its ways of being ill-at-ease.

Patient BC

Eight years into her analysis and looking back, Ms BC, a married woman with children, was much more verbal than she had been when we began. This sequence emerged after a series of difficult interactions about her inability to speak; about a change in her style of dress (silk blouses that showed more cleavage); about her love life; about her fantasies about my body. I had been actively interpreting within the archaically ambivalent maternal register as the forbidder, but also the tempter to sensual and sexual pleasure. Repeatedly, we encountered her wish that *I* bring up body issues, and so allow her to ward off her ownership.

"One of my biggest burdens in elementary school was my breasts. Breasts were such a nuisance. They interfered with baseball. No more baseball. I couldn't find a bra. Mother came with me to a special shop. She'd watch me try on all these bras and reject them. She kneaded my breasts like pieces of dough and pushed them up and into all different bras—it was awful—mortifying. She never spoke to me directly, and I never spoke to her. I just thought I had to stand there, being prodded and pushed about …"

"She'd talk about me and over me to the salesgirls. 'Too big, too little, not enough cleavage.' She'd say over and over to them: She's *big* for her age, she's a *big* girl. She'd snap the bra at the back. Did I come out of it? I never said anything. She needed to be right in the room on top of me. I got the first bra when I was ten. Even at fourteen, I couldn't convince her I could manage by myself. They never fitted right, as far as she was concerned. For my age, I had large ... breasts. It's still hard for me to call them by name."

In this portrait of a typical exchange between mother and daughter, the mother is silently molding the daughter's body as if she were made of clay and inanimate; the daughter silently plays her part by being acted upon. The senior women in the shop are the audience; but they take part in the tableau as well by speaking only to the mother and obeying her orders for different bras.

"Having a woman's body was too complicated. It's too loud—it's too noisy—it announces itself, the female body. I was taught to be quiet. ... I learned that silence and minimalism is best when it comes to my body. 'The less said the better': mother used to say."

Patient L

I supervised the short-term psychotherapy of a 19-year-old student who came in the summer with short, oiled hair coiffed in a cow's lick, dressed in khakis, a white shirt with rolled up sleeves, a heavy belt and dark leather loafers with Carlisle socks. The opening gambit to the therapist was: "I want you to call me Len. ... I've told my mother and grandmother to do this. I'm really a guy ... but my father keeps calling me Lenore. I've told him over and over, but he ignores me."

This student told the therapist that formerly the family had called him "a girl," but since coming to university he had discovered that he was really a man. He was transgendered now, felt good about the discovery with peers of this new identity, felt at last true to himself. Len wanted help with his fury at how people outside his transgendered group were not adapting readily to treating him as a male. He carried a copy of *Bodies That Matter* by Judith Butler, and read it as a Bible. He was doing brilliantly in school, had no psychiatric symptoms, and no engageable complaints except about others' puzzlement and slowness to respond to the changes in him. His mother had said, "Whatever you do is OK with me," an exaggeratedly hands-off response that convincingly conveyed a posture of nonengagement. Len experienced it as an appropriate parental response—which led the therapist and me further to suppose that he was quite used to a policy of silence about bodily feelings and changes. This is obviously an extremely complicated case. Still, Len is a sketch of another way that a body mime happens without access to commentary. There was a suggestion that Len's body language was aligned with his mother in their combined silence. The therapist tried to interest him in a discussion of Butler's "performance of gender" given that he carried her book to the office more than once, but as the therapist had conveyed that this theme may be relevant to Len personally, he summarily dismissed the exploration as hackneyed and political. "I only want your advice on how to talk sense into my rigid father," Len instructed her (rigidly).

Clinical theory

In these three cases, few words pass easily and directly between daughter and mother about their sexed and gendered bodies. Nonetheless, these are intense, emotionally laden tableaux charged with implicit meaning and the mothers' vigilance over the daughters' bodies. I would argue that even Len's apparently uninterested mother enacted a mutual silence with her/him which I believe involved a collusion that requires a powerful unspoken bond.

Lerner (1976) and others have illustrated and documented how infrequently little girls are taught a name for their own genitals. The academic psychological literature reveals that boys are not taught a name for the girl's genitals either, though both sexes are taught "penis." If we needed any more even concrete proof of adults' lingering inhibitions with sex and gender, we have it there in a nutshell. Once girls possess a body vocabulary, their communications about their sexed bodies become more open and available. Patients AB, BC, L, and Maryam from Iran, and Augustine from Paris have in common much personal body experience, yet are still sadly limited to communication through "dumb shows," graphic tableaux, or play-like wordless demonstrations. These tendencies create them highly vulnerable to the outside world's innuendo, interpretation and most importantly, subtle and gross misinterpretations if not frank abuse. I have shown here some elements of *how* such body silence happens. *Why* it happens particularly with females is explored also gradually throughout the following chapters.

Note

1 Obviously, there are sadly too many heartbreaking episodes of female oppression from many other countries that one could choose as a similar example.

Chapter 2

Women talking

I now want to think about what happens when a purposely receptive climate is nurtured in the culture, or individually in psychoanalytic treatment, for the verbalized detail of a woman's body experience that is unique to her own life.

Portraits of the pleasures and joys of existing in the female body have been slow to emerge in the literature because, when seen through the phallocentric lens of inevitable female pain, pleasures are understood as defensive. Becoming more acquainted with a far greater range of female body anxieties than foundational "castration anxiety" opens the way to beginning to try to find a genuine place for pleasure. Looking more closely at the nonpathogenic aspects of female exhibitionism, as I do in this chapter, for example, can contribute to this study. To display the body can be a great pleasure and experienced as such, but women can also be in conflict about it. Emerging slowly as we are from a theory that centers primary body pleasure on the male, and creates female pleasure merely by derivation, it is vital that we investigate the nature of female body pleasure free of the constraints of gender comparison. I will exemplify the "classical" view of female exhibitionism first, to show up the problems that I believe have been subsequently dealt with by ignoring them, and then go on to offer some alternatives with illustrations that are quite compatible with modernizing the ego psychological point of view.

Exhibitionism and the literature

There is actually only one paper on the topic of female exhibitionism revealed in a search of the PEP CD Archive up to 2007. It is quoted as a reference in many other papers. It is called "Fetishism and Exhibitionism in the Female and their Relationship to Psychopathy and Kleptomania"[1] by George Zavitzianos (1971) from Montreal. Female physical pleasure is a rare topic in psychoanalysis, addressed by few (Kulish and Holtzman, 2002; Elise, 2000, 2008).[2] There are a number of papers mentioning "female fetishism," which symptom is unsurprisingly generally not interpreted from the point of view of anxiety about the female body per se, but rather with a maximal emphasis on the need for a missing phallus. Close examination of the texts, however, reveal inviting but untouched and ignored material that directly relates to the patient's horror-struck reactions to fantasy pregnancy—the anxieties of body belly expansion, fears of how a baby emerges, memories of mothers' pregnancies, etc. Once aware of how male-type body interpretation covers over the female, it is surprising how frequently one detects it. A good example of these omissions of the female body in favor of male interpretation would be Raphling (1989).

Male exhibitionism is frequently studied, and readily acknowledged. It concerns public display of the naked male genital. However, analytic writers, Zavitzianos says, interestingly do not categorize female body display as "exhibitionism," even if used descriptively in a clinical text. I suggest that this may result from the following logic of theoretical gymnastics. Straightforward female "activity" can have no referent in Freud's male libido from whence sexual activity comes, other than being dubbed "an active pursuit of *passive* aims" (Freud, 1933). Passivity being over-equated with adult femininity, female activity becomes would-be male behavior. Such an opinion indeed is rendered by Zavitzianos. "The very fact that the woman has no penis, and feels this as a narcissistic mortification, makes her replace the infantile desire to expose all other parts of the body, with the exception of the genitalia. Since displaced exhibition cannot reassure against castration fear, it cannot develop into an actual perversion" (1971: p. 298).[3] The writer explains (without any self-consciousness!) that females are extremely fear-inspiring, repulsive, and produce castration effects on the male (referring to Freud's 1922 insight that the decapitated head of Medusa represents the frightening female genitalia, and Ferenczi's 1919 insight that a woman can use her nakedness as a punishment to produce terror in a man). Fetishism in women, he says, has been noted very rarely in the literature. Exhibitionism has not been noted at all, he says. His case report was a 20-year-old college student with "traumata" (as I read it, a highly traumatic set of parents). The mother had masturbated her; she had been exposed to primal scenes, and the father beat her ferociously at the age of 12. The author traces the following "fetishes" to the father's penis. The girl sometimes masturbated while reading, or while alone in a car borrowed from her father. The book was seen by the analyst as a fetish, as was the car. (Virtually ignored in the material is the fact that it was a comforting memory that mother used to read a lot to the girl.) There were also ignored accounts in this text of the girl's 3-year-old acute reactions to the mother's pregnant body, with clear desires expressed by her to imitate her shape. This material, while creditable in its recording, is ignored in favor of the axiom that if a 3-year-old girl were unhappy with her body shape, it simply *must* relate to her mortification for having no penis. That was the basis for Zavitzianos's thinking. The patient once drove her father's car after a sexually arousing analytic session, while showing off her genitalia for passing truck drivers. This was her exhibitionism—quite a historical moment as the only female exhibitionist recorded to date! Moreover, it was interpreted by the analyst as motivated by terrorizing the truck drivers by her lack of a penis. This section speaks to theoretical erasure of the highly significant interaction between mother and daughter surrounding the girl's body and her mother's pregnancy.

Had Zavitziano accessed this aspect of thinking about the student, he might have developed an alternative interpretation about what influenced her exhibition, right after a session with him.

Further problems for the theory

Why do we not hear more about exhibitionism in women? Yet another restraint on analytic thinking about pleasure is that, by now, in front of the patient public, the academic and psychiatric worlds, and the lay community, we analysts have become embarrassed by the old psychoanalytic terminology with its all-too-obvious phallic bias. Embarrassment in turn leads to avoidance of thinking through and updating the existent ego psychological take. Younger analysts are filled with stories of our analytic forefathers and even foremothers having pained their female patients by their Freudian certainties of compensation for a missing phallus, or paternalistic advice to content themselves by sacrificing their own desires for their husband's careers in the public eye. We analysts wish to disidentify with that past as traumatic. We often split off these contents from our theoretical minds. We deal with it by radical condemnation and elimination, and search for brand-new theory rather than working through this embarrassing era, trying to understand it however angrily, trying to sift out anything that still holds, while roundly rejecting the inaccurate aspects in the interests of reformulation. Newer theories that emphasize object relations, say, or the self, or complexity theory, or attachment, often denounce drive theory simply as outdated. If drive theory and conflict/ defense operations are dismissed as irrelevant, penis envy and castration anxiety and denigration of the clitoris do thankfully disappear as focal to a developmental theory about women. Yet, the proponents of the alternative theories do not offer any developmental theory that pays as close attention to the body as Freud did. No arguments to date have settled once and for all the demerits or merits of these psychosexual markers so important to Freud. Running afoul of many American female patients and feminists in the 1960s onward (e.g., Millet, 1963; Friedan, 1970), some analysts were defiant, garnering support from Freud's dim view of feminism, and some made guilty re-evaluations and dismissed what they'd been taught in training. In reaction, sex and gender have gradually become incidental to most current theories (except in the relational school, which has been most actively developing gender theory with a marked postmodern influence, but where this progress has happened by squarely putting the biological body in the back seat). Leaving out embodied sex and gender, an analyst need not recall or revisit his or her embarrassment about Freud. We can think freely and without embarrassment about interior attachments, or "containers," or splitting, or voids, or cocoons, or fragmentation, or being schizoid, or being grandiose, or internalizing, or seeking recognition, or being narcissistic, etc., etc., etc. These days, we may note and talk about "female power" as a positively charged inferred intrapsychic dynamic, or we can analyze gender inequality without mentioning any of its physical components. The arena of female body pleasure qua female, unexamined from the beginning of analysis, even seen as a *defense* seems gradually to have gone by the wayside, lost under the rubble of Freud's male vision and the rightful corrective, but by now less consciously over-reactive push to suppress it. To bring up "penis envy" these days is to be greeted by rolling eyes and a sigh of "not *again*." However, there is far more at stake than "penis envy." A contemplation of female pleasure in its fullness has been lost to view, and with it an opportunity for a genuine struggle to improve Freud's drive theory beyond its beginnings (e.g., Schmidt-Hellerau, 2001, 2006, one of the few thinkers whose critique still sees its abiding virtues, its unexplored dimensions and its majestic capacity to encompass in a potentially satisfactory fashion the mind's workings). It is impossible to think adequately about the mental impact of sensuous and physical pleasures, including their vicissitudes, if the field loses touch with authentic physicality.

Showing off, past and present

"Showing off" has often been looked at askance amongst women who regard themselves and hope to be regarded by men as "classy" in Western Society. Other societies too are marked by this feature. For example, in a recent newspaper article, an American journalist reported watching an anxious immigrant Chinese-speaking mother (one of many) relating to an interpreter during a parent–teacher conference in an elite New York high school, and noted that the interpreter was protecting the mother from a teacher's complaint that her clearly bright daughter was too quiet in class. The interpreter explained to the journalist that there is a word in Chinese that is very positive about girls being quiet, closer to "ladylike." A complaint about this was not information that this frantic mother could cope with just then and try to decipher cross-culturally.

Showing off the body to public display has been denigrated as the bailiwick of strumpets, hussies, call girls, and women of the night. Dancers and models, of course, are encouraged to "show off." Their body shapes, however, are hardly typical of physically mature women, owing to the youthful, flat abdomen, small buttocks, full ski-tip breasts as in pole dancers, or no visible breast tissue at all as is favored in ballet dancers or catwalk models who also must have stick-like legs. My thesis that follows is that these are the only safe females to look at publicly, because on the surface they create less anxiety and do not remind us of the female body's procreative aspiration.

Highlighting society's struggle, *The New York Times* had an article on 14 November 2004 about how the store mannequin industry is experiencing modern difficulty coping with increased ethnic, especially Latina, influence. It is challenged to begin recognizing different body types and standards of beauty by making newly rounded shapes, "closer to a shopper's own" larger buttocks. They said, "mannequin manufacturers ... traditionally stuck to low, single-digit sizes for beauty ideals, reflecting the supermodels tottering on runways ... in Paris, a very tall size 2 to 4." These days, though, apparently, women have been flaunting "more girly, hippy, curvaceous" posteriors in spite of the Parisian ideal.

One high-end skeptic in the industry observed, "It's not creating an image of woman as an elegant creature. It's a little bit down and dirty, a little bit crass." However, "down and dirty" they say, also "[may become] good business." It is interesting that they report that, in a store window, "the sight of a voluptuous mannequin can come as a shock. ... people seem bewitched by them .... Men, women and children wanted to touch them." There is obviously turmoil stirred in all age groups by this change that promises a window display closer to a real woman's body. This reminds one also of Leopold Bloom, the "new feminine man" in Joyce's *Ulysses*, who, when trying to avoid running into the man who cuckolded his wife, famously scurried into a museum to look at the statues of Goddesses— later revealed in the book to be searching their rear-ends for the presence or absence of the anus!

Scopophilia is nothing new, and its origins were persuasively situated by Freud (1905) in early childhood body exploration and experimentation (for an update, see Mahony, 1989). Many women turn out to be quite conflicted about their exhibitionistic desires, especially about the issue of being looked at by others. Many strongly wish to protect themselves or feel they need to be protected from other human beings' scopophilic gazes. One hears a great deal on the couch about these discomforts, and the anger that women experience in being "objectified," felt as a shameful humiliation. This phenomenon can occur side-by-side with a woman dressing in very revealing clothes, as if signaling that she is fully comfortable with her desire to be looked at.

Another lens reveals the acute discomfort of many people at actually observing a woman expose her body. In hospitals, the scene of much socially acceptable medicalized nudity, busy emergency room senior male and female physicians with their harried junior helpers often cannot wait to get rid of drunk or coy female patients whose come-on behaviors such as opening their gowns to display breasts or pubes is categorized angrily as "seductive" (not as descriptive, but as a pejorative signaling disgust), because such women readily provoke conflicts in others by their invitation to be looked at.

Showing off the mind, or worldly accomplishments, also has been a tricky scene for women. When Elizabeth Blackwell, the first woman medical graduate in the United States, was invited to join the procession with her male classmates from Geneva Medical College in upstate New York in 1849, she apparently declined, saying that it was not ladylike to "parade" herself. She found it one thing to study medicine, but completely another to handle the celebrity tag attached to being *seen* as a pioneer. To "parade," to show off her accomplishment and risk either the admiration or disapprobation of the onlooker was intolerable. Instead, she said demurely that she would wait inside the chapel, to be called up along with the others. Not for her the display of robes and pomp, and exposure to the then equivalent of the nineteenth-century paparazzi. Display of her intellect had apparently broken the bank of her resources to be seen in the flesh, sinfully rejoicing in public and violating her internalized sense of what was appropriate to a responsible, respectable Quaker woman.

A folk saying from the Scottish Calvinistic communities rawly delivers the following message:

A whistling woman and a crowing hen;
Is neither good for God nor Man.

The woman who draws attention here by making a noise by blowing through her protruded mouth is perceived as impersonating a show-off *male*. Were she a cock, crowing would be designated as "good." Such manly behavior would be beloved of God (that show-off male who created the earth!) as well as all humankind—who join to repudiate this sinful, blowing, attention-getting female with the pursed-up protruding lips. Men have pronounced such behavior to be sinful for a woman, and women themselves have felt it to be so.

Problems for theory

There are problems for psychoanalytic theory in the area of "biological essentialism" that bear on exhibitionism. Modeling the "passivity" of "femininity" on how Freud believed that, in conception, "the ovum is immobile and waits passively" (1933: p. 114) while being pursued by the active, aggressive sperm, he (and many other followers, including contemporaries such as Kurt Eissler,[4] 1915–1994) believed that women were more dependent than men, more in "need" of love (1933), and naturally self-absorbed in their own beauty (1914), and *therefore* that narcissism was a normal feminine condition—"... we attribute a larger amount of narcissism to femininity" (1933: p. 132). "The effect of penis envy has a share, further, in the physical vanity of women, since they are bound to value their charms more highly as a late compensation for their original sexual inferiority" (1933: p. 132). Briefly, "biological essentialism"—a questionable construct that has existed since the 1800s—means that *because* women and men have different anatomical and physiological characteristics, their personalities *therefore* are necessarily different and *matching* these characteristics as a result, and that the resulting differences can be (over) confidently designated universally as essentially "feminine" or essentially "masculine" traits. Freud (1933) sometimes struggled against this convention, as in "... the proportion to which masculine and feminine are mixed in an individual is subject to quite considerable fluctuations" (p. 114), or where he points to lesser aggression in females as not a *biological* essential characteristic, but a result of social suppression. His main thesis in this same paper on femininity swallows whole, however, biological essentialist attitudes. For example, his attempt to render straightforward female activity deteriorates into a circuitous notion of what subsequent ego psychologists too were to dub the inherently feminine "active pursuit of passive aims." It would have been so much simpler to allow the female in her own skin to be active, but the latter descriptive would have disturbed the uber-notion that libido had to be masculine. Hence, Freud's baroque reasoning. Accentuating the *passive* in female activity of course derives from Freud's conventional image of females passively awaiting impregnation by the "active" male in sexual intercourse. "When you say 'masculine' you mean 'active' and when you say 'feminine' you ... mean 'passive' ... it is true [that] the male sex-cell is actively mobile and searches out the female one ... [which is] immobile and wait[s] passively" (p. 114). Nevertheless, he notes that this feminine passivity is not always the case. He goes on to explain, "A mother is active ... towards her child ... [and still] one might consider [this as] characterizing femininity ... as [still] giving preference to passive aims ... [This] is not the same thing as passivity. ... [T]o achieve a passive aim calls for a large amount of activity" (p. 115). This thinking was rampant in analysis till it was debunked in the 1970s and 1980s, and the advent of the intellectual interrogations of postmodernism (e.g., Flax, 1990) that stressed the importance of theories being subject to the biases of their creators. Unexamined biological essentialism can still persist, however, even in the writing of many who view themselves as liberated and have long decried penis envy as central to all female inner lives. For example, Patrick Mahony (1983), writing about Erikson, an otherwise enlightened academic, elaborates that, "For Erikson, anatomy is destiny to the extent that 'it determines not only the range and configuration of physiological functioning and its limitations but also, to an extent, personality configurations' (Erikson, 1963: p. 285); accordingly ... the contention [is] that the richly convex parts of female anatomy suggest 'fullness, warmth, and generosity' and that 'the very existence of the inner productive space exposes women early to a specific kind of loneliness, to a fear of being left empty or deprived of treasures, of remaining unfulfilled or drying up'" (p. 453). Erikson's suggestion of awareness of inner body space, I believe, proves valuable to explore in the talk of women themselves, but other unexamined attributed nouns like "warmth and generosity" smack of wishful projection toward women. Mahony (1983) adds a footnote about follow-up from Erikson: "Over a decade after his first article, Erikson (1975) resumed his thinking in 'Once more the inner space' Life History and the Historical Moment, New York: W. W. Norton and Company, pp. 225–247. Although he is now more cautious, I believe that he is still guilty of overstatement and metaphorical extension. However, in one place he insightfully supplements the Freudian penis envy assigned exclusively to women with inter-male penis envy as well as 'probably ... a deep envy for the maternal capacity'" (p. 238). The point is well taken and serves to correct a Western prejudice as old as Aristotle, which gives a one-sided male description of woman's insufficiency. I think it would not only be amusing but profitable to turn the tables around and define man exclusively in negative terms, as lacking maternal inner space, and then to measure the impact of a discourse extended along these lines. At any event, the envy of penis, breast, and uterus exists in both sexes. Erikson speaks inconsistently of body part (penis envy) and function (maternal capacity); were he to have drawn a tight logical parallel and thereby to have spoken about penis functions, he would have realized other complications in his linkage." Mahony, in contemplating the contribution of nature and culture in gender as reflected in language, draws attention to potential distinctions about the use of language. "Genderlect," a term he coins, is attributable to cultural learning. In also considering "nature," proclivities for the use of certain primitive metaphors may well reflect the primitive mind's inner registrations of body morphology at the time of learning to speak. The female body could play a role as distinguished from the male body. This kind of exploration, I believe, exemplifies a way of furthering exploration and expanding gender theory by correctives that *include* the body, as opposed to ignoring Freudian physicality.

Advances in contemporary theories about female development and sexuality have hopefully gone beyond the original Freudian conceptualizations in which the male body dominates—such as the indiscriminate use of "castration anxiety" for *female* fears of body damage. There are many different kinds of genital and female body anxieties that we have learned about over the years since Freud. There are anxieties about the loss of hymen and virginity (Holtzman and Kulish, 1997), penile penetration (Horney, 1926), or rape fantasies, for example, which latter Bernstein (1990) and Richards (1996) believe to be the female counterpart of castration anxiety; or those arising from loss of control of flow in menstruation, to which Ritvo (1976) alerted analysts in his studies of adolescent females. There are anxieties about pubertal and pregnancy expansion in the breasts (Balsam, 1996); or about anticipating and grasping in fantasy the elasticity of the abdominal cavity (Chapter 4), the uterus and the vaginal canal during natural childbirth (Hall, 2006, Chapter 3). Some attention has been drawn to some of these by Deutsch (1945), Raphael-Leff (1995), and Pines (1993), but their work has remained focal to the moments of childbearing and not generated the logical and necessary revision of developmental theory that I would like to propose is necessary in fact, in Dr. Raphael-Leff's many publications in this area , her critiques of psychoanalytic theory have always proposed and sustained a hope of generating revision. Yet, in spite of all her brilliant work, and also the increasing numbers of papers on the problems of procreation encouraged by this work, the acceptance of the centrality of a procreative body has not filtered into theory building abut the mind. The many specifically female body anxieties, widen the scope well beyond the specific anxieties associated with the classical fantasized loss of a personal penis. Pretending that these anxieties can be subsumed under the rubric of "castration anxiety" nowadays has to be a form of defensive reductionism. Many of us (e.g., Goldberger, 1999; Long, 2005 reporting on an APsaA panel about changing the language of female development) have argued that the newer theories, alas, can still be impeded by our psychoanalytic lexicon, which abidingly memorializes and rigidifies older, culturally shared ideas that have been passed on from generation to generation.

Problematic aspects of theory that directly relate to exhibitionism

"Femininity" is often used as if it were an objective phenomenon or scientific term, or a term that we all agree and are clear about. This is utterly misleading.

"Femininity" in fact inevitably encodes many implicit personal and societal value judgments (Elise, 1997). Freud, upholding Enlightenment aims of scientific objectivity and his knowledge of the biology of conception, employed "femininity" and "masculinity" as scientific terms and equated them with libidinal "passivity" and "activity," respectively (as described in detail earlier). This language should be retired for good. It creates confusion. I can demonstrate that it contributes obfuscation to the theory of female exhibitionism.

Logical extrapolation from classical libido theory (the latter as exemplified by Freud, 1933) suggests that, if passivity is the essence of mature femininity, then anything active in a woman, such as a display of herself, must encode masculinity. Elizabeth Young-Bruehl, in her 1990 introduction to *Freud on Women: A Reader*, points to how if libido is active in Freud's narrow male terms, it therefore cannot, in these same terms, belong to women. Even though he toyed off and on with considering all humans as bisexual, Young-Bruehl says that Freud never did call the libido "*bisexual.*" He could find no way to link the concept of a bisexuality that related to objects and aims, to the theory of instincts that he had already proposed. Passivity, therefore, was inherited into ego psychology as "held-back" activity: femaleness is "held-back" maleness. Showing off with another person in mind is necessarily "active." A bisexual libido theory would not have required this forced gender dichotomy, imposed almost for theoretical neatness. Female exhibitionism or female activity could have been investigated in its own terms without nefarious comparison to males.

A contemporary shift in female theory

Let us entertain the possibility that showing off the naked genital, or another part of her body or mind, might have meaning to women different from those of the old read of females through the eyes and bodily possessions of men. What then? For one thing, an analyst unencumbered by theoretical comparison to men finds it easier to expect that a woman on the couch will surely talk about her body just as man will talk about his. "Held-back qualities" would then be recognized as inhibitions, and an accruing social value of silence could be analyzed as a problematic form of hiding from, say, the woman's own pathological shame and desire to hide (often internalized from traumatic environmental handling of the girl child's body and aspirations). One can use a technical focus on helping females to talk freely about their own bodies and be surprised at the content, rather than colluding with their traditional silences for whatever reasons, or interpreting "absence" as an inherent part of the female condition, as do the French, or, say, interpreting "psychic retreats" from a knowing but "other" point of view, such as assuming excessively archaic underlying physically metaphoric constructs, as do the Kleinians. The opportunity for increased free association results often in portraits that reveal that the mother's and other's female bodies, such as sisters (Kuba, 2011, Chapter 7) and aunts, are often far and away more significant as an icon of comparison than males. Males can also certainly be a focus for triumph as well as envy, remembering that there are important differences between a young girl's comparisons with the bodies of boys as brothers (Chapter 8) or cousins, or grown men as fathers and uncles. All kinds of sexed bodies can act as a stimulating motivator for a female's draw to joyful showing off. Conversely, "holding back" in therapy sessions often encodes especially female body–female body conscious and unconscious fears of inferiority, and enactments, especially with a female analyst, of fears and wishes to be eclipsed and out of the limelight. One can appreciate that female-to-female dynamics give an altogether different arena from female-to-male dynamics in which to explore how the female body is mentally encoded during childhood, adolescence, motherhood, and aging.

Five clinical vignettes

Here are some alternatives to the older point of view that I will demonstrate with clinical vignettes. My attempt is cogently to build on and expand highly viable aspects of Freudian ego psychology by theorizing about the content of what the patient says, finding accurate and helpful Freud's emphasis on the sexed and gender physical aspects of psychic functioning, while rejecting his obsolete formulations. Female body pleasure in exhibitionism will be taken for granted as a function of baseline female libido. Negativity will be read as defensive[5] to the freedom to think about exercising the body's potential.

(1) The first will show a lively business woman's outgoing excitement in giving a PowerPoint presentation that pleasurably and spontaneously reminds her of being physically exposed while giving birth. (2) The second shows a male analyst's "classic" male misinterpretation of a young girl's criticism of her mother's showing pot belly, mistaking it for rivalry over her father, whereas the obvious alternative was an identificatory comparison to her mother's body that expressed anxiety about her own procreative potential. (3) The third shows a woman patient's use of comparing her own and her female analyst's bodies to fantasize about herself being inside a womb and anticipating delightedly showing off a large pregnancy herself. (4) The fourth demonstrates a mother's need for a patient to exhibit her body by being a model, for her own erotic delight. (5) The fifth shows regressive competitive desires among young adult sisters to show off being physically big and beautiful enough to get married, and thus ultimately displaying body desirability and maturity to the matriarch, by besting recollections of early awe at the mother's sensuous display of her own "married" glories.

(1) An adult woman who was a successful business woman and a divorced mother (reported at length in Chapter 5 as Ms. HJ) reported a fantasy of taking off her panties, lying down, opening her legs, and feeling erotic as she imagined showing her vulva—as she said, "pink, pouting, slightly open and damp"—to some male to whom she was relating. The fantasy would occur when she was excited, as she said, "doing a PowerPoint presentation" to clients to attract their business. She felt playful and elated about it, if

concerned with pangs of the forbidden, as she told it to her analyst. Sometimes, she would go afterwards to a nearby bathroom to masturbate. None of her associations concerned the male organ in any sense of a classical "compensation" for a body wound or gap. Instead, she recalls being thrillingly sexually stimulated by the examining fingers of her obstetrician while in the lithotomy position during prenatal examinations. Her associations led to all kinds of feelings and sensations about giving birth—the "show" beforehand in the bursting of the waters, the stretching, pushing, "crowning" of the head (interesting language for childbirth, certainly suggestive of the celebration of body power, and not female abjection!). Listening to memories such as these, and to the accounts of many other women with similar experiences and fantasies, one begins to appreciate how the focus on specifically female aspects of the body, multiple erotic and physical excitements of visiting gynecologists, and undergoing obstetric care stoke the memories and fuel the impulses to display in the ongoing mental life and fantasies of adult women.

(2) During a case presentation, a very senior male child analyst commented constantly during a description of a young girl's intense dislike of her mother's potbelly, that the girl clearly had an "oedipal" problem. He meant that the girl, because of her rivalry with her mother for her father's love, had a negative opinion of her mother's belly and her mother's bodily attractiveness. In order to defend against her stirred forbidden rivalry with the mother over the erotic wish for the father's attentions and baby, she instead criticized the mother's body to diminish her as a rival. This is an example of listening to female body material with the primacy of the male in mind. One could wonder instead about what this means for the little girl's erotic and procreative interest in her *own* body comparison with her mother. One could wonder about her anxiety about her fantasy of her girl body's future destiny to become a woman, which is being expressed as a repudiation of mommy's abdominal girth. She may fantasize a destiny to bear children and suffer anxiety and confusion about how a baby gets out and in. Freud's 1905 "Riddle of the Sphinx" ("Where do babies come from?") translated for this little girl could be: "What happened to mommy's belly anyway to make it like a pot?" A growing girl studies her mother and compares herself in future effigy. The sincere comments of the senior male analyst, imbued in classic theory, because this is the only one that is articulated fully for sex and gender, is an informal example of the way that the primacy of female-to-female body interaction was and is still ignored.

(3) An adult patient talks about her own body in relation to her mother's (and preconsciously to her female analyst's) in a way that is relevant to my topic of showing off. This daughter, in showing off her "female stuff," includes a comparative awareness of a fantasy of the adult female as a body in which once she herself was enclosed. This pleasurable exhibition is for the delectation of her mother (much more than for males): "In this dream, there is an elephant. Or is it a whale? I think I'm in its belly. I'm suffocating and

struggling and struggling to escape. Suddenly, it's like a cave. There's plenty of room, I think. There's plenty of food—nice food, too. It's not so bad in here. I can live here for a while. ... Then I turn into an elephant. Like the ones in parades you see in pictures of India. I'm ambling down the street with a beautiful silk gold paisley cover on my back and a gold and scarlet rope loosely around my belly. I feel content..." The patient had ready associations to pregnancy, to the stories of her mother and to comparisons where her own bodily experience was similar, and where it was different (she had a bigger frame than her mother, for example). She carried her baby low, whereas her mother carried hers high. In the treatment, I understood her to express an activated fantasy of a strong desire for fusion and one-ness with mother and me. "Just like I want to be in your belly. ... You could be my mother."

(4) An art student, Ms. CD, with a "stage mother," had spent her sixteenth year being a swimsuit model. "It was perfect for me. I thought of myself as being entirely a grown-up. I was showing—showing off gloriously—I was display-ing everything I had—and I knew from mother it was good—that is the other side of those warnings about being sluttish and sexy and show-offy. It dawns on you that she thinks you are powerful and that you are incredibly, unbear-ably enticing. I longed to be pregnant—I used to push my smooth little belly out a little bit, daring to display—here folks, this is what I have ... look at MY lithe little belly ... it'll grow big some day ... look at my crotch ... it's pretty, it's wet ... dirty thoughts ... I knew I was safe on the runway. Mother liked watching. Look mother, everybody's watching me ... THEY think I'm good. They want to feast their eyes on me." And of course, at this moment in the process, the "everybody watching" was also me. CD was excited to display herself to both her mother in the past and me in the present, even if old guilts and anxieties of competing with her both adoring and punitive mother image would emerge.

This patient's stated and unstated questions in the therapy were: Can I compete with you? Can I show my sex? Can I display my body to you—in image, in metaphor, in words? Will you admire me, permit me, encourage me, get anxious, angry, retaliate? Do you need to insist always that you are bigger than me—weightier/more fecund/bigger-breasted? "Let my show you my stuff," she'd say to me when she brought in artwork.

(5) A young woman in her late 20s was sadly breaking up with her boyfriend. Her reason was that he just kept avoiding proposing marriage. In the midst of her tears, she shared a scene that had happened the night before. She was on her evening job in the box office of a theater. A bunch of his female coworkers came in looking for tickets. They exchanged bright hellos. My patient was miserable—desperate—yearning to screech out to the women that Bob was hurting her, jilting her; and she was desperate for their comfort to her tears. She thought of her older sisters. All the sisters would unite to shame him publicly. He would never be invited to their parties again.

Then, however, another miserable thread entered. In her imagination, her older sisters start to tease and ridicule her. They'd dance around her and chant, "He won't marry you–you–you! And you can't marry him!" She focuses on her oldest sister—the beauty. She has two babies by now. My patient's weeping becomes distressing. She suddenly remembers her mother heavily pregnant and looking resplendent and bejeweled and "hugely breathtakingly gorgeous" in a white velvet dress going to a Ball, leaving her with the babysitter.

My patient weeps and weeps. Other women are more powerful than she is. They are bigger/more beautiful/more powerful/older/have some magic/are winners—something she does not have that *enables* them to get a man. Here, there is an important distinction from older theory. For my patient, it is not *having* the man necessarily, as in penis envy interpretations, but having the *female essence like her mother to attract the man* that is her concern. She says, "You need a man to get pregnant. But it's the big, powerful mother-person you want to be yourself." Other women are hence compared for beauty, breast size, and body proportion.

The burning question is, who is the biggest and (unconsciously) the ideal, best mother-person? This vision can be enacted in exhibition and body display as in the impressive show to the little girl of the mother's large, bright velvet dress emphasizing her large pregnant belly. Not surprisingly, the radical opposite of these images can operate, as the "mother-person" body imago can be also frightening to contemplate. The sight of this body carried a future threat of ever-increasing, potentially out-of-control expansion, which a girl knows awaits her one day. As an avoidance of the fruits of femalehood, a burning question among a family of females can be, who is the smallest, thinnest, most straight, thin? Who can show off ascetic restraint best? A girl compares and contrasts herself with other girls and women to measure who can occupy (or radically avoid) the senior seat of matriarchal power. Exhibitionistic desires, pleasurable and painful, often encode female-to-female competition. Ongoing envies and jealousies that carry fantasies and images of attaining the body pleasures to which she is heir, far beyond early childhood, have been little explored in our literature and thinking. Newer formulations about females are strongly interested in "What does my mother have that I, a little girl, don't possess?" Mothers, in other words, seem to have a lot to "show off" that little girl children do not—breasts, hips, pubic and underarm hair, babies in the belly—as well as a mysterious and magical opening somewhere that can be hidden yet revealed, and can let out a whole baby into the world.

In this chapter, I have tried to show what topics become displayed when women open up from inhibition to their delight and pleasures in exposing body talk, free associating to these images, and thus allowing a self-display and attention in particular to the derivations and drive derivatives of their rightfully exhibitionistic procreative pleasures.

Notes

1 I am not claiming that this is the *only* work on female exhibitionism. The PEP archive does not include book chapters, for example. My point is that the topic has drawn very little attention. Contemporary work that is especially in tune with my own interests in this book is by Nancy Kulish and Deanna Holtzman (2002, 2008), who also emphasize missing theory about female body pleasure, such as in their writing on "Baubo," the old nurse whose playful genital display to the Greek Goddess Demeter, bereft after losing Perspehone, made her laugh joyfully and recover from depression.

2 A figure like Baubo (see preceding note—Freud actually had one of those on his desk!) is familiar from carvings on Irish and English Gothic churches—most are in Ireland. "Sheela-na-gigs" were eleventh–twelfth-century carvings of naked females holding open their exaggerated spacious vulvas. They are said to be fertility symbols or symbols of female power.

3 In my chapter, I do not take on a discussion of the related (but pathological) topics of female perversion or fetishism, because I want to separate out exhibitionism as a normative element in female functioning.

4 As a candidate generously invited to Dr. Eissler's beautiful apartment once for a class, because of his leg fracture in the 1970s or perhaps early 1980s, I was aghast to hear this powerful and otherwise highly sophisticated man seriously expound at length on how female humans were biologically inferior, because they had only one sex cell as compared to the millions possessed by men! This fact seemed to him to "explain" a lot about women's problems! The women argued, of course, but to no avail.

5 An ego "defense" is detected as evidence of an unconscious process that tries to reduce the anxiety associated with instinctive desires.

Chapter 3

The vanished pregnant body

When women can talk openly about their bodies and what interests them, topics about their own body experiences as adults emerge. Illness and wellness themes abound, including the themes of sex and gender that are intrinsic to their development as females. This means that women begin to talk not just about sex per se, but often about their children, and not just as individuals, but also as the fruits of their bodies.

The general argument of this chapter will be that, for a very long time, the fact of a woman's pregnancy body capability was completely wiped off the slate. I will illustrate this with ancient medical pictures of female body parts depicted as male. Eventually, the concrete realities of female anatomy were elucidated, but the importance and implications of them for both men *and* women were pushed out of awareness. Then psychoanalysis came along and explicitly co-opted women's fantasies—first by Freud into a monolithic male-based scheme of female development, and by Klein, into a monolithic archaic scheme (albeit two-sex), based on alleged "originary" body "phantasy." (Jung and Adler should be included here too, but my spectrum is narrower.) On these bases, we psychoanalysts shifted more into judgmental confusions about the desirable "normal" woman. That era was later exploded by the feminist theorists. The latter trend created other vicissitudes for emerging theory ... and on and on, where the female body keeps getting re-lost. This is the story that I am slowly unfolding, but I ask the reader to be patient with my highways and byways, because the details of some of these moments can be quite arresting. As with psychoanalysis itself, at times the pivotal moments connect with similar ideas, rather than proceeding in an orderly linear chronological fashion.

Analyzing with splits

If a contemporary analyst listens in a way that splits off the sex act from its procreative aspects (and most do these days, for the complex theoretical and sociopolitical reasons unfolded in this book), then his or her interpretations will evoke solely *either* literally a sexual aspect of the person's experience *or* attitudes about the person's children as individuals, or her "mothering." Thus, nowadays, one finds progressive analysts such as Joyce MacDougall, in 2006, making fractionated and inadvertently theoretically dichotomous statements, in her blurb on behalf of an edited book by Alcira Alizade, *Motherhood in the Twenty-First Century*. She says, "Alizade underlines the importance of recognizing that women's psychic organization is *independent* of its maternal function thus implying *necessary dissociation* of femininity from motherhood" (italics mine). Or, we have Daniel Stern's popular concept of a "Motherhood Constellation" (1998), which theoretically splits off an allegedly brand-new mental state called "motherhood" from a woman's sexuality and certainly her mentalized psychohistory of her body. There is widespread confusion even among the most seasoned analysts about "femininity," "sexuality," and "motherhood." This is partly because of the plurality of perspectives that are represented in psychoanalysis. However, these compartmentalizations have occurred in our modern thinking partly to cope with some of the theoretical problems of previous eras. A contemporary therapist can thus easily miss an opportunity to hear connections between a woman's sexual body, its implications to her, and the productions of her sexuality, i.e., her children, by focusing *separately* on talk of her "mothering" as a more "out-there" phenomenon to do with "out-there" children. A therapist can forget that her own and her mother-patient's bodies and interior corporeal memories are constantly taking part in this experience in the office.

Binding these topics of so-called femininity, sexuality, and motherhood together and integrating them can be achieved through considering that the girl/woman's *body* is the common denominator. Her physical body needs to be taken into account in every era of psychological development and psychic elaboration—her sexuality, asexuality, motherhood, or no motherhood, gendered "femininity" or "masculinity" or somewhere in between. All aspects are in dynamic reverberation at all times at some level of consciousness. Deconstructing reactions and ideas about a female patient's body psychoanalytically, should not be confused with our often overdone need to advocate either a necessarily positive or negative view of her physicality (even though our history may be influenced by the still popular 1970s feminist helpmeet, "Our Bodies: Ourselves"!).

Female physicality

The pregnant body—as a psychophysical entity—turns out to be a highly problematic image for both female and male analysts' contemplation. It is so problematic that it has actually been *omitted* in important aspects of theory building to date. Since it seems obvious that this icon of female bodily maturity should be included in a complete discussion of female body image development from cradle to grave, some theoreticians who agree with me suggest that the omission constitutes a persistent "erasure" from the literature (Hoffmann, personal communication 2001). "Erasure" implies that there is both conscious and unconscious motivation in this omission. The word "erasure" also links suggestively to gender politics of the 1970s, and beyond that bears on the role of who is wielding social power in the composition of theories in general. Gender critiques of literary, historical, or scientific texts point to the history of the exclusion, erasure, and other absences of female identity, carried out in relation to social power dynamics (Bordo, 1999); or Freud's erasure of female desire in delineating a unisex "male" libido; or the denial of female representation in the perpetuation of laws of patrilinear descent; or the effects of the ancient struggle to keep the female voice "silenced" (Weisner-Hanks, 1999).

No matter how this crucial omission has come about in our particular psychoanalytic theories, it has kept us from achieving a cohesive theory of how a growing girl develops mental representations in relation to her own body. Using small boys as a basic model for females has failed, not just because it is inaccurate, but because an entire theory of body development over a life cycle cannot be centered on a sporadic childhood fantasy, no matter how important it is to any individual child, or how intense. Horney understood this in the 1920s. Many post-1970 analytic writers have also attested to this flaw in the original Freudian scheme. Phallic body developmental theory for males, while it has other flaws[1] (Corbett, 2011; Lewes, 2009; Fogel, 1996), has nevertheless more potential for cohesion, because from the beginning of psychoanalysis the male biological situation was fully taken into account. This male base can therefore act as a solid foundation to allow for a complicated gender construction to be elaborated as a complex psychic mix of fantasy and subjective reaction to inner and outer experience (Fogel, 1996, for example).

The terminology of the clinical theory graphically demonstrates the depth of body confusion about women that we encounter and collude in maintaining. "Castration complex and anxiety" is cogent for males, because it is a fantasy based on their particular body form. "Castration anxiety"—as commonly used by psychoanalysts to refer to a fantasy about the penis (and sometimes testicles) being cut off—has no cogency for females, because it is not based on a girl's anatomy, as Freud himself allowed (1933). However, Freud's claim that a "castration complex" or masculinity complex was *foundationally* shaping to females' inner lives and their oedipal relations has to be flimsy as a putative cornerstone for any gender theory. It is merely a fantasy construction based on another fantasy. Importantly, it willfully ignores the female's anatomy. Many analysts have known this (Klein, 1928; Chasseguet-Smirgel, 1964; McDougall, 1964), but many have also gone out of their way to grant major normative importance to Freud's so-called "castration complex" (e.g., Deutsch, 1944, and a host of American ego psychologists, as well as Lacanians, Rose, 2005, or Mitchell, 2000). Based on body accuracy, a female "castration complex" would logically either refer to a reaction to fears of castration of *her own* organs (e.g., Quinidoz, 2003), or it would refer to a pathological end of the spectrum of mental possibilities, where the grown female had *an awry* fantasy of having a "penis" in place of a vulva. (The latter imaginative bisexual pluripotentiality, of course, is ubiquitous at the level of early childhood.) These divagations are vital to understanding the psychological details of gender issues. It would help if analysts could establish more of a consensus on such issues.

Some analysts have made logical suggestions in the last few decades. The term "genital anxiety" or "female genital anxiety," for example, has a clear meaning (see Chehrazi, 1986; Bernstein, 1990; Shaw, 1995; Dorsey, 1996; Goldberger 1999). Special varieties of a female "genital anxiety" may then refer to elaborations, which will encompass the complex internal dilemmas, say, where a girl cannot mentally grasp the limits of her own anatomy for lack of maturity, or cannot tolerate or disowns her own genital for other reasons and instead shifts the focus to the male genital as central. Using the latter framework that acknowledges the current terminology to be inherent to a secondary elaboration, "penis envy," or "castration anxiety," or "phallic castration" issues can become comprehensible as female variants of a basic "female genital anxiety." The female's gender elaboration then—the psychological working-over of such fantasies into more stable compromise formations—will be free to express complex mixes, misfires, attempts at, or successful integrations derived from internalization of what she makes of the basic body forms and attitudes of both female and male sexes. Light can therefore be shed clinically on how most adults simultaneously are clear about their sex, as "I am a female" or "I am a male," while simultaneously "performing" (to use Judith Butler's word) her or his gender elaborations in living their lives.

"Pregnancy and motherhood" are commonly treated as one subject in the literature, but I want to differentiate my present topic from this general topic. The actual pregnant body and the way it is mentally represented is not the same as the experience of "pregnancy." Nor is it the same as "motherhood." Since Deutsch's crucial work of the 1940s, there has been an increasing interest by psychoanalytic authors in both pregnancy and motherhood. Schuker and Shwetz (Schuker and Levinson, 1991), introducing their chapter in the annotated bibliography on "pregnancy and motherhood," noted the pioneering work of Bibring (1973) and Benedek (1961) in these areas. Pregnancy is viewed as a normative developmental "crisis" that offers "an opportunity for reworking unresolved conflicts from all phases of development ... to facilitate the transition to motherhood" (p. 239). Papers dealing with "role conflicts, elective abortion, ... miscarriage, infertility" (p. 240) are also summarized in this section on pregnancy and motherhood. The authors note in 1991 that these topics are "still infrequently explored."—even avoided (p. 239). Fortunately, there are more papers these days on such themes, and along with it, there has been much more work on the impact of a therapist's pregnancy upon psychotherapeutic work (e.g., Fenster, Phillips, Rapoport, 2010). A series of three books edited by Alcira Alizade of Argentina (2002, 2003, 2006) represents the work of the committee which she chaired, COWAP (Committee on Women and Psychoanalysis) of the International Psychoanalytic Association) (founded by Joan Raphael-Leff in 1998). This committee studies "sexuality, interactions and relationships between men and women" (2002: p. vii). The papers, in the three volumes about "femininity," "the embodied female," and "motherhood" show the open, questioning discourse that has taken hold in psychoanalysis, and inevitably represent disparate perspectives. The female body and its psychic representations are charted, for example, by Lieberman on stereotypic attitudes to the body, Myers on the menopause, Sellig on a genital aberration, or Raphael-Leff on reproductive technology and egg donation. However, as far as the state of our field — specifically in theories of mind — is concerned, roping off these "women's issues" into loosely linked themes that are contained in the work of a roped-off committee, very valuable as it is, speaks to psychoanalysts' apparent general desire to keep theory about discrete "women's issues" compartmentalized. Books on the theory of transference, for example, expected to be of general interest, likely will have little truck with attitudes about egg donation. Nevertheless, whether or not an analyst has external signs of potential fertility affects how a patient will fantasize about her or him. I am not claiming that (especially) contemporary psychoanalytic colleagues *never* think of the condition and state of mind of "pregnancy," particularly in conjunction with "motherhood." It is the specifics of the bodily details about pregnancy and childbirth, and the attendant fantasies that they give rise to, that have been left on the drawing board, "silenced" or, at best, marginalized.

In their sociocultural history of photographic images that also includes medical images from the late 1800s to the 1990s, Matthews and Wexler (2000) encounter the same suppression that I am talking about, in the field of photography. They were "astonished at the shortage of visual images of a bodily event as fundamental and important as pregnancy" (p. 1).

Vanishing mechanisms

In the rest of this chapter, I will address three themes. First, I will outline a startling historical dimension of the problem, showing that full registration of pregnancy has been elided over many centuries to the point where the female body was depicted as *male* in early anatomical drawings.

I will then review some evidence of how psychoanalytically the pregnant body has been "vanished"—and a few of the implications of this. Finally, I will tackle the anatomical and physiological female body's plasticity of form during development and the girl/woman's experience of it: this is a novel notion that I believe relates to the widely observed difficulty of adult mental integration of the female body image. Inhabiting this plastic body form, I suggest, is part of the sequence of the mental expectation of becoming a woman with the possibility of one day expanding and contracting in accommodating a pregnancy and giving birth. Brief case material will show what I mean. I do not mean to imply at all that body plasticity is the *sole* factor, but plasticity of form introduces a more psychophysiologically mobile body image than those we are used to thinking about. One reader of this chapter commented (aptly, I thought) that it seemed like a leap into calculus from the more static algebra!

The early anatomical history of the vanished pregnant body in medicine

I would like the reader to look at these sixteenth-century drawings. The first one (Figure 3.1) is by Vesalius, 1538, and it shows the first anatomical drawings of the (male) medical profession's vision of the female body, dating from the sixteenth century.[2] Figure 3.1 is taken from Thomas Laqueur's 1990 book *Making Sex: Body and Gender from the Greeks to Freud*. Figures 3.2 and 3.3 are taken from Rudolph Bell's 1999 book *How to Do It: Guides to Good Living for Renaissance Italians*.

Note that, even with the visual aid of a cadaver, the anatomy of the female is portrayed by the male illustrator as basically male. This is apparently the most reprinted image of the vagina being portrayed as a penis. The uterus is depicted and described as an inverted scrotal sac.

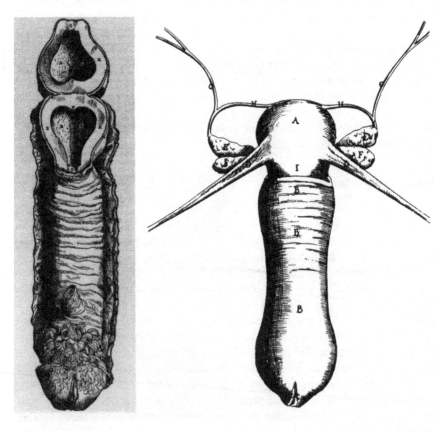

Figure 3.1 (left): "Vagina as penis" from Andreas Vesalius, *Fabrica* (1543), and (right): "The vagina and uterus" from Vidus Vidius, *De Anatome corporis humani* (1611) "De Humani Corporis Fabrica Libri Septem", and "De Humani Corporis Fabrica Librorum Epitome" (1543).

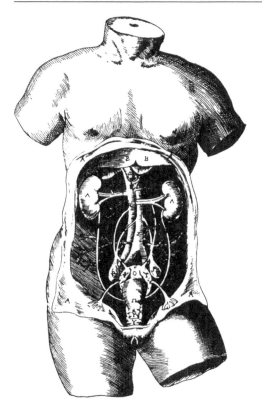

Figure 3.2 The female torso, in the form of a piece of broken classical art from which Figure 3.1 was taken.

By this time in the Renaissance, dissection of the human body was openly permitted, but it was still relatively new. Nevertheless, the drawings are particularly peculiar when one thinks of the doctors' familiarity of looking at and palpating female anatomy in its most distensible state in attending to childbirths, even if they had never dissected a dead female body. They knew somewhere that the vaginal cavity is not perfectly the size of an erect penis, and that no penis could expand so. Such data might suggest that it was a different organ! Laqueur's explication of the penis/vagina drawing is sociocultural. He shows that the anatomical representation of male and female was dependent on the cultural politics of representation and illusion. Laqueur also states that he does not think that it testifies to a blindness or inattention on the part of Renaissance anatomists, but rather an imperative to create images of male and female within the language— the only genital language till the eighteenth century being male. Psychoanalysts, intrigued by unconscious motivation, might infer powerful internal anxieties on the part of the males who created these pictures. Presumably, for example, these drawings support the male's belief that orgasm can be generated only by a phallic mechanism (the "vaginal" canal in the picture), and that an internal empty

LIBRO PRIMO.   33

Sito del parto naturale, nel quale naſcono coſi i maſchi, come le femine per lo più.

C   *Del*

Figure 3.3 Normal birth position, facing the mother's rear, for both boys and girls. From *La Commare* (Venice, 1601) by Girolamo Mercurio.

scrotum (the "uterus" in the picture) became filled up with a baby. From the second century teachings of the Greek Galen onward, of course, women's anatomy was said to "lack perfection"; the theory was that because female embryos were too cold, they "retained" the male structures within, instead of extruding them in proper male fashion. That is, women were inside-out men. That theory developed before dissection was permitted, but interestingly it lingered, as an example of how one can become misled by trying too hard to fit one's observations to an established theory.

The preceding phenomena of anatomical distortion are also present in Figures 3.2 and 3.3.[3] These drawings are odd female forms, "objectively" rendered by the artists. Among other things, these *static visual* representations of the female body seem to highlight the makers' psychic resistance to its imagined mobility and functions.

To the anatomists (and to the colluding populace), male parts alone were essential for the orgasm necessary for the production of a consciously longed-for, but unconsciously dreaded, female pregnancy. These anatomists seemed to imagine a baby being born via an "internal penis". This distortion could be an elaborated form of the psychoanalytic male fantasy of a "phallic woman"—a fantasy that implies a reactive unconscious anxiety about seeing the female as having a "castrated" genital. Surely, massive anxiety about pregnancy and childbirth, given the miniscule birth canal granted to the female in depiction as a male urethra, rather than a more focused anxiety about the female genitals alone, may inform these pictures. One might infer visual evidence for splitting as a defense, where these men both "knew" (from their sensual proprioceptive evidence of sexual intercourse, and also from obstetric experiences) and "did not know" (as shown in the limits of their figurative representational skills).

Vanishing psychoanalytic ideas

Over centuries of philosophy and science, "male reason's" dominance over "female irrational" elements has been read into human nature. There is distaste for what is thought "irrational" (e.g., Lloyd, 1984; Balsam, 1994). The study of medicine has often been party to this philosophy (Fox-Keller and Longino, 1996, and many others). A pregnancy might be viewed as female/inferior/irrational, being that most earthy of states, a symbol of woman as "body" to the man's "mind," the fruit of guilt-laden sexual intercourse, the result of unseen meshing of ungovernable genetic codes. Even modern psychoanalytic clinical observations could be thus unwittingly affected, so that the pregnancy remains invisible in theory (or marginalized and bracketed) in spite of the blatant presence and visual command of any pregnant woman who walks into a room of children and their richly evoked fantasies.

The history of the medical vision of the female body suggests a speculation on an abiding tendency in Western culture—in both men *and* women—the need to distort the female bodily configuration while making theories. My own speculations about how this may come about involve universal unconscious fears of *pregnancy* that are held by *both* men and women. This differs from the usual psychoanalytic view that the primary confusion about the anatomical distinction between the sexes resides in concerns about phallic primacy (for both sexes—in their castration anxiety). We may not need to choose between the biological male or the biological female, because major fears appear to involve both/and rather than either/or.

Early anatomists' view of the female

Thomas Laqueur is a contemporary historian from Berkeley who spent a year in medical school learning about the body through anatomical dissection. His father was a pathologist and had allowed his young son to accompany him in the morgue. Laqueur began to research the history of female orgasm. He reports that from the fifth century to the Age of Enlightenment, it was popularly believed that conception could not take place without orgasm—that "apart from pleasure nothing of mortal kind comes into existence" (1990: p. 3). Every medical and other effort was therefore made to help women achieve orgasm. Frigidity was consciously feared by both men and women, and in fact fantasies about voracious female sexual appetites seem to have been consciously greatly exaggerated, presumably as a way of advertising the desirability of a fertile woman. Orgasm and erotic play were at the forefront of activity up till the eighteenth century, when, regrettably for women, it dawned on the medical profession (and others) that it was possible to become pregnant without experiencing sexual pleasure (see, e.g., the difficulty in psychoanalysis with theorizing female body pleasure that I discussed in Chapter 2, or Kulish and Holtzman, 2008). For the purposes of my argument, I would like to underline again that *fertility and the capability of the female to become pregnant* seem to have been the actual engine that powered medical and social interest, even when it appeared on the surface that female eroticism was the prime locus of attention. The need to create a pregnancy was front and center as it were.

Laqueur's 1990 study shows how deeply the "scientific objectivity" of medical science has been affected by sociocultural and politically driven phallocentric attitudes toward women. Though this is not Laqueur's interest, the psychology of the scientists' internal climates likely contributed to these distortions, as they sincerely and meticulously recorded on paper their findings for the medical profession that were passed on from one century to the next. The concrete implications are startling. Laqueur describes a "one-sex" theory, which existed for thousands of years from Aristotle and Galen through the end of the eighteenth century and beyond, where the female genital was actually "seen" as a male organ. He also shows how Freud, being a doctor, naturally evolved within the traditions of this scientific medical milieu. The one-sex theory refers in early analytic theory to the notion that libido is male, or that the girl is a little boy, or to Freud's notion of the necessity for a woman to abandon her clitoris and exchange her wish for a penis into a baby, for example. Freud, possibly medically also abreast of the discovery of hormones in the 1930s, later moved slightly more toward a "two-sex" theory where a female was not an exact mirror image of a male. (However, the notion of a baby as a substitute penis was retained in psychoanalysts' normative developmental scheme for women.)

One-sex fantasies, two-sex fantasies, and possible merger fantasies

Clearly, it is unwise to impose a modern sensibility upon medieval life and claim certainties that are historically unwarranted. However, on the grounds of a shared engagement that we moderns have with past would-be healers in the task of trying to understand, interpret, and treat others, I will risk here some psychoanalytic speculation about the apparent blindness of these medical people. The confusions of the anatomical text may suggest possible merger phenomena between the observer and the observed, fueled by the anxious impact of the apparently taboo act of actually *looking at* as opposed to just theorizing about the sexual and child-producing parts of the female body, to do these first drawings. To appreciate the intensity of this taboo, one would also need to factor in the elevating and terrorizing power of the medieval Christian Church's teachings on sex and gender; its view of the dissection of (especially the female) cadaver; and its attitude of mixed dread and titillation about the exposure of forbidden secrets to which God alone should be privy (Kemp and Wallace, 2000).

During the pre-Enlightenment era, Laqueur says, along with the popularity of equal-opportunity orgasm, there existed a physiological theory of "the fungibility of fluids." All body fluids, male and female, arose from a single source, blood. Blood could turn to semen or milk interchangeably. This suggests an unconscious fantasy of merger to one-ness. From clinical psychoanalysis, we know that merger fantasies can occur as an attempt to obliterate an overwhelming unconscious anxiety generated by some aspect of separateness. Anxiety about looking at and learning the functions of the female body may have contributed to a male coping device in perceiving the female as blended with him, in order to reduce the anxiety of her otherness. For the male who holds the pen, to draw a woman as an inside-out man suggests at least anxiety about sexual intercourse. It also may suggest possible terror about how a baby can pass through the birth canal. The depiction of uterus as scrotum seems the product of a possessive fantasy to gain control over the female organ. If "he" controls it by possession, then it is "his," and "she" need not exist on "her" own count. Omission or erasure can thus occur in the picture. "He" controls m/other. Such fantasies and desires have an oral or anal cast that echo the social versions in which woman is chattel of man. In Mahlerian separation–individuation terms, we recognize the archaic bases for these fantasies within the separation anxieties of the early child–mother interaction.

Babies were born all the time in the sixteenth century. The birth canal could be observed and palpated by doctors and midwives. It did not require dissection of a cadaver to see the anatomy in its function. These men were superb artists. They were delivering babies and having sexual intercourse with women. They were adults in full consciousness directly scrutinizing women's bodies for the express purpose of making careful drawings meant to inform and factually enlighten others who were working medically with females. Their frank and direct access to female bodies makes this demonstration of the one-sex principle more graphic and compelling than it would be in the more intellectually distant texts of, say, philosophers.

Dissent from the one-sex theory

Janet Adelman (1999) refutes Laqueur's claim to the lingering Galenic one-sex theory of the Middle Ages. The late Shakespearean literary critic asserted, "A random sampling of those who have assumed the hegemony of the one-sex model reads like a Who's Who of prominent ... Renaissance literary critics" (p. 43). She provides evidence that there were then other attitudes about sex and gender abroad too—for example, an English manual called "*The Byrth of Mankynde,*" from 1612 by a Thomas Raynold, whom she avers, "when he looks at the uterus ... does not see a defective or inverted penis: he sees an organ perfect in its own kind" (p. 35). "When Raynold writes about the congruence between male and female sexual parts, he does so not in the service of an argument about homology but in the service of an argument about function. ... in Galenic terms ... if the neck of the womb is the penis inside-out, then the two should be roughly the same length. But Raynold reads this similarity ... as evidence of nature's wise management of ... generative function." Continuing my own psychoanalytic take on the situation, we might infer that Raynold had less anxiety about sexual difference than the medical illustrators whose work I have displayed earlier. He further argues, quoting from Adelman, "...nether is woman to be called (as some do) unperfecter than man in his kind" (p. 33). He is able to apply his cognition with less interference from ego splitting. However, when it comes to men with "woman like" qualities, his attitudes become excoriating and denigrating, as Adelman shows us. She admits that, for him, "admiring women is clearly not without its attendant anxieties" (p. 34). He sees himself in opposition to his predecessors and contemporaries such as medieval Churchmen like Albertus Magnus. These men were, as Laqueur pointed out, much influenced by upholding the foundational misogyny of Aristotle (see, e.g., Kodera, 2010).

From a psychoanalytic vantage point, invoking the idea of the unconscious (which is not of interest to Laqueur), one could see Laqueur's evidence as a powerful and strong *tendency* to resort to a primitive mode of coping with the female body which seems to have held sway. It need not be absolute. Adelman's case for influential exceptions portrays her authors also as being intensely burdened with anxieties about the sexual differences, while their *tendency is* to be defensively positive about female bodies.

Until notions of unconscious thought are invoked, Adelman and Laqueur appear to be on opposite sides. From a more clinical psychoanalytic vantage, however, they seem to be noting the same underlying conflicts and attendant anxieties in the expositors concerning sex and gender that manifest themselves in either a strong adherence to a one-sex theory, or the need to battle against it. The two opposing sides take the measure of a deep ambivalence that is connected in turn to the phenomenon of "knowing" and "not knowing"—a general state that I contend still clings to our own theory (albeit in a diluted way, compared to the Renaissance and tempered by increased scientific knowledge) right into the twenty-first century.

Freud and pregnancy

Freud waxed and waned, as it were, on the issue. There are about 30 references to "pregnancy" in his 23 volumes of work. (This is about a quarter of a column in the index, compared say to "masturbation," which commands two columns of reference.) Freud (1918) was, of course, aware of the taboo of pregnancy, and lists it without privileging it amongst the other horrors for males who encounter the mature female body. He says, "primitive man ... fears some danger ... [a] dread based on the fact that woman is different from man, for ever incomprehensible and mysterious, strange and therefore apparently hostile" (p. 198). The paragraph ends prophetically, "In all this there is nothing obsolete, nothing which is not still alive among ourselves" (p. 199). I will treat here Freud's contribution to the subject only minimally because of concerns about focus.

The most body-based paper I believe that Freud ever wrote with excited curiosity and exploratory openness was the "Three Essays on Sexuality" (1905). There, he points to the component instincts and the infantile drive for deriving bodily pleasure by physical exploration of the erotogenic zones and body parts. He speaks of the child's pluripotential sexuality and his "Riddle of the Sphinx" as the abiding question of all humans, "Where do babies come from?" The reaction to an *actual* pregnant mother, however, he strangely elides, even as he seems to me to be asking *the* central question. He says: "Children also perceive the alterations that take place in their mother owing to pregnancy and are able to interpret them correctly" (p. 197). How suddenly strange! This is a curt and strangely foreclosing statement. It suggests to me a cognitive Freud who has suppressed his capacity for dwelling on the sights of and curiosity about the pregnant body. Freud's imagined child "sees" only in his mind's eye or otherwise imaginatively intuits an infant within the large body. By *looking past the body* itself to the "truth" in the form of the baby hidden inside, the famous Riddle of the Sphinx may seem cognitively solved to a child or to a grown-up in denial. Freud's child's information gathering is incomplete without a visual and affective reaction to the swollen belly and its immensity.

In the "Three Essays," the genital organs themselves, mouth, anus, thumb, childhood fantasies of conception, and birth fantasies hold center stage. Yet, even in Freud's most earthy, passionate, and physically explicit developmental exposition, girls' and boys' reaction to the mother's body in its massively altered pregnant state remains almost imperceptible.

Newton (1995) calculates that when the 41-year-old Freud writes to Fleiss about how his "libido toward *matrem was* awakened ... seeing her *nudam*" (p. 40), and therefore records for posterity his first sexualized glimpse of his mother, the incident must have occurred during the winter of 1859–1860. Little Sigismund was then three-and-a-half years old, and traveling by train from Leipzig to Vienna. His nude mother at the time must have been heavily pregnant with Rosa, the fourth child. The adult Freud only remembers *something* sexual, but fails to mention to Fleiss her body condition and its gravid metamorphosis—which may tend to support my thesis concerning his unconscious anxiety about the sight and about pregnancy in general. During his self-analysis in 1897, he also wrote to Fleiss about the long-standing puzzle about a memory, which revealed itself as a repressed memory that surrounded a suspicion of his mother's pregnancy and her absence during the birth of his sister Anna, the third child (Gay, 1988: p. 7). In childhood, Freud was certainly surrounded by pregnancies up to the age of 10, his mother having seven more children besides him. Much more detail of his sporadic references could be examined, but suffice to say here that it is possible that if he had anxiety, there was good cause.

In the case of Little Hans, Freud (1909) does attend some to the mother's pregnancy and childbirth. Hostility against the new arrival was well noted, as is usually the case when pregnancy is the subject. The understanding of procreation was male-directed: "With your big penis you 'bored' me and put me in my mother's womb" (p. 128). Freud is admirably sensitive to all kinds of metaphoric references to Hans's body preoccupations that involve his conscious and unconscious concerns with pregnancy and childbirth; for example, "The falling horse was not only his dying father but also his mother in childbirth" (p. 128). However, few comments or interpretations involve direct reference to Frau Graf's body. If one reads the text asking oneself, "What details are developed here about Frau Graf's pregnant body—considering the child had observed, handled her pregnant body and regularly "coaxed" with her in bed—and what was elicited about the recorded events of the bloody childbirth that Hans had witnessed, according to the vivid narrative?", one does become aware of the lens through which the boy's experience is appreciated. The connections made by Freud and the father are brilliant, enlightened for the time, unobjectionable but limited. They are mainly the fantasy fate of Hans's own penis; his erotic masturbatory fantasies; his fear of his father because of his love for mother and his wish to possess her sexually; and his body theories of childbirth as his own anality. An explanation of a child coming out of a woman's body as "lumpf" is one based on the boy's own body. (For the theory's sake, I am just situating the sexed and gendered body status of this explanation.) Hans's wish to imitate the care giving of his mother is the only direct reference to mother where the mother forms the center of the interpretation. The primacy of Hans's own maleness holds sway and any, say, perceived deficiency of his body (e.g. his often mentioned smallness) in relation the mother's actual physicality is absent in the text. The dates are unclear, but, for example, it may well have been due to the sight of his heavily pregnant mother that Hans postulated that she was "so big" she would have a "widdler like a horse." Hans *did* express desires for the men in the story to deliver babies too (see later articles), but this interpretive slant requires an ability to shift without bias between male and female body imagery. Freud, as is frequent, records meticulously material that is not centrally used in the argument at hand, but only later emerges in the development of his theory, as it becomes available to contemplate. Hans's "pregnant" preoccupations are a good example.

I think that Frau Graf did not mislead Hans in saying that she had a "widdler" (p. 7). I gather that "wiwimacher" in the German refers only to an organ for micturition. It is a word that can apparently be applied to either sex.[4] The little boy understandably thought only about the organ he knew best—his own penis. A less concrete mother, even in that era, might have grasped his desire to compare genitals and thus display his underlying confusion to her. That boy's perplexity about the mother's genital remains the main point of the story, regardless of how the word is translated. If "wiwimacher" is not specific to the penis, Frau Graf seems to have been thinking straightforwardly about her own body openings and was merely answering directly the question asked. A mother can urinate too! It was perhaps Freud and the father who inadvertently added to Hans's confusion in this detail, even though, side-by-side (showing his conflicts in these matters), Freud is very much on the side of promoting a child's anatomical education about the vagina and copulation (p. 145).

Later authors have indeed drawn attention to Hans's preoccupation with the feminine (e.g., Silverman, 1980, Ross, 1987, Frankiel, 1992). Freud, who did not elucidate the negative oedipal complex until 14 more years had gone by, did, however, offer a comment in a footnote here that would seem to indicate an arbitrary (if temporary) closure to the openness he had demonstrated earlier in his *Three Essays*—"There is no necessity on this account to assume in Hans the presence of a feminine strain of desire for children" (p. 93). An intriguing disavowal. It is strikingly similar in quality to his foreclosing moment recounted earlier about the mother's pregnancy in *The Three Essays*.

The continuing omission of the pregnant body

It is now fully documented that males and females have separate lines of development. Tyson and Tyson (1990) is one text that summarizes and frames much post-Freudian work in this area. Notman (1996) also states the situation simply: "The experiences and endowment of the girl are ... inevitably different than those of a boy. One component of the girl's experience derives from having a female body." Even though this statement seems so obvious, has the integrity of lay commonsense, and is by now consciously accepted by all but a few psychoanalysts, psychoanalysis still has much more to explore and contribute to this particular knowledge from the inner vantage point. Little attention has been paid, for example, in the child analytic literature to the growing girl's mental representations of self and other as they involve her vision, kinesthetic sense, and touch of the mother's body, especially of the adult woman's pregnant body, which a girl child inevitably will relate in fantasy to her own body and its future.

Elsewhere, I have derived questions, clinical theory, and clinical evidence from far more adult analyses and psychotherapies than I can report and publish, concerning patients' mothers' pregnancies. These women patient's latent *physical capacity to become pregnant* (what in medicine is known as her potential "secondary sex characteristics," or her physically mature body) seems to have registered in her *earliest* fantasy and body memories, and to affect all of her bodily experience as she grew from being a little girl who was first reactive to the bodies of adult females around her (Balsam, 1996, 2000, 2001). Psychoanalytic literature, reflecting the surrounding culture, has too often mired itself in generalizations and moral values concerning how "truly feminine" women "ought" to be as a group, and paraded these judgments as "facts" (Elise, 1997, and others). A developing girl's or woman's free fantasies about her biological self can be fruitfully separated from (1) claims that these are in any way essential to "motherhood"—that is, to an identity that evolves in relation only to actually having a child, or (2) a claim to an originary essential "maternal instinct," or (3) any social necessity to bear children. Confusions rationalized on biopsychological and social grounds—such as the open belief of many past and a few contemporary psychoanalysts (such as De Marneffe, 2004), and the covert belief of some moderns, that a woman could scarcely be fulfilled without bearing a child—have been rightly and widely shunned in gender studies and repudiated as "essentialism" (Chodorow, 1978,1994). The theoretic psychological elaboration of the body apparatus can be freed from a moralistic essentialism.

Children use adults of both sexes and genders to aid them in their fantasies about, and their ultimate discovery of, the futures that await them. The analytic literature is full of accounts of how females react to the male bodies in the surroundings. Females reacting to other females is less common. Same-sex sibling body interactions—boy-to-boy, and girl-to-girl—have gained the least attention (Kuba, 2011; Mitchell, 2001). Psychoanalysts know most about children's reactions to the bracketed male or female genitals. This fact of our theoretical life is deeply informed by, but is not solely a result of, Freud's original if skewed vision of female development. Freud's genital vision, though, is in a way in tune with the general populace. In all cultures, from the moment of birth, the genital is the defining anatomical differentiator to tell male from female. Stoller (1968), first suggested that a "core gender identity" is initiated at birth on behalf of the child by the adults, whose visual perception of the baby's genitals determine the sex, and therefore begin to set in motion the child's mental registration and perception of herself. He also says, "... gender identity implies psychologically motivated behavior" (Stoller, 1985: p. 10); therefore, the concept of gender encodes not only the sex biology but also the psychological development of the individual. Ultimately, development will be processed internally to yield individual positions somewhere along a spectrum of psychosexualities—in the plural (Chodorow, 1994).

Throughout analytic literature, the vagina, clitoris, the strains of puberty, sexual intercourse, the many meanings of love, and the role of the early mother have commanded most of the attention to women. However, the *specific* capacity to become pregnant and give birth, as well as the pregnant body itself, has been curiously missing here, though it actually may be the most important icon of all.

Consider pregnancy. The living belly of gigantic proportions, containing mysterious new life within, is at least as arresting as the psychoanalytic legends of the erect phallus, the storied "castrated" vagina and its "dentate," the female child's "lacking" flat pubis, or even the archetypal "bad" and "good" breasts, and the womb packed with hordes of fantasy foeti. The pregnant body of a grown woman is for little girls an awesome glimpse of the future. Girls frequently envision adulthood as "being a mommy." This is usually taken as a reference to a mentalized identification with the *caretaking* aspects of the mother. (There are multiple well-delineated examples of this in child literature, side-by-side with random samples of case histories that show a marked tendency to pass over entirely specific female pregnant-body fantasies in little girls.) Yet, children probably mean something more—something about their bodies too—when they make such statements. Nevertheless, we have to listen for them specifically.

Pregnancy per se has not captured a focus in the original drive-based theory, in object-oriented theories, the post-1970s self-psychological, or the intersubjective theories. In Klein's theories, a response to adult pregnancy is not privileged as a harbinger of the body upheavals of things to come for a girl. The mother's womb, looking right into her pelvis as if by x-ray, is utilized by Klein as a focus of originary fantasy concerning baby production, a site of archaic massive aggressions against the maternal object, the stimulus for envy, guilt, reparation, etc. However, Klein in no way privileges pregnancy as especially significant among any of the body phantasy phenomena such as breasts, "internal phallus," vagina, anal and oral cavities, or the conjoined parents in the act of sexual intercourse. In some way, the playing field of these phantasies is flat when it comes to her sense of individual functional bodies.

The pregnant body would seem to find a natural place in the structural theory, which claims as axiom, "The ego is first and foremost a body ego." Yet, "the body" in the structural theory has been eclipsed by the genitals. The American ego psychological theorists, more interested in establishing and defending psychoanalysis as "science," and being more interested in trying to fit in gender to generalizable metapsychological theory, have not been enough troubled by the phallocentric bias. Women in analysis in the 1970s objected to being formulated in male terms (Richards, 1999, among others), but the field at the time remained largely unquestioning about the terms of the theoretical understanding or the terminology of the psychosexual phases of the original instinct theory. Anna Freud was very helpful to actual mothers, as they coped with children, and to children as they coped with a new baby, but she was neither especially focused on the female body nor in eliciting a child's responses about the pregnancy in corporeal terms. Miss Freud accepted her father's phallic developmental formulae for women, as did her followers and admirers. Analysts who were very influenced by Anna Freud, and also by the American ego psychologists such as Greenacre (say, 1950), were especially interested in the trying to map the tiny girl's pre-oedipal era to emphasize female development in relation to the mother, but there is not much said there about the little girl's comparative take on this large, fecund mother per se. The political clash between the Kleinians and the Anna Freudians in the 1941–1945 London "Controversial Discussions" was sorted out into amicable territories under one umbrella for educational purposes with analytic trainees. However, a sharp division in written articles still exists between Kleinians, who have been more comfortable with the idea of female qua female, and the Anna Freudians, loyal to the father and retaining the female-qua-male primacy (Sayers, 1989). To this day, the contemporary Kleinians and the contemporary Freudians rarely quote the work of the other in their respective bibliographies. The self-psychologists tend to quote each other also. And now, a reader notes that the American relationists, who earlier had the best reputation for bibliographical cross-fertilization in their journal *Psychoanalytic Dialogues*, increasingly seem to confine their bibliographies to their own school. (I too regretfully am not immune from this criticism.) Especially the female body, never well secured in theory even by Freud's interests, tends to fall further and further away among the cracks and divisions of all the schools of psychoanalysis.

The changing forms of pregnancy: a suggestion about body confusion

A significant source of deep anxiety about the female body may be derived from its *plasticity*, and the experience of the notable instability of its form throughout the life cycle. Sometimes the shifts are subtle: due to hormones and fluid balance regulation during the menses, for example, or weight gain and loss, or the engorgements and deflatements of sexual excitement. Sometimes the shifts are far from subtle, as in the growth of breasts and hips at puberty, the weight gain of pregnancy, the larger or smaller body forms of menopause, or the rapid changes after birth when the breasts fill out for feeding and then empty again. Each external shift reflects shifting internal states that engage images and mental representations of the whole body, and not just the genitals. Simple examples are when small women describe themselves as "huge," or thin women feel "flat," when they do not have much breast tissue. Obviously, the climate of psychic reality is what is most determining in the description. Perceptions of the dimensional shifts lead also to thoughts about the body's function, and internal dynamic representations of how organs work and what their purpose is. All of these physical registrations are open to fantasies that in turn affect the description. Both women and men respond to the shifting shapes of the female body and tend to distort its configuration, apparently more than with the male body. Here are some clinical explorations of what I have come to think of as *the relationship of psychoanatomy to psychophysiology*.

Case example

I will take a narrow view of this case, limiting myself to the patient's preoccupations with the changing forms and shapes of her various body parts. I want to show how this female body plasticity emerges often in the patient's associations with references to pregnancy. This is a case in which anxiety can be seen, but not a real dread of pregnancy. The patient's illumination of these anxieties' significance as representing aspects of the building blocks of her body image as a whole will be the focus of the parts of her story that I tell. The purpose of the material is to demonstrate that it is not her genitals alone that assume importance for her body image. In addition, she tells about her reactions to her mother's pregnancy and its impact on her growth fantasies. As my purpose here is to extend the reader's interest in the history and dynamics of body image, I will not comment on my own analytic technique, countertransferences, etc.

Ms DE, a 50-year-old married woman with two grown-up children, came into analysis because she was feeling restricted in her creative work.

Shortly after we began, she lay on my couch, holding up her hands for our mutual inspection as she quietly talked. The afternoon sunlight glinted on a simple gold ring, dotted with tiny chips of diamonds. She wore it on the middle finger of her right hand. A wedding band of thick gold was on her left. They were well-used working hands. A few joints were thickened. One thumbnail was ridged and irregular, betraying the scars of an old nail-biting habit. The rest of the fingers were tapered into unpolished newly manicured points. The skin was soft with a few age spots, the freckles of sun damage.

"My mother always said, 'What beautiful hands you're blessed with!' She'd put her large square hands in mine and say mine were lovely, so artistic, so soft and white. She'd worked in factories all her life... I still love my hands, in spite of the arthritis and the age spots. When I bit my nails short I knew they'd grow again. Isn't it odd that mother's appreciation in the end is still what makes them lovely to me?"

It was her internalized mother's view that lingered over the passage of time, more enduring than the external world that shaped her hands from her internal gaze. In that moment, she was inviting me to caress her hands through her mother's eyes. "This ring was hers," she said, and I knew before she told me. It was as precious to her as the crown jewels, a talisman of her mother's love for this part of her body, the seamless circle of treasured attachment.

In the transference at that moment, I was blended with her appreciative mother. The mother had gladly given her ownership of her own hands; a compliment borne out of intimate visual and tactile comparison, accepting of difference and without apology for her own factory-worn hands. It expressed a primal pleasure in giving her daughter life, but a life with difference, a life tinged with her own yearned-for ideals, a life of more ease with more avenues of expression of her artistic talent. The patient expressed no urgency to compete with others for the most gorgeous hands in the world. Her mother's reaction to her was a psychological gift tailored like an elegant glove to the hands entwined in hers, in this tender moment.

This clinical moment seemed to me a window into the creation of a building block of substantial and positive self-regard for a body part. Attending to remarks about the periphery of the body as a window for exploring encoded internal perception, and as a route to unconscious fantasy lends renewed interest to separate body parts as they may relate to a whole configuration, in what is registered as an asset or a liability and how it also becomes gendered. It therefore becomes more problematic to make global statements such as, "The patient turned away from her femininity," or, as was frequent in the older writings, to conceptualize a woman's ambition to work outside the home as necessarily "masculine." This analysand, for example, was a highly successful graphic designer. She put these valued hands to work, as had her mother before her, but in a professional context, as it were with the mother's blessing, for the making of a work identity. She elaborated later an unconscious fantasy about my holding her hands from time to time, in conjunction with the wish to create together, and in association with a desire to have a baby with mother/analyst. This was a recognizable pre-oedipal derivative of earliest female-to-female experience.

Early in the analysis, the patient talked of other parts of her body. "Mother didn't say much about my rear end!" she laughed. "And I know she didn't like my hair. She liked short, permed bobs, and I always wore mine in a full dark fuzz all over my shoulders." She'd say, "Take your hair out of your eyes! I can't see your face. You're like an owl looking out of an ivy bush!" "I wanted to hide from her at times. I think she worried that I was trying to be too sexy, especially in adolescence."

Later in the transference, this woman often compared her body shape to mine. One day, she saw me bending over from behind, picking up a book off the floor as she entered the room. Shyly, she hesitatingly told me of a sense of relief that I had a big fanny too, like hers. She had been aware in retrospect that she had avoided looking at me from the back during the entire previous 2 years. Nevertheless, while walking in her world outside, she confessed, she always glanced at women's backsides. After addressing her hesitancy and guilt about the desire to look at me, she spoke of the meanings. My large rear end in her view meant to her that I "knew" what it was like to be pregnant. The dread of seeing my contours, despite her overwhelming curiosity, was connected to a fear that I might have a thin, small rear—a sign, she feared, that I would disapprove of her sexualized preoccupations. In the too-thin version, I was the thin "forbidding" mother of her adolescence. Fat fannies led to images of her mother's body when mother was pregnant with her sister, when the patient was three. Her mother had complained of putting on weight then. In further exploration, it was not really a fixed image of a female big backside that my patient sought as she perused other women. Preconsciously, she was actually looking anxiously for shift and change in the body contour. Backsides that could swell and get thin again were her focus. She remembered then her 3-year-old's view of the wobbling mounds of flesh that were her mother's buttocks. These seemed to match the swelling breasts that became like melons in front. In associating to a dream about an elephant in the zoo, she recalled the huge abdomen of the pregnancy. Anger in the transference that I was "pushing" her away because of an unexpected absence, helped her recall angry feelings of mother pushing her off her knee at what was probably the height of the pregnancy. This felt like a sudden change too, because her mother was generally affectionate. Growing bulges and bumps of the body, and anxiety and anger about anticipated negative shifts of affect in loved women were for her all in conjoint association. The patterns were discernible as transference neurosis, circling around the time of mother's pregnancy, and also detectable in her life outside.

As she expressed all her fears of changing body shapes and moods, her graphic design became more abstract and adventurous. Her work inhibition was relieved.

Analysis is not a linear process, as we know. This patient developed paternal transferences to me and themes about her father's body and sexuality, which she wove in and out of her concerns about the maternal swelling and subsequent flatness after delivery. Although, in general, she liked lovemaking with her husband, she was reticent to begin foreplay, and she was curious about this. Considerable anxiety emerged about the sight of his erection emerging, and his subsequent detumescence. She preferred to have intercourse in the dark. "Once he's inside me, I'm fine. I can really let myself go as long as the lights are out." This meant that she would be protected from the exciting and anxiety-provoking visual cues regarding his penis growing large and then changing dimension. The concerns about his penis growing large led to associations about her father's penis, about her parents "going at each other" in the dark," "the beast with two backs" under the sheets, and her own masturbation fantasy at night as she lay in her room down the hallway. Sexual arousal made her genitals and body feel sensations of swelling and changing. One fearful and exciting fantasy was that she could swell up like Alice in *Alice in Wonderland*, and end up towering over everyone in a frightening way. The fantasy became so uncomfortable that she stopped masturbating in latency to get rid of it. The Alice fantasy recurred in adolescence, when she resumed. This time a section was added where Alice returned to ordinary size. As a teenager, the sequence was no longer frightening.

The construction of this fantasy was based on compromise formations, involving perceptions and mental pictures of her own sexual arousal, admixed with partial elements of wishes and fears from the primal scene fantasy, visions and responses to the penis as a part-object, and also, importantly, responses to sexualized registration of her mother's pregnant state. Young DE was utilizing this creation, among other things, to master her anxieties about body parts of each sex changing shapes.

Her long bushy hair had a different significance. It had been the focus of pubescent fights with her mother to "Stay out of my hair!" Her mother had short hair. Her father admired short hair. The young girl wanted something to mark an unmistakable difference to mother, in part to help curb her homoerotic attachment. No one in her family had hair like hers. It signaled, "I will grow in my own way." She could master her fear of uncontrollable change by deciding when, where, and how she wanted it trimmed. She needed to test out for herself the autonomous surrender to her own physicality, to see for herself if ungovernable forces in her nature could turn her into an Alice. Once, she let it grow for several years in adolescence, and was delighted that it slowed down of its own accord. By that time, she knew well that her limbs would not grow endlessly till she hit the roof, like Alice. If there was a classically described "phallic" significance to her hair, and "castration anxiety" about getting it cut, I missed it. Her mother in this regard did not seem to DE to be a "castrate" with her short hair. She referred to my short hair in terms of a possible womanly envy that she hoped for, and thought that I might have, toward her abundant crowning glory. The endowment of lovely hair seemed presented to me as a body asset of which she was proud, and which made her attractive to men.

Much more could be said about her reactions to her menses, and subsequently to the pregnancies and deliveries of her two children. However, I think I have made my point. Every aspect of the possession of her waxing and waning female body was deeply and importantly interwoven with the body of her own mother. The male body was important too in its capacity to wax and wane; but DE's chief body preoccupation lay with her mother's expanding and contracting body. Often when a female patient such as this is described as in close internal connection with the mother, the summary phrase used is, "fixation on the mother," as if that state must be "gotten over" before a female can progress to an oedipal stage, and the eventual ability to enjoy sexuality with a man. Undoubtedly, this linearity can be discovered in a given case, but insistence on a rigid oedipally progressive theoretical system may also serve to restrict our explorations about the vital nature of female-to-female connection in the growth of a girl. This woman was, in fact, more heterosexually than homosexually inclined. Her sexual object choice was male. DE was understood by me to be in a close inner dialogue with her mother and yet simultaneously satisfactorily involved with males. She was capable of triangulation in her object relations. The so-called "pre-oedipal" and "oedipal" unfolding here to me seemed on a par.

Discussion

This patient seems fairly typical of many adult women whom I have analyzed, who are as deeply concerned, if not more, with the bodies (and personalities and minds) of their mothers and sisters, as they are with those of their fathers and brothers. The experience of having a pregnant mother is especially prominent as building elements of a female body image. There is a puzzle about how girl children in the analytic literature are not *reported* to talk to their therapists about their mothers' pregnancies. I think that this is a significant professional erasure— given that, even in the lay press, such cute conversations between mothers and children (not just daughters) take place! For example, in *The New York Times* magazine section of September 5, 2010, in the "lives" section, in a story called "The Origin of Jonah: an adopted boy begins to wonder how he got here," by Melanie Braverman, a 5-year-old adopted boy of lesbian mothers is reported patting one of his mommies' tummies and asking if she will be making more babies in there! He is described as quite preoccupied with whose belly he came out of. Why does this material rarely come out in children's reported analyses? Could this be an example of how our favorite theory drives what we actually record for each other as analysts? Another question that may be worth thinking about is: is it only in adulthood, with all the developmental attainment of more complex object relations and ego growth, that a female can communicate the earlier registration of how the mother's body, personality, and mind feature in her psyche? These are questions still to be explored.

Notes

1 Working this out for males too is helpful. However, for the moment, my own subject is females.
2 I am not making general claims about how pregnancy was or was not represented in art during this time period. I have not studied this subject. My comments apply only to medical illustrations. The drawings by Leonardo da Vinci (1452–1519) might be included here too, even though their purpose was not for medical enlightenment aimed at treating women, and few people saw them at the time, but because they were based on cadaver dissection. "To make drawings directly from a cadaver was an enterprise never previously undertaken" (Nuland, 2000: p. 120) Leonardo too shows confusion in dealing with the genito-urinary system of females, even though all his drawings of the "non-sexual" parts of the body are so painstakingly accurate in structure and in relation to functional mechanics. His exquisite drawings of the fetus and baby *in utero* were disembodied from the women, except for the depiction of a containing uterine outline. He was most concentrated upon the baby and its growth. The famous 'coitus' drawing that he did (c. 1497) demonstrates an amazing confusion of the relation among all the anatomical parts (see Nuland, 2000: p.159). Leonardo was guided by Galenic ancient theory.
3 A suggestive connection to the ancient but ongoing fantasy that women are "empty" or that their genitals are "nothing"?
4 I am advised on this by German native speakers Professors Herbert and Annemarie Arnold. He is a Professor of German Studies and of Letters at Wesleyan University,

Middletown, Connecticut, and she an Adjunct Professor of German Studies at the same university. They are not Freud scholars, and thus have no vested interest in either upholding or challenging Freud. They are simply familiar with the German vernacular, and are interested in the translation of these words. They read the German text and were amazed that Freud or anyone else would not take as accurate even the first communication reported between Hans and his mother: "Hans: Mummy, have you got a 'wiwimacher' (trans. widdler) too?" "Mother: Of course. Why?" Denying this anatomical fact leaves in a very strange position indeed the male grown-ups in the story who tell the boy that the women have "no wiwimachers" in an attempt at sexual enlightenment!

Chapter 4

The pregnant mother and her daughter's body image

The vast belly, the bounteous breasts, and the swayback posture of pregnancy create an arresting new outline for the common form of a grown woman. It requires hard work to ignore a pregnant woman in the environment. To a layperson, it seems obvious that there will be necessarily a strong link between a girl child's experience of her own pregnant mother and her eventual potential experience of also being pregnant. Yet, for many curious reasons, within the theory of psychoanalysis, this connection was and is treated as far from obvious. I want to concentrate on giving clinical material first before approaching the theoretical tangle. I will, however, explore the highways and byways of this obfuscating thinking in our profession, throughout the book, but especially in Chapter 11. It is as if psychoanalysts took pride in not believing or being somehow seduced by the obvious! Says Freud (1933) "... a solution of ... simplicity ... we could suppose ... [where] children are following the pointer given them by the sexual preference of their parents ... the power of which poets talk so much ... but ... we have found an answer of quite another sort by means of laborious investigations" (p. 119). Poets might believe such obvious things, but certainly not *we* wiser analysts! The power of pregnancy and actual birth falls into this category. But because there is little actually written to support my simple claim of a close and vital physically comparative constructed fantasy connection between a mother's body and her daughter's, I believe it therefore important to show evidence directly from analytic or in-depth psychotherapy treatments. I feel almost apologetic about how obvious the associative material is, but this just serves to deepen the mystery about how these materials are not referred to by theory builders, and to what lengths they go to twist out the logic of this fundamental developmental connection.

Especially in the nude, the outline of the body captures in a moment's glance the epitome of female biological prowess. The erect phallus of the grown man is a familiar, visible, similar, nude icon of biological power, promise, and destiny. This symbol, however, has been granted much more focus in the minds of both female and male analysands reported in our literature, and in our clinical and developmental theory, especially about gender differentiation.

The topic of pregnancy is virtually absent in written accounts of psychoanalytic treatments (except in the Kleinian tradition). Yet, many were witness to a mother's or aunts' or neighbors' pregnancies in early childhood, and surely this experience was not insignificant. What then does this absence mean? Assuming that the material may have "disappeared," or that it may be unrecognized or glossed over, rather than that it is fundamentally unimportant, how may it manifest? If encountered, how does it yield to interpretation? Moreover, is it indeed important in the formation of body image? I differentiate exploration of and attentiveness to memories of pregnancies and their impact from any implications for "desirable normality" or "fulfillment" in womanhood. The latter are value judgments best arrived at by a woman for herself. One longer and two short case vignettes will be offered here to examine and suggest the place in mental life that a mother's pregnant body can assume, as demonstrated in the analyses of adult women.

Freud

Of Freud's few references to pregnancy, one of the most intriguing (besides those in Little Hans) are in his 1920 paper on the lesbianism of a "beautiful and clever girl of 18" (p. 147). The mother's third and last pregnancy when the girl was 16 was, in his opinion, a formative experience. He claims that this girl expressed a wish at 13 or 14 to have a baby, and displaced her motherliness onto a friend's little boy. He also notes that a boy sibling was born to her mother when the girl was 5 or 6, but that this "exercised no special influence on her development" (p. 155). (One wonders about that event in retrospect, as the original traumatic experience.) Then, when she was aged 16, her mother became pregnant again and delivered a son. After that, Freud, says the girl fell in love erotically with "a substitute for her mother" (p. 156), though not a mother herself, and with a thin and boyish figure. He wonders why this girl did not grow contemptuous or envious of her own mother and thus distance herself, as many teenaged girls might. Instead, he thinks that her "lady-love" (p. 156) combined boyish and girlish physical features satisfying both "her feminine and her masculine ideal … [combining] the satisfaction of the homosexual tendency with the heterosexual one" (p. 156). Freud then attributes the girl's turn away from heterosexuality to oedipal disillusionment with her father and her wish to have had his baby rather than the mother. Freud notes nicely the girl's fascination with the physical looks of the ladylove, but he is not really curious about this girl's preoccupation with her own mother's body—or her pregnancy, or birth experience, or indeed her own body. Apparently, it was after this brother's birth that the young girl "entirely repudiated her wish for a child" (p. 158). The case is complicated by the fact that, apparently, the mother did not like her, and greatly favored the boy siblings. Freud was very sure of these speculative oedipal dynamics, as well as knowing the ambivalence toward her mother, but one wonders how much this young adolescent girl, having "'retired in favor of' her mother" (p. 158), might also have been traumatized by something about the physical intensity of her reaction to her mother's body experience, perhaps experiencing fear or repugnance. Much was made in the story about the girl's virginity, also with her "ladylove." We shall never know the role her body played. Freud viewed her as having "changed into a man" (p. 158), which foreclosed his exploration. In a footnote on p. 169, he expands on a declaration she made to him during the analysis that pregnancy and childbirth were disagreeable to her, which, he suggests to the reader, is because of "the bodily disfigurement connected to them" (p. 169). Freud regards this negativity as her girlish narcissism. His footnote contains an explanatory Wagnerian reference, where Kriemhilde says to her mother that she "would never allow a man to love her since that would mean the loss of her beauty." This is an interesting reference to pregnancy too—as unmentionable. The vicissitudes of the daughter's relations with her parents and older brother—oedipal and otherwise—take center stage, and Freud considers female body issues only at the periphery of the case. Nevertheless, he does speak promisingly of her fascination with other women, in her case, mothers. However, her homoerotic trends alone are split off for attention, leaving behind her procreative sexuality.

I believe that this kind of listening has been fairly typical, where female patients have riveted their attention on adult women in their stories. The analyses of their concepts of "beauty" have been underexplored, other than in the 1960s as comparison to the male, or as compensation for penis lack.

Case I

Ms. EF was a 48-year-old interior decorator, divorced 5 years previously. She had two daughters, professional, single women in their late twenties. She was a fresh-faced, crisp little woman with a pear-shaped figure, dressed in a business suit. In repose, she had a grim expression but was able to engage and smile, if in self-mocking wit. My clinical sense was that she was a socially well-functioning woman in mid-life, with good-enough object relations to sustain analysis, but a person who had lived in a chronic depression. The depressive cast to her personality, tinged with mild sadomasochism and the implied underlying troubles, especially with her aggression, possibly accounted for aspects of her difficulties with intimacy. Her 5-year analysis dealt with many issues common in the lives of women—wavering self-esteem, relationship problems, inhibition of aggression, inhibition of sexual feelings, and body image concerns. After previous practical therapies, she had turned to analysis to address a few questions that had long irked her. Why, she mulled, did she turn out to be the "spitting image" of her mother, replete with short temper, a perfectionism that drove others to drink (a wry reference to her ex-husband), a need constantly to nag her daughters about their weight plus a grumbling obsession about her own weight, and an uneasy sense that her work was never good enough? She had hated these characteristics in her mother. EF believed that she was hard to live with. "I pick at people. I pick and pick. When my mother was dying and she was half-conscious, I was sitting up with her during the night. I was stroking her hand. She opened her eyes for a moment—just long enough to growl at me—For God's sake, Eliza, you're putting on weight again. Your hands are pudgy." I felt so ... so ... (she gasped back a sob) ... hurt. It was 4 a.m. She died at dawn." EF did not want to continue to be enslaved to this relentless ritual of complaint.

Her mother was domineering and critical, yet not devoid of warmth—especially for babies. The mother loomed over EF's analysis: her character, body habitus, and fate were deeply imprinted upon her daughter to make her the woman we both encountered upon my couch, and with who together we became acquainted. The father was a steady workingman—a "man's man," mildly patriarchal, with ideals of "betterment" for his two daughters and one son. My patient was the oldest. Her sister, Estelle, and brother Eric were 2 and 6 years younger, respectively. EF and Estelle were born during the Great Depression, when times were hard. The moments of peak developmental significance, as we analyzed EF's character and interwoven depression, circled around the births of her siblings, one when she was struggling with her mother over constipation, and the other at the height of her oedipal striving. EF married at 18 years of age, perhaps an effort at mastering earlier traumata of displacement from mother due to her pregnancies. She precociously pushed on grimly into adulthood.

The opening gambits in the analysis suggested a transference where I was a female friend and confidante. It was not a twinship transference, nor was she worshipful. Excitedly, she shared with me her secrets—hopes for contracts at work, hopes to impress clients, and disappointments. A woman friend was also included in this circle of intimacy. I heard about the details of her 25-year marriage, the high-school romance with the football hero, and her social success as Queen among the seniors, deteriorating to her gradual disillusion at how hard it was to have babies with a husband terrified that domestication would undermine his manhood. Fighting, backbiting, and his alcoholism marred their years together. Their sexual relationship was poor to non-existent latterly. She attended art school in her 30s. As soon as she could support herself, and her daughters were independent, she fulfilled a long-held promise to herself—she separated and subsequently divorced her husband.

I watched the sting of her tongue at first from a distance. This neighbor was callow in matters of taste. That co-worker lacked a sense of design. The other was laughably obese. Another was a circus dwarf. This man preened like a rooster proclaiming himself at dawn. How long, I wondered, could her contentment with me continue? She seemed to experience the three of us (her, me, and her friendly enemy) as if we were a high-school clique of "popular" girls. Boys and other girls would be verbally torn down in the group chat. Mutual allegiance and solidarity operated within the inner sanctum of her (our) approval. High school had been her favorite time in life.

One day, about 9 months into treatment, she saw me make my way toward my office, hunched against the cold, with an old hat pulled over my ears. Picking my path with caution over patches of ice, I did not notice her at some distance behind me. Once established in the room, she said that I had slammed the front door in her face. What was wrong, she wanted to know. Hesitatingly at first, and with my help, pointing out how she was holding back criticism of me, possibly sensing danger, she began to elaborate. How could I wear that old hat? The coat too looked worn and awful. It was too big for me. Or perhaps not, maybe I had put on weight? It was hard to get a good look at me because she had hit the couch so quickly. At the beginning of the analysis, I had looked neatly dressed, she thought. I seemed bigger now. Bigger and fatter than she, she reflected. I looked like a bag-lady. What was I hiding?

This episode turned out to be a paradigm, a pattern of the way her inner conflicts unfolded. First, "You ignored me. Then you slammed the door in my face. You hurt me and make me mad. You disappoint me." And then: "Your body has changed. How does my body compare to yours?" The conscious aspects of this sequence appeared over and over in the analysis. The unconscious underpinnings belonged to the eras of the mother's pregnancies.

Maternal preoccupation

Later in the analysis, the patient was exquisitely sensitive about any failures of mine to see her in public places. She disliked any evidence that I might sometimes be preoccupied with my own inner world. For her, I was "dreamy and far away," "not attending to the environment," "spacey." I was "in a fog," "out to lunch," "distant," "in a world of your own."

EF's language interested me. The imagery implied spatial elements. In addition, she was conjuring up in the transference a creature adrift in internal contemplation. I asked if my actual attention to the details of her associations in the sessions had shifted. She said "Not really." The accusation of inattention as I crossed paths seemed to be the stimulus, because then she could readily view my whole shape. Indeed, I am not particularly tuned into the sights and sounds of the street as I take breaks during work hours. However, my patient built many scenarios about my "troubles" and mental state based on her own convictions about these moments. She worried that I was short of money. Was my husband out of work?

This was the first clue to the time frame of the regressive material that was emerging. Imaginatively, we were back in the Great Depression. The following dream also alerted us both further to the events of the time of her own childhood depression.

"I am walking in a street and the lights are bright. It seems to be Christmas. I am very happy and expecting Santa Claus. I have on a green velvet dress. I smooth down the front nice and flat. My parents were around some place, but not right there.

"The scene changes. Somebody in a big brown cloak has her back to me. I'm in a toilet, in a stall sitting on the toilet and feeling all swollen up. My mother turns out to be in that cloak, bears down on me, and starts screaming at me. I start to cry, and I wake up with my heart pounding."

The associations began with the figure in the cloak—like me, she said, turning my back. This was a symbol of my preoccupation. Given the way the cloaked woman behaved, EF began to wonder if her worry about my inattention was in fact "cloaking" a terror that I was in fact enraged at her. She recalled sitting on the toilet before Estelle was born, trying to "poop" while her mother, with her own "fat" belly got frustrated. She was sensitive to my preoccupations, because they reminded her of her mother's "distraction" when she was pregnant.

At first, the little girl had been mother's inseparable companion, helping her to tolerate the loneliness of her young husband's absences as he combed the streets looking for a job. My patient used to stay up late at nights until her mother went to bed. Her mother was, however, always irritable about physical closeness. "You had to watch her hairstyle, or her lipstick. I did sit on her knee—it's just that I had to be very careful. I liked to sit and play with her necklaces, and touch her breasts, and I fiddled with the buttons down the front of her dresses. I believe she did breastfeed me for a bit—not long—she threw me off her knee when she got so bulky, and told me I was too heavy." We had evidence that my patient was allowed a period of close physical proximity and many opportunities for affectionate scrutiny. We understood it to be a blow that the mother's pregnancy reduced her lap, and that the wrangling over the constipation created a distance between them. "Mothers who change shape can change mood too, and get very, very mad!" she averred. "You have to watch out." EF no longer felt safe with me.

The changed body and the mother–daughter comparison

In the first "girl-to-girl" transference, EF related to me as if we were separate but equal and perhaps not so different from each other, even if these similarities were not brought to consciousness in analysis. Implied was the notion that "we" were not obese like this woman, or crass, ugly, and big-mouthed (as a displacement of being "big") like that neighbor. The subjective realm of "shared" feeling tones, outlook, and imagined experience dominated the associative field. Others were outsiders, and unconsciously also compared to her own body too as bigger and brasher as compared to daintier and well behaved like "us." However, once I was cast out of this circle of intimacy, as it were, the differences began to concern her, and these differences were couched in concrete body talk (similar to the observations of Lieberman, 2000). My clothes were the first emotional trigger. These, she felt, had changed. She had pained feelings, and I looked bad to her in a newly different and in a disturbing and negative way. Her own miserable feelings and my perceived ugly looks seemed meshed within her associative response. "I feel closed out and hurt and you are in a big, ugly coat" came together. In her dream, her mother's vast cloak of brown ("a color I really hate") featured side-by-side with the patient's constipated/unconsciously anal pregnant sensory discomfort—a large swollen belly, and weeping. The phrase she used ("she bore down") yielded associations of the births of EF's own children. The dream mother figure was furious, screaming, and conveyed an image of pushing something down upon her—giving birth herself in a child's view? The dream child was crying, overwhelmed, and afraid. One can see in these sequences inter-changeability among the affects, fantasies, and body experiences of the blended adult woman and the girl child. In this instance, the patient recalled the episodes of constipation when she was two-and-a-half, and how she had to sit on the toilet for ages and very much against her will to convince her mother that she was trying to push out her bowel contents. She engaged in bitter fights with her mother, whom she knew (in her child's way) was pregnant with her sister. Later, we understood that these episodes, as her response to me at the front door, probably were designed in part to pull her mother out of her pregnant dreaminess. The patient also recalled her fascination with the tailpipes of cars. She would always bend down to look up them. What monster was up and hidden inside these dark, mysterious spaces? What insistently needed to be pushed out—of rumbling car engines, of swollen and distended abdomens? The patient thought that by the time she was six, when her mother was pregnant with her brother, she was sure there was a connection in her mind between that big bump in mother's previously soft belly and something that needed to be pushed out.

When EF spoke of her dream green dress, she used her hands to smooth down her abdomen as she lay talking, a gesture cueing the kind of current liveliness of the topic in my presence which signals that transference is in play. The velvet dress had been a precious Santa gift from her father. Mother's baby was a "gift" of another sort. Little E looked gorgeous in her new dress. "Then I was so nice and thin. Not like that heap of a mother. I was so flat in beside mother in bed, feeling very superior to her soft, rubbery, blubbery, cushiony form … not like I am now." Everybody in her house, she thought, admired tall, thin women. Her mother was tall, and by her own self-description had always had a weight problem. When they took showers together, the mother would compare their bodies, telling the child always to cherish her slender lines. EF recalled uneasily crawling into bed trying to snuggle into her mother. She would poke her mother's body and say, "Lumpy, gooey, ucky," and her mother would push her away, telling her she couldn't help it.[1] The unconscious ambivalence toward her mother's belly, and her increased weight and breasts, could be appreciated in her memories.

Another rich theme over the course of the analysis was her mother's dresses. There was a red silk one with dots. It sounded like a formal cocktail dress, slinky and long, with a frill around the hem—"like a mermaid." The shape was crucial, and EF particularly stressed that it was flat in front. She imagined herself, this time enviously, watching mother put it on to go out with Father. "She pulled it up from the feet. Did I mention that she had great slim legs? Like a ballet dancer. My father, she told me, loved her legs. We both looked in the mirror, and thought she was gorgeous."

"That word again … and being flat," I reflected.

"That makes me think of another dream. I'm a grown-up. I am preening in a mirror and smoothing down the front of myself, in a blood-red satin dress and I like what I see—slender hips and abs of steel," she said wistfully, "so far from this pudgy shape I'm stuck with ever since my babies came." By the conjunction of these references, we began to appreciate again the merged favored internal vision of her own body with an admired shape of mother probably between mother's pregnancies. Womanly beauty for EF was sharply differentiated early from the pregnant state, which was associated with ugliness and negatively tinged affective states. This was reminiscent of Freud's 1920 18-year girl's reaction to her pregnant mother that I mentioned earlier in the chapter.

The fate of the red dress was telling. Sometime after the birth of the brother, when the patient was maybe eight or nine, her mother banished her to the parental bedroom without dinner. It was a punishment probably for fighting with her siblings, and a "time-out" for getting over her anger. Silently, after her tears had dried, the child took her mother's sewing shears, opened her closet, pulled out the red dress and systematically cut it into shreds. She had no memory of the repercussions. This deliberately destructive act was a vengeance wreaked on both herself and the mother: "I hate you for banishing me. I hate your babies. I will kill any chance for your body to be admired—the body that can bear those hateful siblings. Only I can be flat and beautiful."

Throughout the analysis, EF regularly noticed and spoke about my clothes. Ninety-nine percent of her comments would be followed by references to her own wardrobe, which suggested to me ongoing scrutiny and body comparison. It seemed as though she (as with many other women) perceived her own body by contrast or similarity, and she often measured who was superior and who was inferior in terms of thin and fat. Tent shapes on her or me were "like haystacks." A-line dresses were "cutsey little girls playing at being pregnant." Long skirts were fine, as long as the waist was visible. If the blouse flowed to the top of the legs without definition, it was deemed "frumpy." Trouser suits were "not in my league."

Male influences in body image

The comparisons for her, as has been often noted in case studies, also focused on the genitalia. Mother's genitals too were of interest. EF was able to remember confusions from her early life. Mother's genitals seemed vague, she thought, like the tail pipes of cars, with perhaps another hole for bowel movements (similar to a cloaca perhaps.) Her father's penis was clear to her and also large. In her husband's drunken, disinhibited states, she had seen him late at nights in underpants, with his large, flaccid organ hanging out as he dozed in the living room. Memories of her father came back. She used to sneak peeks of him in the bathroom, as he shaved, in underpants, the clear bulge of his penis and testicles being her fascination. Disgust, fear, as well as excitement were registered. EF was less concerned about what she was missing from her own body, but about how he poked it into her mother's tail pipe to make babies. Again, as with her mother and other adult females, her emphasis was on largeness, bulge, sexualized fear, and ugliness. I looked in vain for some connections for awe and admiration of images of the erect phallus, perhaps leading her to more classical ideals of a "phallic" body image as she certainly admired a tall, thin version of the female body. Women are not all the same in this way.

However, her brother's tiny penis was the major focus for her male-oriented envy and longing when she scrutinized their respective endowment. She thought it would be fun to play with such a dainty, small, and perfect little stick. Secret genital play had occurred with the brother. Masturbation fantasies involved "taking" his organ and putting it on her mons pubis. She admired latency boy figures and connected her aspiration to be thin and flat also to acquiring brother's body outline. These conflicts were vivid at puberty for her. As she struggled with breast growth, growing hips, and putting on weight at age 13, and her initial horror of menstruation, his 7-year-old body seemed enviable to her. It was in her early adolescent closeness to peer girls, when characteristic female-to-female body comparisons came into fruition for her, that she assumed significantly more comfort with breasts that were envied by other girls, and a nubile body that brought excitement from peer boys. Issues about the technicalities of sexual intercourse and her power to promote arousal and popularity with boys went side-by-side for her with temporary repression about the implications of her body for procreation and pregnancy, which as we saw in the analysis held a rush of horror, ambivalence, and expectation of ugliness.

When EF described her own experiences of pregnancy and childbirth, there was a flavor of their having been "visited" upon her. At times, she blamed her husband for his wishes to prove his manliness by impregnating her. Once the girls were born, she was a passable caretaking parent. It would be an oversimplification to call her experience of pregnancy or motherhood a denial of "femininity." An amalgamated picture might have led to this old formulation, because she did harbor resentments. However, she could separate her bodily feelings of grotesqueness from her interest in the children's welfare. The larger she became, she recalled just "waiting out" the pregnancies, feeling depressed and hiding from company. She was grateful for spinal blocks so that she would not have to feel "ripped apart." Imaginings of the comparison of her own tiny "hole" and the old fantasies of her father's large penis penetrating her, plus memories of her constipation struggles around the time her sister was born emerged as likely forerunners for her dreaded imaginings of childbirth.

In recalling the births of her children, EF reported a dream of herself running through the rain, in mud puddles, tearing the hem of a fancy pink dress, evoking thoughts of her defloration, which she had feared. In her associations, she discovered an unconscious fantasy that she must have a ragged and torn vagina, as had her mother, and now she herself evoked in her a sense of being bleeding and torn from intercourse and birthing babies. At one point, while working over this material in analysis, she decided to use a mirror to examine her genitalia as a reality check. She was surprised at how intact she looked! I felt that her "castration" anxiety represented fears of the fate of her female vaginal canal. This kind of data from women makes one sure that "female genital anxiety" is a far more accurate term than "castration anxiety" (referring to an absent penis) ever was.

The outside and the inside baby

For EF, the wish to have a baby seemed to be expressed in two modes, which existed in uneasy alliance. For this reason, speaking generically of a singular "the wish for a baby" in girls seems inadequate. I will explain what I mean by an outside mode and an inside mode by leading us there clinically.

While her mother was pregnant, little EF, as with many other little girls (and boys too), engaged in doll play. She had a baby doll that she brought once to show me during analysis. It was a standard plastic doll with an imprinted navel, a closed genital slight groove, and round, imprinted cleft buttocks. She showed me where she had tried to open two holes—one for pee-pee, she thought, and one for babies. These were anatomically accurately placed. She laughed at the pinhole she had managed to poke into the pelvic cavity in the vaginal area. We agreed that only a miracle baby could have passed through that! The pinhole additions, made at 6 years of age, however, had coincided with the mother's pregnancy with brother. This suggested to us that, by then, she had some knowledge of the vagina as separated from the anus—an advance on the cloaca theory. The female doll's name was Gloria, likely an allusion to sister "Estelle," the star, and likely a female body reference. Not all women crave a boy baby! This girl wanted a girl. Its "skin" looked grey and worn from many baths. While she showed it to me, she held it tenderly, with a gentle hand behind its head, a display of "motherliness" for me. Gloria used to sleep in a cot beside her bed. It was her own baby. This phenomenon I will call the "outside" baby derived from modeling and identification with mother as caretaker. She rivaled her mother's skills. Her baby Gloria did not cry like Estelle or Eric. She envied her mother's power over the new babies. (As an adult, she still could feel resentment if the mother's advice prevailed over her own to her siblings!) She also felt jealous of the attentions of both parents to Estelle and Eric, and the constipation episodes helped fuel this rivalry. We wondered together if her overt disgust at mother's pregnant belly served as repudiation to express rage at the contents and to keep her envy and even her admiration at bay. Most of her envy was about how the adult woman got to take charge of the littler ones. A vision of mother's harsh and critical stance as associated with power and control, therefore, became an *admired* quality for her, to match her childhood view of a mother's desirable power. As the analysis deepened, we could appreciate that her proclivity to "pick" at others, to criticize and condemn, actually held a positive valence and was part of a strong childhood picture of the behavior of any competent mother worth her salt. Turning out "the spitting image" of mother, in spite of stated contrary wishes, encoded the "spit" and the "spite" of her early vision of mother with three children under 6 years of age. EF used to yell at her doll Gloria too, roughly potty-training her, for example. This would alternate with soothing her, to make up for the bad treatment.

Classical oedipal wishes, that Gloria was daddy's baby with her, also were manifest. Her father played with Gloria with her, responding to requests to admire an outfit. The father seemed to have an ability to affirm little EF in "motherliness."

This brings us now to the baby "inside." For EF, this set of unconscious fantasies nearer to informing body structural images, were more conflictual than her desire to express motherliness with a baby. I will relate these "inside baby" fantasies to the transference, as it unfolded later in analysis. Previous work had pointed to her unconscious longing to be pregnant like mother. The spatial position of EF, lying supine on my couch in the office, was central to understanding these fantasies. Consonant with her profession as an interior decorator, the patient seemed visually compelled by the decorations on the walls. Her eyes would travel from picture to picture while she critiqued the merits and demerits of each piece of art. Over time with her, she seemed to shift her gaze from the exterior position of me in the street, to a close-up, and then an interior view that involved fantasies about the interior of our bodies. I will relate the most regressive moments.

A Matisse poster from his Moroccan period particularly captured her eyes. As she stared at it, she reported a swelling sensation in her abdomen, "coming up like a balloon" and a tingling sensation of growing very large, extending over the end of the couch. "I feel myself inside the room in the painting, with you, looking into the distance. How can I get through the window and onto that beach below? Those annoying bunches of flowers on the windowsill in the foreground are obstacles. Would I push them aside and jump? Are there stairs hidden and leading down to the beach? The outside is sunny and there are little people on the beach below, but inside the room is blue and dark." She sighed, sounding sad. I wondered out loud if she felt trapped. Her eyes traveled to a watercolor. "Now I am going through the woods and pushing through the underbrush. I could swim down that brown river." Her gaze moved on. "The path down over there is hilly. The landscape is covered with little round hills. Maybe I could scramble down the bank. It's so hard ..." and she sighed again.

I found myself in a responsive daydream. It was no accident that I, too, should have experienced my own regressive pull at those moments. For the landscapes in which she was now wandering were ones from our family place where I grew up in Ireland. There is not an inch of the territory that surrounds me in my watercolors that I have not trodden, and there is not a "little round hill" (they are called drumlins, and are the heritage of the glaciations melt after the Ice Age) that I have not clambered upon. I am, in effect, surrounded by my own Mother Earth, belonging to my father. The whole room seemed to become my own vast imagined pregnant belly. It was as if she were imagining herself as my internal fetus becoming too big for the space, as if she were viewing from the inside the obstacles of my womb, inspecting the territory, and wondering how to escape into the world.

Earlier in the analysis, EF had reported a dream where she was first in the basket of a hot air balloon, hovering uneasily over the earth. Then she became transfixed with the primary colors of the balloon and in the dream became anxious, being gradually sucked up into the cavity of the balloon, being first long and thin and then expanding again. In her associations, she had referred to the vivid primary colors of the Matisse painting and spoke of a parallel feeling of being "sucked into" the painting.

Based on the memory of her balloon dream and my regressive experience, I offered an interpretation. I spoke of her wish to exist inside my body and look at it from the inside. I offered that she feared the power of her wish, because it would mean that I could suck her into myself to make me big, and she feared it would be very hard to get out. She was quiet for a bit. "I do want to become like you," she said slowly. "I want to BE you. I want to be your baby. I want to be part of you. But I want to be your big girl too … It will be very hard to stop coming here."

She recalled days on the couch when she would sit up slowly, experiencing dizziness. "I was angry then. I didn't want to get sucked in and be dependent. … Now that's okay. … But I also want to be free. I can imagine you looking at me through a window now. It is sunny and I fancy you'd approve of me playing on the beach." We translated this experience as previously repressed fantasies embodying both her desire to be in the big belly and her desire to become the possessor of the big form and belly herself.

At times, in the termination phase, EF would wear bright blues and reds. She adopted more of a Bohemian style, with looser and flowing pants and dresses. It was an era of less form-fitting fashions. However, she and I interpreted her responsiveness to this shift as consonant with more ease about her underlying shape. It mattered less to her to appear flat all of the time. We terminated as she approached menopause. Her depression had lifted, in the way that it does when the mind becomes more agile, the affects become more available, and the patient tolerates the meanings of her communications and can decode them. She feared less the body changes that she anticipated in advancing age. "Some day, I hope my daughters will be pregnant and that I'll be a comfortable grandmother. I hope I'll have a granddaughter, and I suppose I'll re-do the history of my body all over again." As I trudged through the snow in my old hat and coat, I hoped she would have the opportunity.

Case 2

Ms. FG was a 31-year-old loving, if anxious, mother of a 2-year-old boy, and wife of a scholarly graduate student of physics. She was a high-school teacher. She suffered from a sense of chronic underachievement, and wanted to explore her urgent competitiveness in analysis. Compared to her academically successful husband, she felt inadequate. It was a functional marriage with mutual encouragement and passion. They were both entranced with their little boy.

FG's parents were a traditional couple from the mid-West, and her father was a businessman. Her sister, Frances, was 4 years younger. Her analysis lasted 4 years.

The first year unfolded themes about her competitive feelings with her husband. She felt her father had wanted his oldest to be a boy, to keep the business in the family. A tomboy and athletic, she still enjoyed coaching field hockey. There was evidence of a classical phallic oedipal striving, as she tried to become father's best boy, while covertly wooing him simultaneously to become his best girl. The route to a fantasy boyhood seemed more open (if naturally thwarted by her obvious girl's body as she went into puberty), because, as she said, "There seemed to be too many females to compete with in the household." The birth of her own boy, and her marriage to a man her father admired, provided an outlet for some transformation of these issues, if at times she felt rivalrous with them both. Unconsciously, she had fantasies of attempting to possess a penis, one way or another. As with others, she wanted to be both genders at times.

However, eventually her female body took center stage in the analysis, and male body themes became more peripheral. Even from the beginning, FG's breasts had been a matter of pride and hope for body self-esteem. They held some phallic significance too, for example, in comments such as," Why should I care what the men have, when I have two beauties of my own?" All curves of her female body were of interest to her too, but the breasts were predominant. I will discuss here only issues concerning her breasts as they related to her avid competition with other women.

FG was of medium height, trim and muscular, with a blonde bob. There was a bouncy air to her carriage, and she possessed large, D-cup breasts, which she talked about initially as needing special "cradling" in athletic support bras when she ran on the hockey field. The words she used for them first attracted my ear, because they were so tender, like the words she used for her little boy, and they also seemed to me to be offered in a slightly yearning tone. "My boobies," she called them affectionately. During her periods, when they became engorged, she declared that the slight ache was pleasant." My great big titties are really gigantic today," she would giggle, "I'm glad I'm on my back here—they look like they're sitting up all by themselves today." "Do you look at them? I wonder what you can see from where you sit?" And she would push them up further, inviting my fuller inspection.

As these moments were full of teasing giggles, one day I ventured naughtily, "All the better to see you, my dear!" Entering into her playfulness. "What big eyes you have, grandma!" she flashed back. "Oh I do feel like Little Red Riding Hood with her goodies, coming to see grandma…" "I feel like I'm offering you my breasts—maybe to eat, but more to show them and take them away. I have something you'd like, but they're mine, and I can take them off home." " I guess you're teasing me with your goodies," I said. This led to associations about being teased at school by the teenage boys.

In part, her female display served to get the upper hand over the "drooling," aroused, provocative boys and their own tendencies to exhibit their genital endowment; in part, it was a reference to her "drooling," competitive, Grandma Wolf/analyst/phallic mother. We were shifting ground between male and female. She grew sad and serious … "I used to use every excuse to watch mother breast-feed Frances." FG used her breasts in compensatory and competitive fantasies at first (thinking of mother's superior capacity to give milk, or mine to give interpretations), but unconsciously she was fascinated with the seductive potential the "giant titties" symbolized for adult womanhood. FG's flirtation and cheeriness always markedly ceased when these themes came up. Talking about women was less playful.

In the last 2 years, we spent most sessions on herself, on me as woman (as opposed to me as father or phallic mother), on her own mother, and on Frances, who was a stereotypically "frilly" girl. FG told of looking at women's magazines and other women in the gym, as she worked out. She searched the torsos for the "boobs": the bigger the better. She constantly looked for the size of the rear-ends too. Spandex and skintight workout gear were her specialty. She watched my body especially for low necklines and the declivity between my breasts. Her gaze also included my lower body. "You sit all day. Your behind is big, that reminds me of a dream. I was in a zoo. There was this mammoth kangaroo. I was like a huge pyramid. And it had a little baby in its pouch. How do they give birth anyway? Do they have a big hole under there? Ugh! Imagine they'd lose all their control—they're such athletes jumping round usually. They must pour their 'do' when they give birth—so gross! (A cloacal theory of birth, I thought.) Maybe their little Frankie—no, Joey…. God, that's Frances! Comes out of their belly-buttons, right into the pouch? It would be neat to have a pouch in front like that. You could see everything then."

I reminded her that she had been worried that the nurse would forget to let her see in the mirror when she herself was giving birth. "It used to be a mystery what was hidden down under," she said. (I refrained from interpreting the meaning of the choice of kangaroo as Australian, for her "down under" references. The mood of the moment was somber and pensive. Countertransferentially it felt to me as though it would be competitive to offer that, and I fancied that any such word play would invite her back into her own teasing competitive mode, as in "who's wit is bigger?")

After a pause, she went on, "My father used to distract me by taking me to the zoo to make me laugh when mother was pregnant."(I realized that I had been about to do the same, now that mother's pregnancy was in the atmosphere. I noted to myself that there really is something anxiety and guilt provoking about staring at mother's pregnant body and fruitful breasts in a sustained way at close quarters. Perhaps this may be more universal than with FG and me, I thought? Perhaps this was a clue to why people do not note the material much?)

FG went on in many other sessions to recall her views of mother's pregnant body—in varying lingerie, in colored large dresses, in the bedroom, etc. She wanted to touch her belly and breasts all the time. Instead, she thought, she had eyed her constantly, with a vision of her whole body, but with special attention to her huge breasts and also hips. She thought the buttocks might grow out in two mountains, to match the breasts. She connected her current attraction to looking at the female behind with a hope to see varying buttock sizes. "I used to look at myself when I was 7 or 8 and worry that I would grow big, big buns. The big boobies were okay. How I yearned for the day when my little nothing chest would grow. I waited and waited. Yet, I had a very unstable sense of what it would be like to change. Mother grew; I thought it would never stop. And then she got flat again–but she still had those big, delicious breasts for a long, long time. God, how I wanted to be her, and have those pillows myself."

Nature was kind in providing little FG at last with what she wanted. She beat her analyst in the body contour competition, and apparently her mother and her sister too. FG's spirited competitiveness was therefore importantly fed by her female connections, in my opinion even more prominent than her male connections, but woven together. Female-to-female competition is less often elaborated in adult analyses (except for the phantasical archaic aggressive elements of envy and reparation, etc., of infants toward their mothers, ubiquitous in Klienian everyday language). More integrated forms of fierce competition are easier to see and hear if the therapist attunes to the building blocks of body image with many patients.

Case 3

Ms. GH was a 25-year-old graduate student who could get "neither in nor out "of a relationship with a man, the third such relationship she had had since high school. There were cycles of arguments, in which the man pushed and verbally denigrated her, and then subsequent reconciliations. Her analysis lasted three-and-a-half years.

GH had grown up in the West. Coming to school in the East represented an attempt to escape a strict Roman Catholic background. Before long in treatment, while speaking of the insults she endured from her boyfriend about her mild acne, she revealed a relentless ongoing fascination and horror with skin blemishes on herself and others. At the time, I was having some sun-damage spots dermatologically treated on my face, which resulted in some redness and two small spots on my forehead that crusted and healed over a couple of weeks. She noticed them, but when they began to heal, she seemed even more involved, tracking their progress. "Will they leave a dent? Will they always be red? Are they bumpy? Are they smooth? Are they blue in the cold? And, finally, are they white now?" The texture of the skin was a particular focus.

Interwoven in these associations, I heard all about the history of her acne. In the rhythm of her associations—the alternation between my blemishes and her own—and the rhythm of her affect—first anxious then relieved followed by a patterned steady sexualized enjoyment in dwelling on the "horror" of the detail—crusty, oozing, and pus-filled—and in the pain and pleasure of squeezing her sores, she betrayed the sexualized sadomasochistic relation she had to her own body and especially to the bodies of other women. As she walked in her world, descriptions of women she watched had the same flavor. She was taken by the sight of women of color. It became clear that preconsciously she searched their skin for signs of wounds. Male-type "castration" concerns were unconsciously present for her, relating to masturbation and worries about what the apparent "bleeding wound" of her genitals meant. Could it be that once she possessed a penis? These wounds were of the open kind. Male body comparison was therefore present. This is an example of the apt understanding of "castration" fantasy, when a patient provides evidence. "Phallic castration" is not universally present in women. It is a specific fantasy with specific meanings such as in this case. As such, it is one variety of "female genital anxiety."

However, beyond these concerns, there were others. Her fascination with the healing colors, and the textures of healing, changing skin scarring had special female-to-female body significance.

GH's mother had had five children, all 2 years apart. GH was the second child and the only girl. She had experienced three of her mother's pregnancies, at ages 2, 4, and 6, approximately. Her mother had talked incessantly about the skin on her abdomen, the *striae* that she called the "stripes of pregnancy." Her breasts and thighs too had the silver stripes of healed stretch marks. The mother also had severe trouble with varicose veins. Mother and little G frequently took showers and baths together, during which the child would scrutinize the mother's body and skin, while the mother continued her narrative of the wonders and agonies of pregnancy. "God's work for a woman." GH vividly remembered her own awe and horror at the bathroom viewings. She particularly remembered the brilliant red and purple stripes covering the huge, hard belly during those last weeks. Mother would invite the little girl's comparisons of her own small pink "stomach" with hers. The smooth young skin on her legs was the object of comparison with mother's bumpy leg flesh delineated by the long purple lines of her varicosities. Mother lovingly related to little G's smooth peachiness. She offered exciting warnings of how all this would change when she grew up. GH in turn, lingered in admiration and trepidation over her mother's flaws—"the flaws of use ... like an old war horse," she said in analysis. She recalled secretly praying every night that God would grant her stripes on her tummy too. GH longed for and dreaded the coming of breasts, pubic hair, axillary hair, and her periods. Her unfortunate acne became a focus for mutual cleansing rituals and doctor visits. GH became aware in analysis that in fact she valued her acne, as a swallow to the spring of her awaited puberty. Pain and pleasure were inextricably entwined for her. The relations with her boyfriends carried these painful yet pleasurable overtones. It was exactly what she had expected of life as a woman.

In the middle of analysis, while breaking up with her boyfriend, she reported a dream. "The Virgin Mary appeared to me last night. I've told you I no longer believe, but I was enthralled with her last night. She was dressed in blue, smooth silk. Baby Jesus was on her knee. He was sitting funny, and then I realized that she was pregnant and he was half off her lap. I started to laugh, but then I felt awful. I seemed to be wearing shorts and no top. Then I was with a baby and I was on my back putting her on top of me. There were red ribbons forming a tent over me and her." (I noted the presence of a girl baby.) The associations were to a pregnancy scare that she had just experienced, through "forgetting" to put in her diaphragm. The play on the floor on her back represented her thoughts about analysis, "where I can play with the idea of a baby and think about pregnancy, but let it slide off too. The Virgin is me too. That fright I just had was as impossible as the Virgin's second pregnancy. I think I laughed with relief."

She went on to talk of her heavy guilt about nearly getting pregnant, and her guilt about defying her mother's injunctions about birth control and sex before marriage. Later associations emerged to mother as the Virgin, and to more thoughts about mother's pregnancies with her little brothers. I, too, became the Virgin; with herself as baby Jesus being knocked off the couch by a new patient she had seen emerging from my office. The red tent ribbons were like my red couch fabric, and represented memories of the striations on mother's skin.

Discussion

Does clinical material exist in the associative process that primarily concerns identification with the physicality of the mother? Clearly, I believe that it does, and I think I have given some compelling examples as to why. I have tried in this case material to separate out and bring into consideration the specific visual perceptions of body-to-body comparison between mothers and daughters as one external starting point from which the kernel of an interior fantasy life emerges. I have been particularly struck by the ongoing and at times insistent same-sex body comparisons that can be heard from adult female patients talking to a female analyst. A male analyst may also hear these themes. Nevertheless, they are inescapable with a female dyad.

My patients EF, FG, and GH, of different ages and life experience, are typical in their concerns about their form and shape and those of other women. It is possible to hear these references, which may be laden with affect as envy or triumph. If one moves back a notch, however, joining the patient on the visual plane and concentrating on the descriptions of *exterior* form and shape, then one has to wonder about the origins of this heightened visual acuity for the human body that many women express. The target of the eye is often other women's shapes, looking and comparing on another's exterior outline. Their interest is in the shape, not necessarily the "contents" of that shape, and the shape-image is registered often in comparison to the perceived outline of the subject herself.

(Dressing with other women in mind is a linked prominent preoccupation.) Because this is a dyadic situation implying "the mother," and a dyadic emphasis as opposed to a triadic one, the analytic listener may assume and expect the patient's material to be more primitive than if the assumption were that the patient operated on a more integrated triadic level. When this happens, I suggest, the therapist may attune almost automatically to merger phenomena and the primitive fantasies that accompany them, and thus be deafer to the imagined and remembered visual and tactile perceptions that I am trying to describe, and which imply and demonstrate more separateness. Lieberman (2000) calls this a "rush to metaphor" and devotes a chapter of her book to this matter in "body talk." In addition, the classical literature has encouraged us to consider a woman's continued internal focus on her mother as a "fixation," a state to be hurdled if development is to proceed (see Bernstein, 2004, who challenges this as old-fashioned and offers a modern view). A therapist's certainty of the patient's "fixation" on the mother, too, could cause him or her to try to "help" the patient too rapidly past the kinds of inevitable fascinations that I am dwelling upon here. The preoccupation with same-sex bodies is another one that is often too quickly heard as primarily erotic (e.g., Freud's 1920 case, referred to earlier), especially as homoeroticism is a difficult subject for people who consider themselves heterosexual. Therapists have learned to be on the lookout for the disavowed and latent unconscious underpinnings, and may approach this "homoerotic fixation" counterphobically. This listening stance too can shift attention away from "surface" phenomena which may contain the disavowed history of this female body too.

EF was searching her environment for flat abdomens. She was preoccupied with shape and form—the curvatures, convexities, and concavities that visually differentiate women, especially pregnant women, from men. Narrowness and width, tallness and shortness—all of these perceptions were constantly compared to her own bodily shape and size, which in turn were integrated in that comparative context. FG scanned especially the torso and the rear. GH too kept an eye above and below the waist. In addition, she scanned the surface for texture and color. Was it red, purple, blue, white bumpy, wrinkled, or smooth? Was it black, brown, or white?

"How do I occupy space as compared to other women?" seemed to be the underlying question that gave rise to the feelings, fantasies, and memories that sharpened in the transference. "How do I shape up?" is a conscious preoccupation that implies built-in comparison. "Who's pregnant, who was, and who is not?" I suggest, is an unconscious dimension.

It is probably no accident that women's magazines are so common in our culture and have such a wide circulation. Women are endlessly fascinated by other women in clothes of varying shapes. Tight forms, loose forms, colors and textures, one curve, or another—all of these render the clothed and made-up bodies of females a draw to women. The naked women in men's magazines, more static in form, are less engaging of women's manifest and latent concerns.

Women are, I believe, looking at other women more as moving objects. I am of course aware that this topic touches upon the matter of male erotic response, and the "male gaze" and how that can be incorporated into the female psyche too. However, although this is a related question to the matter of female's perceptions of shapes and forms, it is a different one. I include it less here, in my attempt to show that women on their own have a need to "gaze" at other women.

The attention to the analyst's clothes, the clothes of other women, and the patient's own clothing that appears in these case examples is testament to the importance of garments and their meaning to many females. There is certainly a competitive element about how they will attract the male gaze. The Queen's "Mirror, mirror on the wall, who is fairest of us all?" speaks profoundly to the intergenerational as well as cross-generational beauty contest that exists for the erotic admiration of the King and the Prince. Dressing to optimize or conceal body configuration can represent this quest. Interior oedipal themes often require little problem to detect when such competition is in the atmosphere. However, dressing for the Queen and Princess attests to another kind of interest.

What emotional valences join the conversation at the exterior of the body? EF ushered in her "body talk" (Lieberman, 2000), by enacting with me scenes of feeling acutely shut out of her mother's central focus—especially, as it turned out, at the periods of her mother's pregnancies. She loved the feeling of closeness to the maternal body in its non-pregnant or "flat," smaller, and narrower state. The pregnant bulge, the tiredness, and the maternal preoccupation joined forces with her anger and hurt. One can note this too as part of a general phenomenon, where patients' moods alter the cast of visual stimuli of the therapist's body toward pleasant or ugly. The same day that EF found me so ugly and ill dressed, for instance, another patient admired my "Irish tweeds"!

These same considerations may be applied to facial cues. EF was more arrested by the image of the body than concerned about the face. The mechanism involved intrapsychically seems akin to projective identification. Synthesia is a concept in cognitive psychology that refers to a joining of the senses—e.g. "the taste of the smell" of something. Grammatically, the phenomenon is known as a "transferred epithet"; e.g., "the green joy … [of the pasture]." The internal affects are negative or positive for the subjects here, and they color the affective response to the shapes perceived in the objects. If this happens even in adults, surely it happens more frequently in childhood, when the attachments to the continuities of form are less fixed and less predictable.

Convexity of the abdomen vehemently retained for EF a sense of ugliness until after her regressive moments of the fantasies of inhabiting and positively identify-ing with me as "pregnant" and "delivering" her toward termination. One can appreciate also how sublimation had turned into professional virtue, as an interior decorator, EF's visual and imaginative proclivities. FG by similar mechanism had positive associations between fantasized delights of breast-feeding and the enlarged arc and circle or oval of the breast. Convexity and largeness of the ana-tomical form accompanied by softness or firmness to the touch were her themes.

Her focus on the buttocks seemed quite similar in quality to the breasts, but her responses were more ambivalent. The rear-end reactions conveyed overtones of both attractive and repulsive anal function. Her dream of the kangaroo, I believe, located her body fascination with pregnancy. As with Winnicott's little L., FG was confused if the birth process would result in the "bottom coming out" for her, a loss of anal control. What a kangaroo hides under its "huge pyramidal shape" was a mystery. "Do they have vaginas or does the baby come out through the belly-button?" She admired the notion of a special pouch in front. One can hear here the often-recorded wish of the girl to actually see the internal genital and womb, a wish that is often associated with envy of the boy's ability to clearly see the penis. FG seemed to have displaced upwards some aspects of the swelling, growing pregnancy in the belly, to her proudly held, twin cupolas of the breasts. Perhaps her anxieties about the birth itself, and how the babies would get out, motivated her vision away from the belly toward the upper torso? Her feeling of having "nothing at all" in front, as a child, as well as comparison to her mother's anatomical display also arose in comparison to her brothers' and father's sex organs. As Mayer (1995), has suggested, FG could be thought of as having two interwoven developmental lines—one in consort with male body comparison, and the other in consort, and to my mind dominant in her case, with the female body, including its capacity to bear children. After all, she was inspired to have a baby of her own.

GH too, studied shape and form, but she also had a visual fascination with surfaces. She was focused on the face, abdomen, and legs, searching the skin for blemishes. Raw wounds might readily be attributed to "phallic castration" fantasy and anxiety. A parallel and abiding concern was about the healing of blunt indentations, a search for shallow, colored troughs on the surface. Looking at women of color assessed possible advantages and disadvantages as to what shade the blemishes would be, and the subtleties of color of a healing scar. As I recorded, her mother had made much of her own colorful emblems of pregnancy. These "female" discussions and viewings occurred with GH, her only daughter. They had an air of the sharing of initiation rites for the physical destiny that awaited her. The girl's yearning to carry the skin^2 geography of this battle map of prowess—the proud and envied scars of the survived warrior mother—was epitomized in her associations to the dream about the Virgin Mary. The oedipal wish was transparent to both of us, but her longing to literally be "in the skin" of her mother suggested also her specific desire to pursue by identification the physical habitus of her mother. She also took in the habits of her mother to compare herself closely with fellow females, preconsciously and unconsciously with (for her) some fantasized postpregnant body state, which would signal procreativity. Her anxiety and longing about the impact of pregnancy fantasy was manifest in her pained but loving attachment to every detail of her troublesome periods while in treatment with me. As with her mother before her, GH was sado-masochistic in her connection to her body. She had had a rich exposure to stories of female Christian martyrs, some of whom manifest stigmata. These figures, whose skin shed blood, but were worshipped for their shallow wounds, also became icons for her own favored body image.

Conclusion

By definition, a mother is the creature who has borne the child, and the child is aware of this fact. A baby labeled "female" by the grown-ups around her is going to be inculcated with visual images of comparison between herself and all the adult women around her. The mother's pregnancy is an aspect more visible and at least as compelling for the growing girl in terms of a show-and-tell as her genitals alone. Granted, the pregnant body is a futuristic image, compared to the immediacy of a little girl's genitals. However, a child's wishful and fearful imagination can easily create a sense of future possibility—no matter how fantastic this may seem to grown-ups in the present, or how distant a future it may seem to the child. The girl's special physical interest in the body that swells up to contain, deliver, and feed a child, solidified by family adults' confirmation of her own ownership of these creative biological entities, is thus of vital interest to her both in the "now" and for the "then."

Notes

1 This is reminiscent of a finding where researchers asked 4–5-year-olds how babies came to be. Overwhelmingly, they said that their mothers had to eat a great deal and get very fat (Freitler and Kreitler, 1966). This was by far the most popular conception theory for both girls and boys.

2 Reminiscent of Didier-Anzieu's 1974 ideas about the skin's function in its early interactive sensual response as encoding ego memory registrations.

Chapter 5

Childbirth

Following my focus on pregnancy, the physical and mentalized phenomena of childbirth seems the logical next topic in the development of my thesis. These female body events are prepared for developmentally, and are instantiated and worked over in the mind of girls and women years *before*, and in women, years *after* the events themselves.

Margarete Hilferding

Dr. Margarete Hilferding (1871–1942) was an early unsung heroine of psychoanalysis in terms of her thinking about women. The 1911 talk that I am about to describe is hidden away in a dusty corner of the earliest Freudian literature. I am startled by her aptness for my own thesis. Unlike Freud or most of his followers (including Klein, who was certainly deeply into mothers and infants in her own, but phantasical way; or Adler, who pronounced that maternal hatred was primary), Hilferding gives pride of place to the role of a sexually mature woman's physical pleasure without defensively needing to theorize it as masochism. Also, she does not shield from pain in childbirth. She unabashedly sees birth's centrality to female physical existence. Had she stayed with Freud, her influence might have made a vast difference in his theories about women. Her refreshing main focus is on the woman herself in her physiological prowess, where the child is more in the background.

Margarete Hilferding was 40 when she gave this talk (Appignanesi and Forrester, 1992). She had then 3- and 6-year-old sons. She was close to early mothering herself and was sensitized to the interplay of the bodies of mother and child together. In this paper, there was a strong emphasis on bald sexual sensations of fetal movement, touch, and suckling. When she talks of how the intensity of a mother–child sexualized bond can be prolonged due to alienation from a husband, one wonders if the alienation from her own husband may have been factored in as knowledge. (She divorced her husband later; Forrester, personal communication, 2011.) Little of the little that has been written about her is yet to be translated into English.[1]

Margaret Hilferding was the first woman member of the Vienna Psychoanalytic Society and was introduced there (against opposition) in 1910. She was also the first woman to study medicine in the Vienna medical school. Being a follower of Adler, she was indirectly extruded from, or otherwise left, Freud's circle in protest on his behalf in 1911 (Balsam, 2003).

The title of this, her introductory talk, as recorded by Otto Rank, was: "On the Basis of Mother Love" (vol. three, 1910–1911, in *Minutes of the Vienna Psychoanalytic Society* pp. 118–125). Hilferding said she had observed in her medical practice (before she practiced analysis) that there are mothers who look forward to the birth of a child, but have no mother-love after the delivery. She saw this "nonexistence of mother-love" in the refusal to nurse; or in the wish to give the child away; or in hostile acts against the child. The first child, she noticed, evokes the mother's maximal hostility (see below the group's horror at this idea). The youngest child, in being spoiled and pampered, she said, suffers from a form of reversal of maternal hostility. Dr. Hilferding's boldness in 1911 was to announce to the group that there is no *innate* mother-love and to point up that the female experience of aggression or love in the psychological bond between her and her infant is intimately interlaced with the bodily pleasure or pain in delivery and nurturing. Social constructs, if you will, for her flow out of this wellspring.

In that era, theorists of gendered human behavior were dyed-in-the-wool biological essentialists. A mother's love was assumed to be biologically inbuilt, instinctual, "natural," and therefore reliable. Freud's group too, in tune with medical ideas, assumed innate mother-love. This unexamined stance (even as they were struggling to understand a psychological inner life), likely drove them to idealize but distance themselves from women's physicality. In turn, this led to simplification in their burgeoning theories about female pleasure and aggression. As we will see later in Rank's account of their discussion, Hilferding's challenge to an inbuilt mother-love went down badly in this all-male group. Recently, for example (before Hilferding's time), they had discussed among themselves as naturally obvious a mother's overweening love and indulgence for her first-born son (see Chapter 9 on mothers and sons for a fuller account).

Therefore, Hilferding maintained that there was no innate mother-love. Rather, "it is by way of the physical involvement between mother and child that love is called forth. ... Certain changes in the mother's sexual life are brought on through the child" (p. 114). For a time after delivery, she thought, the child represents "a natural sexual object for the mother. There must ... exist *between mother and child certain sexual relationships which must be capable of further development*" (p. 115; italics mine). One can see that Hilferding was trying to apply Freud's early sexual instinct theory to her own obstetrical observations, even as she captured a vigorous sense of physically libidinal reciprocity between mother and child that was fresh and original in that group. She did not, for example, think primarily interpersonally, where she might have even struggled with the now accepted notion that different children from the same mother can evoke different reactions in her, separate from their birth order. Hilferding was thinking of a woman's bodily serial experience of childbirths.

In light of current research on mother–infant bonding and the role of the hormone and neuro-transmitter oxytocin, Hilferding's statements and observations were not only prescient but revolutionary. Bonding as a mutual behavior (or lack of it) can be tracked by the release of oxytocin. Oxytocin was not fully understood, but was first discovered in 1909 (2 years before Hilferding's talk to the Vienna Psychoanalytic Society). Henry Dale identified it as a hormone extractable from the human brain that caused contractions in pregnant cats, and it was learned subsequently to help speed labor and lactation. Its significance for human maternal behavior and infant bonding had to await the 1970s. Three decades and more of research ensued, led by C. Sue Carter, a behavioral neuro-endocrinologist, who later found that her research with voles had application to human bonding (Carter and Ahnert, 2005).

Hilferding recognized that there was a great deal of pleasure as well as pain in the sensations of the female body. This too has taken decades to be acknowledged by psychoanalysis as average-expectable experience (Holtzman and Kulish, 2002, 2008, 2011; Dimen, 2003; Elise, 2008 and others). She offered that fetal movements awake pleasure and love in the mother, and she suggested that this might be sexual. The baby's birth caused a loss of all this body pleasure, she postulated, and that for some this had negative consequences for bonding. Milk shooting into the breast gave rise to another pleasurable sensation: "It can be said that the infant's sexual sensations must find a correlate in corresponding sensations in the mother" (p. 115).

Anticipating Loewald in his account of the mutuality of the human crucible of object relations and the drives in the 1960s and 1970s, or Winnicott and others later, or Laplanche (1987), she states: "... *if we assume an oedipal complex in the child, it finds its origin in sexual excitation by way of the mother, the prerequisite for which is an equally erotic feeling on the mother's part* ... (italics mine). The child represents for the mother "a natural sex object," while these pleasurable sexual stimuli coincide with the period of the infant's need for this care. After this, the mother has to "make way for the husband—or perhaps the next child" (p. 115).

Mother-love, though not innate, she thinks, may be acquired either through the nursing and physical care of the first child and may become innate, as it were, for subsequent children by the ignition of these intimate inbuilt memories.

Group discussion

There was much resistance that night to Hilferding's ideas. Universally, the men did not, or could not, enter into this discourse about female physicality of a newly birthed mother together with her baby. The men commonly tended to craft their comments toward male experience as the center of their emotional understanding. For example, the first comment was that it is the loving feeling toward the man during the coitus that leads to conception, that results in mother-love toward that child. They enunciated their own theories about say, child mistreatment; or they expressed observations about a woman's "withholding sex" to her husband at the time of breast-feeding; or they abstractly associated to anthropology, mythology, literature, and nature. Strangely, they wished for more hard science! Adler, who was the most in tune, did address the paper topic directly. However, he too "taught" Hilferding from his own observations, which were all right, about mothers and babies, the effects of the culture, nursing difficulties, etc. He did this, though, without considering her new hypotheses. Friedjung contributed that father love can be deficient too. Sadger claimed implicitly that the sexologist Havelock Ellis knew better than Hilferding, citing that the sexual sensation in the nipple was "the deepest basis for mother-love." He averred that "suckling provides the mother with … a new … unknown, perverse feeling of pleasure." He entirely ignored the emotionally normative element that Hilferding was trying to convey about these pleasures and their impact on the emotional growth of the child.

The extreme emotional distance that the Wednesday men convey in Rank's notes seems tied to their view of how men *ought* to be. Federn (who to his credit was the person who brought Hilferding into the group against opposition about female members), expresses many gender stereotypes that in those days masqueraded as current "science." Fathers, he proclaimed, who have warm feelings for children are essentially "feminized." He believes that there are certain women with a "… favorable formation of the introitus vaginae" (p. 122) who essentially are built in their pelvis and constitution for childbirth with "very strong organ instincts" and that "maternal hatred will be displayed by women who have predominantly masculine characteristics." Quoting some book, he says that it was demonstrated that maltreatment of children "as well as other transgressions" occur with "degenerate mothers … whose organs are not meant for mother-love" (p. 123).

Hilferding's courage in tackling "mother hate" through examining love with the new Freudian emphasis on sex—in spite of her disclaimers about being "physiological"—strike one now as being very psychoanalytic, in light, say, of Freud's yet-to-be-developed structural theory, as in his famed statement, "The ego is first and foremost a bodily ego" (1923: p. 26). These radical concepts, ignored by the group, were a source of Hilferding feeling misunderstood. Not until Winnicott, Loewald, or Kernberg, or the ascension of Bowlby's attachment theory, or relational theory, did psychoanalysis pay close attention to the mutual dynamic matrix from which an infant's psychic emotional life is ignited. What reradicalizes Hilferding in 2011 is her crystal clear view of the body's role in these complex psychic relations.

Talking this way about mothers was more than some group members could bear—One said, "too much has been said about mother hatred!" and moved on quickly to animal kingdom mother-love. Others decried her view that the *first* child (because that is often the most difficult birth) may be the one in most danger of hatred. (In October 1910, the men had noted some emotional dangers of being the oldest child but because he was the mother's *naturally favorite* oldest boy-child—as was at least Freud.) Federn referred to this as "Hilferding's denial of mother-love for the first child" (Nunberg and Federn, 1963: p. 122). Hilferding's material, being focused so specifically on mothers, the mother's body, and the infant in real time was novel for the group. Their discussion topics that year—guilt, magic, myth, and principles of mental functioning—were slanted either toward male experience or were gender neutral.

Freud's response to Hilferding was to hold himself aloof from both the materials about the maternal body and the encoded psychology of Hilferding's commentary on the mother–child bond. He oddly offered, "the only way to find out something about mother-love can be through *statistical* examination" (italics mine)! One has no idea how he came up with that suggestion except through discomfort! I suppose he may have meant that mothers were so mysterious and that this topic would only later be revealed by hard science. Freud tried to be appreciative but was condescending. "It is praiseworthy that the speaker undertook a psychoanalytic investigation into a topic that, as the result of the convention that we maintain, had been held back from investigation" (p. 118). However, he also delivered a potential blow when he added that "those explanations that she arrived at before ... psychoanalysis are the ones that are the most estimable, being original and independent" (p. 118). This could be read as quite a put-down. Appignanesi and Forrester (1992), however, also interpret this comment of Freud's as possibly kindly, by suggesting that he was warning her against too slavishly taking on his psychoanalytic insights. Adler took the position that, in a mother, hatred was more primary than love. Hilferding was a follower of Adler, and she was one of those that resigned from Freud's group after the decisive vote in October of the same year which demanded that members, because of "incompatible theories," essentially choose between Freud and Adler.

Freud offered also a lot from his own ways of thinking—that the disappointment with the baby could be a sharp contrast between the mother's fantasy and her reality; or it could occur in young women harmed by modern novels which stimulated their yearning for a child, whereas they were in reality craving sex; or in a disappointment that newborns are perceived as "ugly"—which, he says, they actually are! He interpreted the mistreatment of children from the point of view of his own contribution about over-reaction to the child's masturbation, and the mother's own infantile sexuality, i.e., where the mother is really the little girl within her, hostile to her new sibling. These are good points but at considerable emotional distance from the topic of the mother qua mother. Hilferding said that his comment on the mother's sibling was "too far into the psychic sphere for it to be able to explain anything to us." She was certainly not intimidated by either the eminence or the insights of any of her fellow group members.

The mother's experience was therefore evoked powerfully by Margarete Hilferding in *mutual* connection with the baby—responsive sensations of fetal movement, milk shooting into the breast, as a powerful organizer of this mother's mental life that reflects the organization of the infant's mental life. She evinced some women's sense of loss in the birth, of her sexual excitement, of her loss of pleasure in and postnatal rejection of the infant. The bond of sensual and sexual feelings between mother and infant were observed by Hilferding to form the nidus of the burgeoning potential oedipal bond. She was long before her time.

Early Freud

Paradoxically, Freud's interest in childbirth was greatest earliest in his career, before he became firmly convinced of his theories of penis envy and the oedipal complex. Actual male and female bodies, and the concrete differences between them, had once been readily acknowledged by Freud. In fact, they had enjoyed prominence in his original conception of psychoanalysis, especially in his 1905 paper "Three Essays on Sexuality." He recognized then that the question, "Where do babies come from?" was as important to the child as the Riddle of the Sphinx was to the ancients (Freud, 1905: p. 195). At that point in the evolution of his theories, he saw children's concern about their physical origins as central. However, later, that issue was allowed to drift into the background of his thoughts. Informally, no analyst or patient would deny the physical realities of childbirth or its importance. Yet, they are repeatedly "forgotten"—as part of the subtle process by which our field continues to avoid integrating the female body into developmental theory.[2] Freud said, "Forgetting impressions, scenes or experiences nearly always reduces itself to shutting them off" (1924: p. 148). As with Freud's patient who "forgets," though, I predict that an average clinical reader of this book will say: "As a matter of fact I have always known it ..." (p. 148). It is known, but kept out of sight by suppression or repression.

Politics and theory

Zenia Fliegel (1973) has drawn vividly to our attention a pattern of recurrent suppression of ideas that challenge Freud's theories about women. Fliegel (1973) says that Horney's first groundbreaking paper in 1924 (in which she proposed that significant penis envy was actually a defense against a girl's primary femininity) implies the existence of "an intrinsic pleasure-oriented feminine sexuality" (p. 388), an idea "profoundly alien to Freud's thought" (p. 388).

Horney's controversial implication of a female libido and a primary femininity lent a freer, less trammeled cast to her view of female sexuality than Freud's. Take, for example, her enthusiasm about childbirth. In her 1926 paper "The flight from woman hood," Horney mocks Ferenczi's view that men and women develop their interest in coitus as a wish to return to the mother's womb. A woman, Horney spells out, is therefore believed to fulfill her own sexual longings by a masochistic conversion to identification with the child she may conceive! Ferenczi had also offered that the real meaning of childbirth was that the male was victorious, having imposed this burden on the female! Horney bursts forth: "At this point I, as a woman, ask in amazement, and what about motherhood? And the blissful consciousness of bearing a new life within oneself? And the ineffable happiness of the increasing expectation of the appearance of this new being? And the joy when it finally makes its appearance and one holds it for the first time in one's arms? And the deep pleasurable feeling of satisfaction in suckling it, and the happiness of the whole period when the infant needs her care?" (p. 329). However, from the beginning, Freud rejected Horney's vision. Fliegel juxtaposed and compared relevant passages from Horney and from Freud's 1925 paper "Some Psychical Consequences of the Anatomical Distinction Between the Sexes." Many of his formulations there directly reverse her theses. Freud insisted, for example, that it was phallic castration anxiety, penis envy, and a rejection of the mother that propelled a girl's baby desires and oedipal interests. Elizabeth Young-Bruehl (1988) points out in her biography of Anna Freud that she was in her second phase of analysis with Freud at that very time. This may have unwittingly influenced Freud's insistent stance about the desired and overly dominant role for the father's penis in female development, which also, incidentally, was set against Horney's added view of the father's large penetrative sex as frightening to a female. It may have been too hard for Freud to think of himself as frightening to his youngest daughter/analysand, or certainly for her to share with her father a negative and frightening sexual fantasy about his penis.

Freud's followers had many reasons to feel protective of him: his cancer; his grief over his favorite grandson's death; their fears of divisiveness in the fledgling international movement; Klein's power and following; and the problems over lay analysis in the United States. They soon relinquished any support of dissenters, and Fliegel notes that, right up to the time of her writing in 1973, views of female development in the literature remained aligned with Freud's.

Political swings still affect the theory of female sexuality. Leon Hoffman (1999) and Dana Birksted-Breen (1993) comment that, after the debates of the 1920s and early 30s, the subject of female sexuality disappeared from the classic psychoanalytic literature for over 30 years. Breen (1993) notes that there was a "spurt of papers that appeared [about women's orgasms] in the late 1960s and early 1970s after Masters and Johnson's (1966) publication of their observations of the female sexual response" (p. 14). Both Hoffman and Breen postulate that this heated discussion of the 1970s diminished again because "the increased focus on object relations in the literature replaced further inquiry into drive concepts" (Hoffman, 1999: p. 1146). This is a point that I too wonder about, and will refer to later. Hoffman, talking about the lack of sustained interest in the once hotly debated clitoris, the only part of the genitals of either sex that appears to have no purpose other than pleasure, challenges, "Is it plausible to hypothesize that psychoanalysts have twice sharply curtailed their study of women's passions for a reason? Did it feel safer to study the vicissitudes of object relations than the impact on both patient and analyst of the intense sexual and aggressive feelings of women?" (p. 1146). This is an open question. Apart from Kulish and Holtzman's (1991, 1996) interest in the hymen and clitoris, contemporary writing analysts have yawned, and we scarcely mention the clitoris any more since its fall from

phallic grace. If a Martian visitor were to come in and use psychoanalytic literature to research the clitoris, its mature joys would certainly not be evident, but
rather its dangers for promoting infantilism. Nobody, of course, believes that
these days, and yet I wonder if many may still hold onto this view nervously.
There must be some good reasons why few analysts these days care about these
details of our patients' sexuality.

Horney was not taken seriously by "classical" psychoanalysis, and until about
the last 15 years was essentially marginalized as a feminist "social theorist."

Many contemporary analysts disagree with the centrality of the drive theory
that was synonymous with "psychoanalysis" for such a long time, but it gave
permission at that time to focus on the body, and it spurred an avid interest in
trying to understand more about the mind's registration of the body's functioning.
It was really *because* of this foundational work, I believe, that the theory's later
cultural lags became evident, as well as the special inequities in the theory of
women's gendered and sexual development. As Adrienne Harris (2000) said, "the
first generation of women analysts ... are striking both for the close obedience to
Freud, who was in a number of cases their analyst, but also for the supple, fresh
experience-near quality of the writing and for the prominent place they give to
female pleasure" (p. 233). I agree, and attribute this to their interest in instinct
theory in spite of its then distortions.

Helene Deutsch remains one of the few writers over the century of psychoanalysis who has written about childbearing. She devoted a whole chapter
(Chapter 7) of her 1945 book *Psychology of Women: Motherhood* to delivery,
following a chapter on pregnancy. If one can maintain some distance from
her dubious certainties about innate female masochism and narcissism, and
from her narrow conviction that a true woman's greatest destiny is to produce
children, her clinical accounts are full of interest, filled with conflicts emerging
and resolving joys, delights, hatreds, and deadnesses—a vivid and heady evoca-
tion of the delivery room. Here are a few random sentences to convey her intense
involvement. On the "conflict between the will to retain and the will to expel"
(p. 212): "the being in the uterus already has his double, who is the subject of
all expectations and fantasized wish fulfillments and whose real existence as
a distinct person is gradually approaching" ... "the realization, through bodily
sensations, of the imminent destruction of this unity, manifests itself in the
mother's heightened identification with the child and opposes the expulsive
tendencies. On the other hand, the fantasy of the child as external love object of
the very near future has been developing during ... the pregnancy and it now joins
with the negative emotions of the expulsive tendencies. If the conflict between the
two tendencies assumes a pathologic character and the expulsive forces win
the upper hand the result may be a premature delivery."

Deutsch's women are rambunctious; they refuse to be passive participants, but
she sees in this a defense against the fear of the birth process. Others are eerily
passive and submissive, and here too she sees fear in the process of stalemated
birth. Her women "fall into joyful excitation"—"I thought I would never have

a child"; others cannot wait to see the infant and describe being separated only by a curtain of the "abdominal casing" from it (p. 237); others turn away from the baby as an alien. Deutsch had a vast work experience in women's clinics that has been equaled by no contemporary analyst, dating back from her earliest career in Vienna in the early 1920s and continuing after her emigration to Boston. She had consultative bedside obstetric involvement. She listened passionately, acutely if judgmentally, for example, observing the effects of anesthesia, bewailing the modern desire for a painless delivery which she associates with a barrier even to loving the newborn, "The [anesthetized woman] experiences the whole process uncreatively," she scolds, "not as giving life to a child, but an operation that removes something harmful" (p. 251).

One point of this volume is to highlight the plasticity of the female body. I have mentioned this also in Chapter 3 with the clinical example of DE. Living through its pubertal transformation and living with the menstrual cycle, females mentally register a rhythm of dimensional corporeal oscillation—a body that tightens and loosens, that contracts and swells, that closes and opens, that expands and diminishes. This happens subtly in tune with menstrual and hormonal shifts, but not subtly at all (as every little girl can see and observe with fear or envy) in pregnancy and then after delivery. Little Hans (Freud, 1909), who bore partial witness to the birth of Hanna when he spied the bloody bowls and bed-pan in the birthing bedchamber on his way to visit his newly delivered mother, captured the drama of these shifting dimensions in his dream of the large giraffe and the "crumpled giraffe" (p. 41). His father interpreted the latter as his baby sister Hanna's "castrated" female genital, but Hans's dream work may have had more to do with his preoccupations about birth, and his attempts to integrate his recent visual experiences of his mother's pregnant and then delivered body. The female body experience is a dynamic and three-dimensional one, and we have never allotted to the process of observing this phenomenon in individuals, tracking it, eliciting its psychic meaning, and integrating it that it deserves. I wish that other analysts too would contribute more material about this element of female physical existence. These processes of inner appreciation of three-dimensional shifts are more akin to an advanced calculus as opposed to simple arithmetic. Efforts one way or another to exert control over and render this dimensionality static do preoccupy many women.[3] Finding out more clinically to fill out this set of ideas for me is still a work in progress. It involves listening with the body in mind and not necessarily focusing on the personal interactions, while a patient talks, say, about how "controlled and controlling" she is; how deeply upset she is to see a half-pound rise in her scales in her morning weigh-in; how she flees filling her stomach when hungry or berates herself for laxity if she feels "fat." Sometimes, we hear these common themes and feel we "know" what is being said. I think often we don't. The exquisite sensitivity that some women have to every perceived swelling and size increase, or every size decrease, cannot usually be explained by her "male" aspirations or envies—though at times this is apt. Being a "phallic" woman or aspiring to a body phallic ideal has been one explanation offered for the distress.

Many formulations exist about the internalized critic, or cases showing various parental or interpersonal conflicts leading to such self-criticism. However, it seems to me that there is more here that encodes physical elements of the female body itself. If women are primed to the interior of their bodies through bowel movements, say, or the stomach's rhythms of hunger, etc., or the ebb and flow of tissue dimensions in the menstrual cycle, why would they not grow utterly comfortable in these ever-mobile body states? Flux is arguably normative for a woman's physical housing, though many do not accept this intuitively; or they seem fretfully to read the shifts with anxiety, as if there is "something wrong." The basal state of the constant flux of the mature female body is peaked by pregnancy and childbirth. Could it be that hidden anxieties about this major personal confrontation with this body flux, accompanied as it is by serious matters of life and death, is a kind of black hole that lurks in many, many female psyches?

Genital anxiety, exhibitionism, and physical pleasure

In contemplating what "childbirth" has meant and means to psychoanalysis, three intimately related body topics need to be addressed: "female genital anxiety" (see also Chapter 3 on terminology) or, what is unfortunately still called by the misnomer, "phallic castration anxiety"; female exhibitionism; and the role of straightforward female body *pleasure* which has been obscured and dominated in theory about the female body by the concept of "masochism," championed especially by Helene Deutsch. Masochism seemed to be the only way open in classical drive theory to think about the possibility of female pleasure in childbearing and the act of childbirth. Harold Blum (1976) pointed out sensibly that masochism in females is a *pathological* variant of pleasure seeking. Analysts nowadays tend to examine a topic such as masochism from angles that are not body-based, such as the object relational aspects of the pre-oedipal era, for example, as in wounded infantile narcissism (e.g., Glick and Meyers, 1993). A linkage between childbirth and masochism is largely ignored, and therefore the original meaning has not been worked through to the point of rejection.

Case vignettes

The following vignettes will illustrate (conscious and unconscious) themes of body adequacy, pride, excitement, and the attendant guilt, shame, and anxiety associated with the fantasy, or the memory, of the body's potential birthing accomplishments.

This first vignette, a long one, illustrates body exhibitionism in relation to ideas of pregnancy and "delivering the goods," whether in the context of having a baby, or having sex with a partner.

Ms. HJ,[4] now in her forties, divorced, a single mother with lovers and a young daughter, was the fourth child of five of Midwestern parents. Her father was a successful and wealthy building contractor, and her mother a schoolteacher. Everyone in her family was highly intelligent; she and her three sisters were always head of the class in school, and all of them went to Ivy League colleges and professional schools. The fifth child, however, "the baby," who was 4 years her junior and only boy, was hit by a car while crossing the road and killed, when he was 8 and she 12 (and in puberty, just taking an interest in boys). HJ had been very close to him. "I couldn't wait for him to be born," she said. "I was devastated when he died." And her eyes still glistened with tears in the telling. She felt rightly that his life and death had a great deal to do with her present difficulty sustaining close relations with "boys," as she called her lovers.

Her lifestyle at this juncture, with a live-in nanny, working in a nearby town in a dedicated fashion for the advertising branch of a big construction company where she was getting rapid promotions, involved presenting her firm and visiting dignitaries with "pitches" for advertising interests. It was fast-paced work that depended for its success not only on her business smarts but also on her public persuasiveness in creating financial deals. Many of the members of her audience were male. "I can tell when they light up, put the spotlight on me; when they gesture toward me, when they avert their gaze one-to-one but still give stealthy glances at my boobs or ass." She said, and giggled, "I can tell the ones that are totally intrigued. And then they phone or text me afterwards, ask me to drinks, and then I know I've got them." I heard that statement as a commentary on her sexualized business come-on and its results; her excitement in the telling and her pleasurable wriggle on the couch caused her phone to fall out of her pocket and onto the floor.

I asked her about what she made of that. "A phone-fall! Just as I was thinking of that last one, Joe, and his phone call … Oh I don't know … Suppose I want you to witness something—like how it is I get them to fall for me." In that particular session about 2 years into the analytic process, HJ had analogized me to her watching mother, fearing my disapproval of her "unbounded pleasures in showing off" as she designated it. Still later, she fantasized envy on my part. She was sure I would want her to be "safely married" and more stay-at-home where, we agreed, she (and I) would imaginatively be protected from these "shameless" adventures. We worked on how she attributed that my enquiry was intended to shame her. She was regularly angry at my intrusions into an inner life she had preferred to keep private from "grown-ups," especially senior women (like me). We thus were involved in her oedipal configurations. Her father had been a dashing guy in her estimate, and she consciously saw mother as "pretty dowdy," and "in truth no match for me." These classically oedipal scenarios led on to illuminate the great trauma of HJ's life.

Albert, her adored little brother, had been born just when she was at the height of excited curiosity about babies in mommy's tummy. He died when she was becoming excited about assuming at last the longed-for shape of a mature woman. She was a highly competitive child both with her older sisters and with her mother (Kuba, 2011), and she began to remember as a young girl actively yearning to be the same shape as her pregnant mother. "I thought her shape was SO great—I still am drawn to doodle these pumpkin shapes over and over in every gorgeous detailed texture with my felt colored pens." The features of the mother's body that she stressed were the big breasts and abdomen, and the feel of the hidden creature's motions and kicks within. Evidence that we were also dealing with materials that were partially unconscious emerged in dreams, or in references right in the office. One such was her reactions to a painting of Georgia O'Keefe. For her, those voluptuous red and purple flowers were associated to images of the vulva, the introitus, and the vaginal canal, and at times images of genitals interlocked in intercourse. Ms. HJ then remembered being both fascinated and excitedly horror-struck by how her baby brother got out of her mother's vulva. She talked intensely to her sisters about this; the girls shared fantasies and giggles, which they talked about in later years, too. They were preoccupied with how the head of a baby could escape out of their mother's vulva. How much did it hurt? Did she bleed? Buckets worth? Did she scream? Was it fun? Oh-my-god … How could they witness this for themselves? Sometimes they lay in bed together at night in what must have been in the first years of little Albert's life, endlessly wondering what it would be like to "do that"—that is, to have sex with a man some day and give birth to a baby. "We looked at each other's breasts and vulvas in fascination, horror, and admiration to see how we grew and changed as one or other of us reached puberty. We endlessly compared our sizes."

As these stories unfolded bit by bit in the context of the daily happenings of her life, or in reference to my behavior or her fantasies about it, HJ both recreated a history of her preoccupations about her sexed body and the successful sublimations of her present work life. Occasionally, she would speak about her fascination with her baby brother's body, but she was far more interested in her father's mature body and attitudes about sex than in little Albert. The familial sexual associations emerged in her associations as she talked of having sex with one of her boyfriends or feeling competition with a girlfriend.

HJ did not seem to me to be very troubled with "penis envy" in a rivalrous way, as are some women who view their brothers more as peers, or as sexed and gendered favorites of the parents. The death of her brother may have repressed this material more deeply than the treatment could reach. HJ had vaguely at first, and then with stronger conviction because of the recounting of various family scenes, remembered having had a "secret crush" on her father. She could easily imagine having wanted HIS baby. In fact, in speaking of her own daughter one day and her similar coloring to her father, HJ touched on the idea that this child was in fantasy like a child of her oedipal longings that proved to her that she was "the head of her class," triumphing over mother and sisters. She came to an insight that her divorced husband and the other males were "boys" because none of them could measure up to dad. Being daddy's girl had been greatly prized, but it was mother's body that had been the richest source of envy and admiration and mystery for these girls to share in this family. The 101% … the grade to beat … the clinched deals … the big pay-off. The measure of success was to be as filled with the power that mother had, the power to get a male sexually interested and so to secure the best prize of all, one's own baby. Each business "presentation" that HJ gave to her audience of men was therefore a vehicle to show her wares, to compete unconsciously with her mother's body especially in its procreative state. Her psyche had the fluidity of an artist in her ability to regress, fantasize, play out a past superimposed on a present, and still utilize the interconnections between the past and present It was animated now as the analysis progressed, this past psychic reality propelling a sublimated and adaptive present tense.

Here follows a pivotal fantasy scenario that demonstrates HJ's attachment to her body and her wish to show it off to gain a pleasurable yield from a male—a yield that was somehow always connected to her female sexual ability and her pride in thoughts of procreating and "producing."

HJ talked many times of being called up to the podium to give a "PowerPoint" presentation. (The phallic reference titillated her, but the associative tilt was to her own female "power point"—the vulva, clitoris, and opening to the vagina—her "cunt" or "hot point," as she felt free to say to me or quip with computer lingo after several years.) She reported a fantasy of taking off her panties, lying down, opening her legs, and feeling erotic as she imagined showing her vulva—as she said, "pink, pouting, slightly open, and damp"—to the male onlookers for whom she was showing off. The fantasy would occur when she was excited by clients "to attract their advertising business." She felt playful and elated about it as she told it to her analyst, and in the early years, there were pangs of the forbidden. Sometimes, she confessed that she would go afterwards to a nearby bathroom to masturbate. In this fantasy, her excitement would culminate with the image of the head of a baby coming through her widely stretched perineum, to be followed by the rest of its slithery form. The sexual excitement that accumulated as she progressed in her "floor show" seemed to "demand" this masturbatory action outlet.

This is by no means the first time I have encountered highly sexually excited orgasmic masturbatory fantasies about giving birth. The contents at times contain pleasurable components of fantasizing about anticipated relief after a wildly exciting orgiastic explosive birth, the yield of a tantalizing prior build-up of tension of "will it, will it not happen? Now? No! Yes … yes!" Anal fantasy[5] is more closely related to these birthing scenarios than male phallic fantasy, as in the childhood fantasy of rectally passing great "gifts"—sometimes for onlookers such as mother, husband, midwife, or obstetrician. Such fantasies are woven into active female body autoeroticism, analogous perhaps to male masturbatory fantasies of pleasurable explosion in orgasm. In listening closely to these fantasies and urges of HJ, I could not detect tonalities of co-existing loss, or the anxiety about being inadequate or a fraud that I've come to think of as associations to the vulval "damage" ideas that characterize true phallic castration fantasies and penis envy.

HJ recalled being thrillingly sexually stimulated by the examining fingers of her obstetrician while she was in the lithotomy position during prenatal examinations. Her associations led to all kinds of feelings and sensations about giving birth—the "show" beforehand in the bursting of the waters, the stretching, pushing, and "crowning" of the head. And, her main memories in this regard would return to her mother and other women's "crowning glories"—their babies.

An analytic reader will appropriately wonder how this birthing preoccupation was influenced by the death of the little brother, and if HJ's repeated baby-making fantasy was shaped by a wish to make up to her parents for the family loss. Therapists could also intuit that the sexually tantalizing elements of HJ's floor-show might encode fears of direct sexual fantasy about her father, or about sex with other males. We might wonder about her homosexual titillation of her sisters (and her analyst as a transferential sister) or her procreative "pregenital" fantasy-systems. Her showing off on the podium, after all, was also filled with sexual tension build-up. We analyzed elements of "tease" and inhibition of heterosexual directness, such as patterns that have been reported about the sexual behavior of exotic dancers, but HJ also was capable of cocreating the "big deal" for her firm. She did not become paralyzed in a teasing mode. Later in the treatment, she actually had a relationship with a male boss; she terminated while pregnant for the second time, with plans to move away from the area. Her great enjoyment continued in her theater of PowerPoint presentations. (I am leaving out how her lovers and this new husband fit together in the story, but suffice to say that the new man was seen by her as a "man" this time around, and not as a "boy.")

Vignettes from case Ms. JK

Four years of psychoanalytic work helped Ms. JK, a 39-year-old divorced mother of two, rediscover enjoyment in her sexuality, and also uncovered the sadistic, sexual, and intensely aggressive mother inside herself. With this work, awareness dawned of her own subtle participation in writing a script for her life that her mother in fact had written for her over the years of her childhood. She was one of the many female patients who dreaded finding out in analysis that they are "just like my mother." This statement, in my experience, always turns out to be prescient! By analyzing the identification with her own mother's sadism toward herself (and others), JK gradually discovered (or rediscovered) previously secret hidden pleasures in her own body. The deliveries of her two children had been pivotal experiences for her in terms of demonstrating her own athleticism to her-self, and in partially overcoming the heavy childhood sexual competition from her mother. Interestingly, she productively made use of a relationship with a European au pair girl to help her accomplish this. (One can see the "good" maternal trans-ferential possibilities here, but I am not going to elaborate on this aspect.)

Here are some of the things she said about her own body in relation to her mother's, which are relevant to the impact of her thinking about pregnancy and birth.

About her genitals

"Mother used to say with that sneer, 'Keep your crotch closed. I don't want to see it!' So I'd try to keep my legs together always. But at night I'd have horrible nightmares that a needle was piercing my labia and I was being sewn up. I'd wake up feeling sick." Mayer (1985), Richards (1996), and D. Quinidoz (2003) have written about the loss of a girl's genital and reproductive capacities as a (maternal) punishment. Oedipal punishment was one strand in the analysis of JK—but the most powerful feature was a fierce female competition with her overpowering mother about her development into an adult woman.

About her developing body

Ms. JK, an only child, pleaded with her parents to let her go to dance classes. Finally, they agreed, but by then JK was 9 years old and pudgy. She was alone in a beginning class of 5-year-olds, and she towered above them and outstripped them in weight. "My naïve excitement turned to disgust as the weeks went on—I saw myself in the mirror—ugh—compared to the others. My mother was right about me. I didn't belong there. It was my own stupid insistence that got me there. They were all like dainty elves. I was a big, fat, pink elephant in my tights and tutu. I was the Mamma Bear at the recital when we did Goldilocks. I remember being in a brown hairy suit with a pillow tucked into my front—I looked just like my friend's mom when she was expecting her little sister—all big belly and clump! I was clumping out onto the stage and I had to try out the "just right" chair. It's all a muddle in my mind ... but I remember vividly the chair broke right under me. Everybody laughed. They were supposed to, I think—but I felt humiliated, so huge and hairy and ugly and protuberant ... yes, protuberant ... like a tuber, a big round turnip, a turnip head—that was me. Turnips make me think 'turn-ups'. ... An image of me turned upside down and someone peering into my vagina and insides to see what on earth is in there. I used to think maybe I was dense like a turnip inside. Hard, like I had a baby in there and couldn't get it out. Stupid idea ... my mother always said I was dense—she always said 'Don't be dense'. I felt ... thick. Actually, I dreaded the day I'd have to carry a baby. I think it had to do with mom ... the idea of her being pregnant with me and me coming out of her was ... it still is ... repulsive. She said I was so *hard* to push out that the doctor had to pull me out with forceps. I must have been like a big rock inside her." One can see in the material all the back and forth linguistic references to her own insides and reproductive organs and the fantasy-contents of her mother's belly tinged with her mother's stories of her birth. She includes old memories of anticipation of pregnancy and childbirth some day.

Some scattered comments taken from different sessions about the actual deliveries of her own children

"I luckily found a wonderful doula, Maria, who was with me both times. She was so positive—she'd say, "You think your body is a poor buy, a lemon—it's not a lemon. Don't listen to your Mamma! It's strong and hearty, and your baby is in there just waiting to get out." She somehow filled me with these strong images and I was as receptive as a sponge—that's what amazed me. She and I would go swimming in the last days of my pregnancy. She actually taught me to swim properly and breathe and use my arms and legs and let my head go in the water ... she'd say, "Now race, as fast as you can! There's a crocodile behind you and I *know* you're getting away free and clear ... go, girl!" We'd make it a keep-fit game. Maybe I loved Maria. I loved her far more than I could ever love my mother. She believed in my body and she had a super-sleek athletic and lithe body herself. She'd also talk about sex in a fun, playful way ... my mother never did. I had a very hard time letting her go ..." And JK wept.

After the births I thought, "My capacious births ..." "My expanding, mind-expanding, girth-expanding, body-affirming births." "I thought I'll never again feel wimpy or too awkward—or that I didn't belong ... of course, I did again, in bits and pieces, but it never was so bad." JK felt "discovered and restored" in her body through the intensity of and her loving responsiveness to Maria's birthing coaching.

She gave an account of Maria's help in the births, being beside her, breathing rhythmically to the contraction pains, soothing her back, massaging her strained legs, helping her change positions, and finally, joyfully urging her to push when the time came. With the chorus of nurses in the delivery room, the two women ended up in tears of congratulations together with the newborn baby on JK's abdomen in a little side-room after the delivery. JK's husband was peripherally present in the first birth, but they were divorced by the time of the second birth.

In a study of her own Yale University 1984 classmate alumnae, Jennifer Stuart (2007, unpublished 2008) found that women whose own mothers loved their mothering role were much less conflicted in their adult lives about possible tensions between work and motherhood. In her case reports, Stuart, like me, reports a subject whose mother was pathologically anxious at every turn, and who had an excellent experience with a doula during her second pregnancy and delivery. The experience long outlasted the doula in terms of the woman's increased confidence.

It seems that the experience of childbirth may be so potent that the regression mobilized in the service of the ego may even make room for an internalization of an alternative mothering experience for a birthing woman. The durability of this internalization would be tested by its ability to withstand the subsequent separation of the doula from the young mother. Can she function at a higher level and with more ease in her body and in relationships in the subsequent years? This novel internal structural shift has been unexplored territory in relation to childbirth.

Alternatively, many stories about horrible experiences of pain and physical torment with anesthesias gone wrong, or insensitive obstetricians or cruel nurses, also readily circulate. One wonders about the immensity of the inner reverberations of such traumatic experiences for a mother. Similar to Margarete Hilferding (1911), I too believe that the mother's experience in childbirth may have a significant impact on her relationship to that particular child. I have never seen a *detailed* psychological account of a woman's delivery, easy or hard, followed by a *detailed* study of her internal relationship with that infant. Is this yet another taboo topic? This is an example of how much in the dark we still are with this common situation, and how open this vast area to psychoanalytic exploration and thinking is.

Notes

1 Dr. Hilferding was mentioned by rank, as after the First World War, being president of the (Adlerian) Society for Individual Psychology; that Rudolph Hilferding, "an outstanding socialist theoretician and Minister of Finance" was her husband; and that after 1942 she sadly died in the concentration camp at Theresienstadt. From the Internet, it appears now that she actually died on a transport between death camps.

   I note that her further writings included "Medical experiences in the war (1918)"; more about "Maternity" in a paper called: *The Female Worker Newspaper* (1922) where there were five articles in different months by that title; "*Sterilization: A problem of population politics*" (1932). Kerr (1994) says that she was well known as a doctor to the working classes in Vienna. She clearly maintained her strong interest in motherhood.

2 The Kleinian school is an exception, of course, centrally concerned as it is with the child's preoccupations with the womb and baby making, as originary fantasy, parental objects, and heterosexual connections (Sayer, 1991). However, individual detail of, for example, childbirth as a body event is not of such interest as it is or could be to contemporary ego psychologists who believe instead that the early ego differentiates gradually from undifferentiated matrices.

3 Body dysmorphic disorders and eating disorders, anorexia, and bulimia fit well in these speculations. To make my point as strongly as I can, in this book, I am focusing in depth on more ordinary women who are in the average expectable range of neurosis and am setting aside the frankly pathological syndromes.

4 An excerpt of this case (HJ) was used in Chapter 2.

5 Lou Andreas Salome wrote of this in her as yet untranslated 1916 paper "Anal und Sexual."

Chapter 6

Childbirth in vivo

It is the obstetrics literature, not the psychoanalytic, that addresses fears and satisfactions about childbirth.[1] Interesting obstetrical reports about women's emotional experience, as well as the physical, seem to come more frequently from the Nordic countries, with their well-developed socialized caretaking medicine. For example, a searching enquiry from Helsinki, Finland, was published on the Internet, an academic dissertation by Terhi Saisto titled "Obstetric, Psychosocial, and Pain-Related Background, and Treatment of Fear of Childbirth" (2001). Saisto comments knowingly: "Fear of childbirth is not an isolated problem but associated with the woman's personal characteristics and close relationships. Women's personal characteristics, mainly general anxiety, low self-esteem, and depression, contributed most significantly to the prediction of pregnancy-related anxiety and severe fear of childbirth." The results of her research showed that "pregnancy-related anxiety and fear of childbirth were predictable not only from the women's personality traits, but also from psychosocial factors such as dissatisfaction with their partnership and lack of support" (p. 50). The author also says that parous women with fear of delivery may suffer from Post traumatic stress disorder (PTSD) or intrusive stress reaction, which both have recently been described after painful childbirth and emergency CS (Wijma, et al. 1997, Ryding, et al. 1998c). She points out that so little thought has gone into the topic that "Little is known about the background factors leading to fear of natural vaginal delivery, and a request for CS." These comments are of direct interest to any psychoanalytic inquiry. The latter, in particular, resonates with my claim that attention to these matters is actively avoided or suppressed. We analysts have access to far more details about mental life than any other health-care professionals, so we above all can afford to be interested in our female patients' experiences of fears and satisfactions. For example, psychotherapists might be able to shed light on this current phenomenon of the frequency of Cesarean section in the United States, and we could help sort out the puzzle about whether it is the women's preference or the doctors' that Cesarean section is so often chosen over natural birth.

Contemporary applied psychoanalytic research

A rare contemporary instance of psychoanalytically oriented attention to the act of childbirth appeared in 2006, in a doctoral dissertation at the Clinical Social Work Institute, Washington, D.C. Caroline Hall was the author (Hall, 2007). The details of this study are as yet unpublished.[2] While the clinical accounts of Dr. Hall's subjects are admittedly limited compared to psychoanalysis, the words and images that the researcher used in the questionnaires and the expressions she sought in the narratives were guided by familiar psychoanalytic ideas about unconscious elements in the female body image.

Hall asked, "In what ways are women's relationships to their bodies affected by the experience [of delivery]? What are their feelings and fantasies related to body vulnerability and pride?" (p. 2). She searched for any contributions to our literature that she could find, which spoke to the concrete "real" body in pregnancy and various genital anxieties. I noticed for the first time, when I was reading her material, that in the papers of the 1980s, 1990s, and 2000s, which carefully delineate and argue for specific female genital anxieties as opposed to anxieties about lack of male genitalia, to my reading, *none* mentions the ultimate connection of the vagina and vulva to parturition, either in fact or in fantasy. Nor does Gilmore's 1998 paper on cloacal anxiety, which restores interest in the proximity of anal sensation to the vagina in girls and women, explore the overlap between anal expulsiveness and childbirth.

Even Judith Kestenberg's contribution from the 1980s (e.g., in Zanardi, 1990), which I find helpful in my thinking about the female "inner genital," stops short of contemplating the fantasy impact in a young girl's psyche of childbearing and delivery. Kestenberg, as a writer who saw the female as clearly female, postulates an "inner genital phase" (1982) which she calls alternatively the "early maternal" phase. This occurs between the anal and phallic phases of development, she thought, at around 3 years of age. She believed that a triangle between the child, the mother, and the doll forms as the beginning of a developmental line of the girl child's maternality. The doll carries the valence of the little girl's externalized projection of inner vaginal sensation. Kestenberg's materials were from child analyses, and her focus was on sorting out an intrapsychic fantasy basis of a primary femininity. The anxieties that she talks about, when the girl turns away from her baby-representations in her doll, shift the girl toward a phallic phase. This is an interesting and persuasive inside story. They may compound a girl's fears and introitus anxieties induced by her immature knowledge of pregnancy and delivery. Kestenberg is not so interested as I am in the girl's registration of a "real-time" experience of adult pregnancy or delivery.

I am not sure what to make of these omissions, beyond that a female's act of giving birth is clearly a difficult topic to allow into consciousness. "Sexuality" tends to be severed from "childbearing" as if they do not—could not—overlap.[3]

Caroline Hall's research

Dr. Hall then created "a project to interview women before and after delivery of their first child to assess changes in their relationship with, and feelings about, their body. ... specifically focus[ing] on genital anxieties and pride in the body ... studying female genital anxieties defined as fear of loss of or damage to the genitals" (Mayer, 1985; Richards, 1996; Olesker 1998). Hall also looked "for evidence of pride or pleasure attained from the experience of first delivery." To this end, she did semi-structured interviews with 31 women with normal pregnancies from local obstetric practices. These women talked to her during the last trimester, and again in the days immediately after delivery. The interviews were audiotaped, transcribed, and the data analyzed.[4]

The aim of the project was to learn more about women's fears of bodily vulnerability, as well as their pride about their body with first childbirth. The experience of delivering their first child provided the focus.

Dr. Hall composed methods of studying "anxieties, pride, and changes in attitudes toward the body [that were] common among women in relation to their first experience of pregnancy and childbirth." Her originality here was in her *focus on the female body* in this key formative experience. She did not become sidetracked prematurely with the presence of the baby. I am just going to pick out observations that serve my own discussion, and will not give a complete or orderly account of her work, because I am hoping that she may publish the full account of this herself.

Women who expressed anxieties about their genitals and fears about what would happen during the birthing process, she noted, as one might expect, were less fearful after the event. They now were appropriately reacting with anxiety to the look and feel of their altered post-delivery genitals. Some worried about the effects of muscular looseness or surgical scarring on future sex. However, one of Hall's outstanding findings was that most of the women—despite long tiring labors and even perineal tears—expressed great excitement, deep pleasure, and even awe in the prowess of their bodies. Most of them "loved being pregnant," and 64% expressed "pride about feeling physically strong, trusting their body and having a more positive attitude toward it after becoming pregnant than before. ... Many commented on their awe of the reproductive process." (p. 40). Comments about the pleasure in having larger and fuller breasts abounded. One said, "I like the bustiness. It's nice. You feel more voluptuous." Another felt "nice and curvy." After delivery, there were such comments as: "I felt proud ... they gave her to me to breastfeed and so I was like: wow, look what your body can do. It's just amazing. ... you can do this ... It's ... an accomplishment." Or, "I just had no idea how adaptive the body was. ... That the body changes based on your baby's needs—that is just amazing!"

Hall was puzzled, however, that *in the days right after the birth* so many women were also preoccupied with what she interpreted as a sense of body "inadequacy." The women had worried, she reported, that they were "not good enough women" in the birthing scene. For example: "Hearing that other women have short labors, I wonder what's wrong with me?" Having an epidural anesthetic or an episiotomy were at times sources of disappointment. After having a Cesarean section, one woman said angrily that she hadn't come all this way just to act like an incubator and be cut open. One woman who'd had a natural birth offered critically, "Women today are wimping out ... I think women are nervous because its something you can't control ... I think a lot of C-sections are just people trying to control every aspect." Most of Hall's 31 women were at the same time exceedingly pleased and proud of their body's general end-state, but in their surprisingly uniform thoughts, many were metabolizing an internal gold standard of "natural" birth. There seemed to be a shared ideal about "natural" birth, without episiotomy or medication. What could this mean, especially in this day of high-tech medicine?

This post-delivery finding is unexpected and interesting. To my ear and experience, this "gold standard" is perhaps *consciously* a worry about adequacy so that I can see how Dr. Hall deems it an expression of "inadequacy." However, *unconsciously*, I think it likely to be a female-to-female rivalry and a competition about female body power, which most experience and report in procreation. Many of Hall's subjects referred to delivery as an age-old initiation rite into the company of mothers. That is a matriarchal expression of proud and awesome heritage, reminiscent of men's same-sex comparisons and fierce competition in the phallic realm. Who can piss the greatest distance? Who has the biggest penis? How many women (or men) has one bedded? How many children has one fathered?

I have written about my own clinical evidence in analysis for marked female-to-female competition that is centered on *both* the perceived body's procreative *and* sexual capacities (Balsam, 2008), where I postulate that intense female–female body admiration precedes an envy that is a more general emotion.[5] Hall's findings in this regard provide further support for my idea. For women, their own birth experiences and deliveries go to the heart of their fierce competition with each other. On this platform, they either "win" or "lose" as females. (This has nothing to do with "femininity.")

One wonders what will happen over time, as the birthing experience becomes a memory; it would be interesting if Dr. Hall were to expand her data about body pride after a year or so. Do the experiences become distorted? Do denial and "forgetting" take place as the years pass? Does guilt over surpassing one's aging mother interfere with the memory of pleasure? Are more patterns of pain left in the residual memory than the consciously overt pleasure and power that the women communicated at the time of the delivery? Unanswered and perhaps as yet unanswerable questions flow from Hall's concrete data. Given the tendency here to report significant body *pleasure* in the birthing experience as a whole, how can we account for our psychoanalytic literature that claims great numbers of female analysands who dislike their femaleness, and suffer one or other genital anxiety, even after experiences of childbirth? Does repression overtake the pleasure? Alternatively, is it that we tend not to want to know about the intense female pleasures and competitive aggressions that accounts of childbirth could yield in the analytic office? Perhaps our theory prepares our minds to load the text with conflict, read pleasure as defense or masquerade, and thus to expect the primacy of pain on behalf of those who are able to have the birthing experience?

Exhibitionism in childbirth

The form of exhibitionism that this act of childbirth triumph requires, and women's comfort with it, can never fit readily into classical libido theory. There is a paradox here. On the one hand, psychoanalytic accounts either dismiss the act of genital and personal exposure in childbirth as so unremarkable as to need no mention, or they focus on and "explain" only the most disturbing and unconsciously pathological aspects of female genital exhibition. Yet, except for the mouth—and followed only distantly by the anus—the vagina is the orifice most frequently exhibited and scrutinized in this society, be it by doctors, lovers, or readers of *Playboy*.

Indeed, many of the parts of the female body that are usually displayed in exhibitionism arouse strong interest in males, females and children of either gender. Once we admit a closer connection between sex and procreation than is customary in contemporary analytic theory, we are confronted with a potentially universal human fascination with not only the sex act, but also with the underlying fantasies about the function of the female body in pregnancy and childbirth. The enlarged breasts, the darkened nipples, the curvaceous posterior, the broad red and purple vulva adorned with hair—all these suggest the fluid simultaneity between the erotic and procreative aspects of sexuality. Obese women, for example, are often highly desirable as erotic objects for scrutiny and clearly are associated with those who have given birth. (This feature may also be the same reason that they are defensively mocked and reviled.) The Internet tantalizes eager viewers on multiple sites with "Hot and Horny Fat Mamas," or "Old fat grannies toying with pussy," etc., etc. Writing on "Sexuality and the Internet," and fetishism in particular, Robert Young, an English psychotherapist, reported ruefully in 1999 that his own website, which offers psychological help for "sexual problems," gets under a thousand hits per day, whereas "all of the top 100 porn sites have 20,000 hits per day." Who knows how that figure has grown since? One can safely conclude that there are an enormous number of people who are very interested in "looking" at and fantasizing about the female body with all of its exciting, arousing, fearsome, or angering stimuli, which (unconsciously) evoke birthing and postbirthing female bodies. Perhaps this is one angle on why (except for homoerotic men) it is generally females and not males who are the primary object of visual scrutiny for both males and females, including children.

Adolescence

Contrary to the suggestion of Freud and others, the dread of the female that underlies the societal oppression of women, and the accompanying unfortunate exercise of sexualized aggression against them, is not the fear of the "Medusa head" or "*vagina dentata*" alone. Surely, it blends with the unconscious fear of the magical power of the female body to contain live humans and to bring them into the world? We see this drama graphically in adolescents. In female adolescence, there is urgent boyfriend competition, suggesting a Darwinian violent desperation in mate-seeking with unconsciously rivalrous procreative motives that are amalgamated with sexuality. Girlfriend rivalries also abound. Physical fighting among teenage female peers who are constantly exhibiting their sexualized bodies for each other and for the admiration of adolescent males is, I suggest, on the surface born of sexual rivalry alone. Bullying behaviors, emotionally abusive epithets of "bitch," and put-downs are hurled at the hated rival. The content of the insult, interestingly, is often an accusation of being a "whore." The victim allegedly has shown off too much of her tantalizing body, or has too much success in attracting the male gaze, in the eyes of the attacker. In a strange atavistic twist, the young girl victim is attacked by peers as if a group medieval conscience is still operating in them, in a pact to keep fellow women concealed and silent—and hence decent and marriageable, and safe to carry a baby and deliver. Girls are apparently abidingly "supposed" to do all these significant physical feats— sex and procreation—in a covered-up fashion, so as not to arouse fear or competition or rage in others (see Chapter 1). In an older era, or currently in some non-Western cultures, we all know that pregnant unmarried adolescent girls hid their shame, and crept off to a convent or workhouse or the equivalent to give birth to their illegitimate babies secretly.[6]

Childbirth in the psychoanalytic literature

The act of birthing involves a level of comfort with the exhibition of the body that is necessary to bring a baby into the world. Some aspects of this are socially acceptable. Exhibitionistic behavior has been rightly written about and accepted in the analytic literature concerning little girls (and boys) as early "normal exhibitionism"—a genital showing that can occur when a child has only a rudimentary knowledge of sexual differences. This is one way that children get acquainted with their bodies, and how they grow into their sexual attractiveness and powers and the ability to modulate the excitement through the emotionally mirrored gaze of mothers and fathers and others (e.g., Fonagy, 2008; Stein, 2008).

A certain amount of exhibitionism is expected of women, but the expected form is a preoccupation with beauty. Female beauty, however, rapidly morphs into the consideration of "narcissism." Narcissism is one of those theoretical way stations that is described as a developmental phase (and therefore normative), but can be confusing because the same term is used for pathology. Females have often fallen into this confusing way station. One example is the famous passage from Freud's 1914 paper on narcissism, in which the description seems to become pathological when he speaks iconically of a beautiful, distant ice maiden as "the type of female most frequently met with" (p. 88). Admiring though he may be— Lou Andreas Salome was supposedly the model—"*lack*" undergirds his statements. In this instance, women lack full humanity. They are, he says, like children who possess the "charm of certain animals that seem not to concern themselves about us, such as cats and large beasts of prey" (p. 89); or when he judges women's object relational capacity as "unfavorable," lacking the "… development of a true object choice" (p. 88). Thus, the whole issue of an adult female's basis for physical self-love, arising from her described observed normative childhood exhibitionism, is cast into doubt. As a grown-up, self-love of her body for its own inherent prowess or beauty is perceived as "a problem." Therefore, any aspiration to theorize pregnancy or the dynamism of delivery and childbirth with an openness to appreciating the woman's self-admiration of her body's aptitude and competence totally vanishes in these statements.

Interestingly, Freud *does* associate to procreation here in a way, but characteristically, as with most other authors, his associations do not go to pregnancy and childbirth, but to their by-product, the child—described by Freud as a "part of their own body that confronts them like an extraneous object, to which, starting out from their narcissism, they can give complete object-love" (p. 90). It is as if he *almost* allowed himself to think about how to apply his statements about female self-love to the female act of giving birth. But then, he would have had to think about what women possess, as opposed to what they lack, compensated for by the child, in this instance. Most of the early women analysts followed Freud's schema. Adrienne Harris (2000) noted their "close obedience to Freud, who was in a number of cases their analyst" (p. 233). This applies also, of course, to Anna Freud who in spite of her creativity, unfortunately, I believe, did not advance any cogent insights of her own about females.

A pre-1970s clinical example of an account of childbirth

There are so very few accounts over the years of *any* descriptions at all, let alone analytic thinking in our field about childbirth, that we might be grateful for any attention paid to it by any of our American forebears, who mostly espoused structural and instinct theory. We can see here, though, some of the problems that feminist writers and clinicians faced later.

Edmund Bergler (1959), a frequent contributor on gender issues, wrote a paper called "Psychoprophylaxis of Postpartum Depression." This is a description of all the fears that may be aroused in a woman anticipating childbirth. To his credit, Bergler writes in a normalizing manner—even if, as likely was customary, he seems to follow without question Helene Deutsch's 1940 certainties that masochism is paramount in mature women. Painful childbirth, Bergler believes, somehow mops up the optimal amount of female masochistic need. To him, this explains why a woman may sometimes be depressed after a painless childbirth! (Painless, that is, because of anesthesia.) Pregnancy, he (rightly) says, mobilizes repressed infantile fears in everyone. Also, he says (rightly) that vomiting in early pregnancy, even though some authors believe there are toxic reasons (which of course there also are due to hormonal outpouring), psychologically the symptom has a component of the fear of being poisoned. From there, he takes a more irritable and judgmental tone, and characterizes these fears as "totally irrational"—for example, fears of being starved, devoured, drained, choked, chopped to pieces, and castrated. All of these show the sufferer, Bergler believes, to be passive-masochistic—in short, a victim. These so-called "undigested baby fears" (p. 362) are interpreted by him as a child's misconception of urination and defecation. He does not take into account the age-old fear of delivery that any adult woman can have; or her fear of anesthesia in the case of Cesarean section; or the unknown of how a surgeon may operate on her; her fear of bleeding and complications; let alone her fear for the infant's life whose birth may rob her of life itself. These stimuli may of course trigger deeper and archaic anxieties such as he alludes to—but there is a dismissal in this paper of the reality of the drama of the situation of a woman about to give birth. Bergler even cites as an example of female irrationality a woman in childbirth who expresses a fear that she was going to defecate. He says confidently that this "irrational" fear is a form of anal regression showing evidence of confusion between the anal opening and the sexual opening. The fear of "being attacked by a lion from behind in the dark" is called be this author a "banal oedipal fantasy.

After enumerating these "irrational" fears, Bergler suddenly characterizes childbirth as a source of public shame: "Added to all this are exhibitionistic fears. The girl's entire education emphasizes the idea of modesty. All at once, during pregnancy, and especially during the process of giving birth, the rules of "decency" are suspended. Not only physicians and nurses but even outsiders are involved, for during the last months pregnancy cannot be hidden" (p. 363).

The history of the tradition of female modesty and attendant intrapsychic conflict that enters into Bergler's comment deserves further thought. Inhibitions *are* frequently encountered, but if they are of pathologic proportions, these are likely to occur as a result of reactions to pre-partum fantasy states, such as in very young adulthood, adolescence, or in post-childbirth regression due to trauma. Bergler's quotation seems to sum up my first chapter on enforced cultural values of female silence and modesty.

I would like to point out that one *very rarely* actually hears a woman who is giving birth express great concern about her "modesty"—the kind of concern that Bergler and also Simmel[7] assume that birthing women *must* have. Bergler's attribution of shame to a delivering mother is likely a projection, the shame evoked in the onlooker at a "taboo" graphic, stimulating, animalistic sight—not to mention the onlooker's possible unspoken reactions to the sounds and the smell, including the frequency of defecation due to pressure on the bowel.[8] Freud, after all, invoked Aristotle and Augustine while talking of disgust at the genitals and their smell, in quoting "inter urinas et faeces nascimur" (between urine and feces we are born: Freud, 1930).[9]

I cannot recall, in my obstetric rotations as a young intern, any of my new mother-patients (either psychiatric patients or obstetrical patients in the days when I delivered babies) telling me that they were horrified by such exposure. I can recall some women who perhaps had spurned painkillers, loudly cursing their husbands or shrieking, bawdily blaming men in general in an outpouring of rage in the midst of a helpless desperation of a strong uterine contraction. One colleague[10] described a patient who was having a very hard time. Her husband was really anxious and was trying desperately to help, but nothing he did made her feel better. Finally she turned to him between yells and bellowed, "Oh honey, will you please just FUCK OFF?!!!" Actually, he laughed, and things got better from there. Sometimes, the excitation can turn to manic laughter at the relief and thrill in the abatement of such a contraction. Many distressed women I've attended wailed and called out for their own mothers. However, I never heard a woman shout out or cry about how humiliated she was. A professor of anesthesiology and obstetrics makes an interesting distinction between pain and suffering in a recent book (Caton, 1999). The former is of biological origin; the latter, he thinks, is due to the meanings that accrue to the pain in childbirth. He speaks of isolation, solitude, and fear, and a loss of the traditional or religious explanations that give purpose to the pain. "Childbearing women support themselves and each other by saying that pain can teach, punish, form social bonds, and increase the love of a mother for her child" (p. 233), he says, and he is continually surprised by the "importance of these ideas and their resilience" (p. 234). Yet, "it is reassuring to realize that patients find ways to preserve the meaning in childbirth even in the absence of pain and suffering" (p. 234). Fresh from bedside attendance to women in childbirth, never once does he mention shame or their concerns about exposure. One newly delivered woman I was involved with exulted, "I showed everyone I have it in me to let go, and give a child into the world"; or about her new son, "He seemed to shout with joy as he squeezed out into the air; or a mother imagining her new daughter's voice, "I'm here, all newly delivered and *she* pushed me into life"; or a religious woman's declaration: "I felt like the Lord, the Giver of Life." Body exposure and genital exposure is highly valued in this context, as well as the appreciation and ultimate love of the organs that have produced this intense unique lusty, exultant birthing experience that will continue as the breasts full of milk will be exposed for the infant. It is said that one of the motivations of exhibitionism in either sex is the seeking of power—but the power that is usually attributed to women is the desire for domination over a man. The exhibitionism of childbirth is larger in scope. It is a uniquely female body power display addressed to the entire world of humans.

Noted authors who have written about childbirth

Helene Deutsch

Helene Deutsch's cases in her chapter on "Delivery" (1945) for the most part confirm the statements above. Deutsch's descriptions are unsurpassed in our small literature on this topic. She captures in her deliveries experiences near-intrapsychic excitement, physical exertion, exhilaration, and an exultation in triumphant physical achievement. The admixture of joy with fears of and mastery over death, the willingness of a mother to give her life for the life of her offspring—all are rendered eloquently in this text, which is freer than other chapters from her usual passion for theoretical categorizations. Pleasurable exhibitionism is paramount in these experiences. Many delivering women talk about the delight of seeing the baby emerge in the mirror. Once the birth excitement is over, some women express impatience at the unnecessary time spent in the lithotomy position for the doctor's convenience, when they feel an urgency to be with the infant and father or partner. The chorus of accolades from those in attendance in the delivery room is a further spur to the woman's pride. As Deutsch points out, "awareness [of a woman in childbirth] is narrowed by her absorption in the progress of the birth" (p. 210). This means that her acuity to her bodily and inner processes are all in an enhanced state.

Marie Langer

Marie Langer was a Vienna-born physician psychoanalyst who fled during the Holocaust to Argentina. Her accounts of childbirth (Langer, 1992) also affirm the joy of giving life. Her background as a physician and as the mother of six children possibly enhanced her interest in this topic. She too points to the preponderance of "pain" stories from psychoanalytic authors who expect women's experience to be pathological. She says, "there are families in which the daughters, following upon their mother's ideas, have little fear of pregnancy and childbirth and, in fact, suffer less as a result than girls raised in families in which they are taught to be afraid of their femininity because of their mother's complaints and fears" (p. 191). In addition, of course, she takes into account each individual's intrapsychic strivings. She uses Freudian and Kleinian theory interchangeably, with a preponderance of Klein. In this rich text, she tends, as with Klein, not to dwell much on the physical body per se, but to "look through it" as it were, to its interpreted psychological function. Thus, she readily speaks of say, infertility, as resulting in paranoid fears, or again, using Klein, "It is as if the mother said to her daughter in labor, 'you wanted to usurp my place and rob me of my children. Now you have succeeded, but you will suffer as I suffered giving birth to you or you will die as you wished me to die giving birth to your siblings'" (p. 222). Langer's account of childbirth is quite focused on the mother's "phantasies" about the child, after Klein. As with Deutsch, though, Langer recognizes the female biological life cycle in dealing with the scope of female internal life from menarche to menopause.

Joan Raphael-Leff

Joan Raphael-Leff's 1993/1995 book on prepregnancy, pregnancy, and childbirth is most akin to the older and unique work of Helene Deutsch from the 1940s in terms of its comprehensiveness and acuity about a women's physical and emotional experience. Naturally modern, Raphael-Leff's work is unsurpassed in our current literature. She deals with the maternal body in its own right. She foreshadows my own intention: "This perspective differs from most psychoanalytic descriptions which take as their starting point *the infant's* developing psychological self. My central focus is on *the parent's experience*—the mother or father as a whole person rather than the object of the child's fantasy or desire. In the literature, granted little subjectivity of her own, a mother is often described in relation to the baby's needs" (p. 1). Given this insight, it follows that there is psychological room in this book to pay attention to childbirth (see Chapter 8). Raphael-Leff's writing on the topic is superb. She does not just say theoretically that this is an important time to recognize the impact of the internalized mother (e.g., Balsam, 2000). In her text on birth, she makes it vivid and understandable that "when the woman—supremely powerful in her goddess-like capacity to bring a new life into being—is also threatened by the human responsibility of bringing that life safely to fruition ... there may be a gravitation toward a soothing mother figure ... which promises to protect both her and the baby, calling the oedipal child into her strong, medicalized arms" (p. 111). Raphael-Leff's background is as a British social psychologist/psychoanalyst. She has years of specialized clinical experience, and of writing about reproductivity. She demonstrates her ease with the theory of the English middle group of independent psychoanalysts— that is, she maintains an object relational orientation that does not lose track of Freud's while remaining elegantly in touch with the life physical and cultural experience of an individual.

Dinora Pines

The late Dinora Pines' 1993 book on women's body fantasies rounds out, I believe, the most important contemporary work on childbearing. Pines too was British. She was a dermatologist before seeking analytic training, and thus has an exquisite sensitivity to and interest in how the body enters the psychic conversation. In the introduction to her book, talking of her special interest in women's bodies and pregnancy, she is explicit that she focuses on underlying pain and conflicts in her patients, which, as a medical practitioner, she found neglected in practice, because she takes for granted the pleasures of reproduction. I personally regret that she passed over bodily pleasure, because her observations are so acute, her ideas so resonant with my own experience, and her writing so available.

The Holocaust and her personal losses also naturally deepened her focus on pain as she analyzed and helped survivors. Pines develops ideas in a chapter called "the relevance of early psychic development to pregnancy and abortion" (p. 97)[11] that enrich and talk about "difficulties concerning a woman's identification with the internal representation of her own mother ... that is bodily reinforced when she becomes pregnant" (p. 98). The pregnant patient carries a symbiotic identification with her mother as well as with the fetus who represents herself as the infant she once was, within her own mother. Pines talks of the childhood wish to identify with her primary object (Deutsch, 1944; Benedek, 1959) and connects it to the first pregnancy as "a further stage of identification rooted in a biological basis ... the final stage in being like her own mother, a physiologically mature woman, impregnated by her sexual partner—and in fantasy her mother's—powerful enough to create life herself" (p. 99). She goes on quickly to contemplate the (psychoanalytically more usual) pained aspects of bodies and relations rather than dwell too long on the "mutual feeling of bodily satisfaction between her mother and herself" (p. 101). For example, she does not dwell on the average-expectable, but on *problems* of the separation-individuation phase where a child is not satisfied by a mother who deprives her. Thus, such a girl "can never make up for this basic loss of a primary stable sense of well-being in her body and with her body image" (p. 101). It would have been interesting to me, had Pines tried to explicate what happens in average "good-enough" circumstances. She has a surprisingly short description of birth (p. 68), before again turning to the dark side—to the anticlimax and depression that follows the "exhilaration and relief" (p. 68). Miscarriage, abortion, and infertility captured more of her interest in this text, which is also wise, imaginative, and highly attuned to her patients.

These are the kinds of observations I think we should listen to (in vivo and in retrospect) from adults in analysis, not just as they deal with pregnancy and birth in vivo, but asking ourselves how the materials are encoded in everyday psychic life. We can acknowledge that the material is subject to the usual retrospective distortions of memory, but recognize the cogency of the patient's psychic reality and how little we know about the longer-term effects of deliveries on either the offspring or the woman herself. How does a difficult delivery echo down the years afterwards, and how may it affect psychic life? We do not, for example, have a theory about why a woman does or does not usually feel shame at these moments of exhibiting. In the early classical formulations, to keep the theory consistent, she was expected to feel only shame, because her lack of a penis was being exposed. My observations, and those of the other authors I've just quoted, point more to a theory of female libido that includes as climactic this opportunity for a uniquely female experience. The procreative body's centrality in childbirth (whether fantasized, anticipated, or enacted) is the same, whatever her gender identity, and whatever her choice of erotic object. It is the same whether she is single, married, or chooses a life of celibacy. Somehow, she has to metabolize these biological facts and images intrapsychically. And it is reasonable to postulate that psychic forerunners of delivery, this imagined scene central to grown-up bodily female life, must be much more lively in the minds of prepubertal and adolescent girls than we analysts have written about to date. We may know more as a group intellectually, about how a mind learns to symbolize, than we know about how a little girl grows to mentalize and encompass these most creative body organs.

Notes

1 Besides work quoted here, there seems to have been a little burst of interest in the early 1950s, with an analyst co-writing with other health care givers. The thrust was advice to the hospitals.
2 Dr. Hall has graciously and generously given me permission to draw on her Ph.D. thesis material "First Time Mothers' Experiences of Childbirth: Perspectives on Psychological Responses to Their Bodies" (2006, unpublished). Doctoral Dissertation, Clinical Social Work Institute, Washington DC.
   I gather that two major analytic journals to date have turned down her paper based on this material. I am actually not privy to the grounds. However, I had a similar experience with my "vanished pregnant body" paper. It was finally published in JAPA by Arnold Richards, and even won a "best paper" award eventually, after being "lost" twice in the journal office! An earlier reviewer, from a different major journal which had rejected it, opined that the author should be told "not to be so critical" of the literature! The name of this reviewer (old, male, and famous) was "accidentally" left at the top of this report. I felt scolded by this man. However, I knew I was in good company—Margarete Hilferding must have felt the same way in 1911—and that I was eerily participating in the very syndrome of erasure that I was pointing to.
3 In African and other countries, where female genital mutilation is practiced, practitioners have no problem recognizing the vulva and vagina as bi-functional—as integrated sex and birthing organs. They cut the clitoris and the surround of the vagina to stop masturbation or control sexual desire, and they stitch up the vagina to make sure no penis or baby passes that way, unless it is controlled and possessed by a particular man. The woman herself has no say. Perhaps there is a clue here for us? Consider this vast aggression mounted against these female organs when they are clearly seen in an integrated fashion, operating both sexually and in childbirth! Perhaps our current intellectual, Western, attempts to keep sexuality and baby-making separate is a defensive maneuver to protect females against the mobilization of even more aggression than they already attract.
4 Quantitative analysis was guided by grounded theory (Strauss and Corbin, 1998). Open coding was used to identify repeating concepts in the data, and axial coding was also used. State-Trait Anxiety Inventories were carried out, and the Wijma Delivery Expectancy/Experience Questionnaire was administered during both interviews (Wijma, K., Wijma, B., and Zar, M. [1998]. Psychometric aspects of the W-DEQ: A new questionnaire for the measurement of fear of childbirth. *Journal of Psychosomatic Obstetrics & Gynecology* 19: 84–97).
5 The ego subtlety of this physical communication as it affects the woman's body image is my interest. This is rather different from Klein, who surely sees envy, but as universal, a massive envy in every girl toward the mother's phantasy internal babies/father's penis.
6 See *Casa de Los Babys*, a 2003 movie by John Sayles that is the subject of Balsam, R. (2011) The Quest for Motherhood: When fertilization Fails Psychoanalytic Inquiry 31: 392–403.
7 Ernst. Simmel, of the Berlin Poliklinik, spoke in a pained way about why poor women, at the height of their miserable public shame in giving birth in a hospital, should be troubled by an array of student onlookers!

8 Dimen (2005) has graphically described a "Eew factor" in common unsavory reactions to sex that encode excitement, shame, and disgust. I believe that childbirth too may hold evocations of this elemental reaction. This is an unexplored topic in childbirth itself. Do actively birthing women also feel disgust at their body fluids along with their excitations? I don't think so, but their onlookers and attendants might, or analysts who hear the detail of the tale afterwards—which might be another motive for vanishing this topic from our minds and the literature.

9 Freud may (inadvertently) have been favorably invoking Augustine's additional notion about birth and "God, the farmer" that was also in that text. A farmer would certainly welcome baby animals on his farm, and the promising smell of the fecund, birthing mothers!

10 Eve Golden, M.D., my editor friend.

11 One of the few contemporary thinkers who ties females' early bodily experiences into their contemporary bodily maturity in an experience-near way.

Chapter 7

Anatomy, desire, muscles, and bellies

Gender identity still tends to be stereotyped and polarized as "masculine" *or* "feminine," in spite of great efforts in the contemporary scene within the social sciences, the humanities and psychoanalysis, to render the construct in a less or nonbinary fashion[1] (see for a scholarly overview of the literature, Gyler, 2010). Conceptual turmoil and confusions abound, and individuals in differing fields write with differing definitions of the related phenomena. "Masculine" and "feminine" to me are adjectives that refer to mentalized qualities. They are related, but not equivalent to "male" and "female," which refer to sexed body morphology. A way out of the confusion in thinking about gender is to conceptualize a gender spectrum from an unattainable (and obviously mentally unhealthy) "pure masculinity" at one end, to an equally unattainable "pure femininity" at the other, and to focus clinically on the lived span in between. This is one way out of the rigidity of the binary trap of categorizing us as *either* masculine *or* feminine. This is not the only way, as attested to by the many scholars and academicians who are struggling with these confusions, and who prefer to conceptualize former binary conflicts as paradoxes and contingencies and look for shared interstitial space in "thirds" (see Kulish, 2010, for a succinct overview of the struggles and proposed solutions). Jessica Benjamin (in Dimen and Harris, 2001) shares working thoughts on the conceptual problems; for example, in her struggle with how to tackle gender polarities as she seeks "...what might be rediscovered beyond the dominance of the active–passive complementarity ... to formulate a different kind of complementarity than the one that emerges at the oedipal level, that of have or have not, phallus or no phallus (Birksted-Breen, 1996) ... true activity does not take the defensive form of repudiating passivity. Activity predicated on the activity–passivity split, directed toward the passive object, is merely action; it lacks the intersubjective space of the potential other" (p. 59).

Because I keep a focus on the body qua body as playing a necessary and major role in gender identity, "sex" and "gender" can be usefully separated, as first suggested by Stoller[2] in the late 1960s. This approach offers the desirable possibility of individual and clinical openness to the vagaries of mentalization, while preserving some clarity that relates specifically to the observable naked biological body. Many, especially contemporary, feminist academics and relational psychoanalysts have chosen to blend biological sex and gender *together* into the notion of "embodiment" (Kulish, 2010) to deal with this problem of the either/or of female or male or any notion of a biologically defined destiny. They see the biological body as either a straightjacket of gender certainty, or else just as elusive as gender. I both agree and disagree with how elusive the body qua body can be. Psychological interpretation and meanings *are* elusive and variable: but biological sex characteristics and trajectories of growth are relatively stable. The latter can be surgically or hormonally purposefully altered, but only by radical external means. I would argue that that kind of morphological alteration does not signify the body's inherent tendency to biological fluidity. It signifies the body's plastic response to being externally manipulated. Such a sex change could therefore be regarded as a new biological construction that can be engineered by minds that are more fluid than bodies.

A gender spectrum can engage a theory of nonlinear dynamics while avoiding an overly rigid ladder-like category of psychosexual theorizing, where one stage fixedly follows another. Freud can be credited for his own style of "nonlinear" thinking that existed side-by-side with his defined overly linear named psychosexual stages. Uneven development, for example, is suggested by his "complemental" series, and the inbuilt role of trauma.[3] The American ego psychologists and followers of Anna Freud following these principles described detectable macro developmental "lines," but individual children were perceived as *not* neatly fitting such linear expectations. They can be read as less "linear" than is the common criticism of them these days.

Freud himself did not explicitly talk about "gender," but the processes of the oedipal situation he thought essentially defined gender. Feminist scholars and contemporary interrelational psychoanalysts in particular have challenged this (see the writings of Butler, Benjamin, Mitchell J, Mitchell S, Dimen, Goldener, as but a few). I am persuaded by them about the limitations of an overly confining and reified Oedipus. I place gender influences combining input from the body and from the environment. These incoming stimuli are intrapsychically influenced by early triangularity (in tune with Klein and the neo-Kleinian view of infancy in relation to both female and male caretakers). These features, in dynamic relation, are far from permanent, especially behaviorally (in tune with aspects of Harris, 2005). Modern nonlinear dynamic theorists who apply chaos theory (Harris, 2005; Galatzer-Levy, 2009) or string theory to psychoanalysis view the concept of "gender identity" as an old-fashioned term that is too stable a concept to be applicable to the mind's functioning. For lack of a better term, I will use it, because I want to conceptualize a *quality of stability* in the body that now risks underappreciation and is greater than the mind's body representations: a stability that was perhaps overly assumed by Stoller and earlier ego psychologists, and that has benefited from questioning, but does not deserve to be ignored. The body has structures, and those structures have functions. To claim that there is no "structure" that is fixed in the mind, works. To claim that there is no "structure" in the body that contains the mind is erroneous. The mind certainly functions with psychological processes, but the structures of the body also function as biological processes.

By "gender identity," I imply a certain repetition and stability *over time* in the psyche's ability to hold a macro-constellation of ideas in mind. By that term, I mean how one, as an individual, subjectively thinks of oneself and enacts life along a spectrum from "feminine" to "masculine" that includes "more feminine than less," "bisexual," "mixed," and "more masculine than less." "Agendered" would represent a complex place in the center. All of my patients in their *adult* patterned psyches have moved in minor ways *internally* from one place to another along this spectrum. I include here those who as adults may entirely change the sex of their partners and their life styles to suit a different place on the spectrum. If the choice is made as an adult, it may seem on the surface that this represents radical fluidity, but these major moves usually have been the culmination of a long developmental search to match the "inside" with the "outside."

I have never met anyone who did not think about their own gender characteristics as some versions of "masculinity" or "femininity"—transgendered people too, who may represent a valid third gender way station. Most can trace their own personal descriptions of "masculine" and "feminine" as valences prescribed or proscribed within their own families. Society counts as model and witness, but is less intense than families. A theorizing psychoanalyst has access to the expressed gendered values that have become highly personalized for an individual in the tales of his, her, or zeer's[4] inner pantheon of objects.

The legacy of Freud's libido theory and articulation of his psychosexual stages offered an unintegratable solution for women. This is because, in order for a woman to claim "femininity" according to this theory, her "masculine" trends in development must be repudiated and "overcome." Clinically, I would now like to demonstrate that an interweaving pattern of paternal identifications and male body representations, together with the female body image and female identifications, is necessary to create a mature gender identity portrait. The female body representation and maternal identifications may well be *enhanced* by male internalizations, as happened in this particular instance. I do not want to seem polemic when I use the divisions "old" and "new." We are clearer about what needs to be left behind as "the old" than we are about "the new." My version of "new" shows my contemporary ego psychological slant and not the relational or intersubjective point of view, although it is in this school where the most vital work on gender has more recently flourished (e.g., the founding of the journal *Studies in Gender and Sexuality* in 2000, edited by Virginia Goldner). My effort is to stick with updating ego psychology, in which I was trained, and which I believe speaks more cogently than relational or Kleinian theory to my own interest in the biological body. I incorporate elements of object relational theory and relational theory because these schools enrich greatly for me the ideas about the ego's internalizations.

Working clinically with women and gender

As far back as 1986, in the midst of shifts in the literature, in a review of female psychology, Chehrazi wrote, "in spite of recently suggested revisions ... it is my impression from seminars and clinical conferences that our diagnostic formulations and dynamic conceptualizations remain more or less the same [since Freud's time]" (p. 22). Nowadays, too, as Chehrazi noted then, the "lack of a revised theoretical framework" may be blamed (p. 22). A continued yearning in our profession for an ideal systematic theory of female development, however, may serve to shield against some changes of focus in clinical work that could be facilitated even while awaiting complete reformulation. Ten years after Chehrazi's observations, Basseches and her colleagues (1996) reported on a study of analytic treatments of women conducted by a group of contemporary female analysts. This work confirmed their suspicion that there is still a "lag between theory and clinical technique"; in the analysts' discussions, they discovered their "collusion with Freud's phallocentric perspective in concert with [their] patients' self-assessments" (p. 515). For example, as with their early counterparts, they tended to view penis envy and the castration complex as bedrock "facts" and failed to consider instead their functional defensive possibilities as body fantasies. The authors believed that the "participant analysts' theories and identifications with their own personal analysts and clinical supervisors did not yield easily to integrating the newer ideas of primary femininity into clinical practice" (p. 516). One female analyst in the group reported automatically interpreting a female patient's denial of her genitals as a sure sign of penis envy—the usual male body terms. The analyst noted that it made her uneasy to shift to an interpretation of the patient's denial in specifically female body terms—i.e., "the patient's wish to deny interest in her [own] feminine space" (p. 517). In 1999, Nancy Kulish and Ruth Fischer convened a panel to discuss primary femininity and its clinical implications at the fall meetings of the American Psychoanalytic Association. Contributors agreed that there was a continuing reluctance to translate more recent ideas into the actual treatment of women patients. One can ask, "Why is this so?" However, one can also ask, "How can this happen clinically?" As part of demonstrating the consequences of a shift of clinical focus that results from integrating some of the newer formulations, I will demonstrate also that unexamined issues from *within the same theory*[5] emerge to "established" theory and then begin to emerge, and the theoretical uncertainty that ensues tends to stay unresolved by being dropped. For example, I suggest that, since approximately 1970, it can no longer be held that femininity or femaleness is "achieved" by renouncing masculinity or maleness. We are free to imagine a different kind of gender solution than one based on an either/or conflict. We can postulate that a female can have a stable core gender identity and yet also follow dual gender developmental lines that need not necessarily be in opposition. The male line can become complementary and even enhancing to aspects of the female line.

The "newer" view

The shorthand designation "newer" that I will use in presenting the following case will refer to the female in possession in her own body. In this system, the female patient therefore considers as "primary" (in the sense of basic) what female body parts and attributes she possesses (see Stoller, 1968, 1976; Kleeman, 1971; Kestenberg, 1982; Mayer, 1985; Bernstein, 1990; Richards, 1992; Frenkel, 1996; Holtzman and Kulish, 1996). Acknowledging a female's *"primary sense of female-ness"* (Elise, 1997), holds many ramifications for a definitive abandonment of old theory (Tyson, 1982), and for far more cogent ideas regarding the spectrum of genders as outlined by Chodorow (1994). New experience-near information can thereby be gleaned about internalizations. New information is needed on the impact of the adult female body on all developmental stages in a young girl's growing mental representations and conflicts about her own body.

Case example: Ms. KL

Introduction

The avenue I wish to take into the primary sense of femaleness (or less preferably "primary femininity") is that of *maternality.* By this term, I want to convey the importance of the body of the mother—not just the general mental state of "motherhood." The maternal body is, for the girl, the most important icon of grown-up physical femaleness, and one she experiences and revisits imaginatively at all stages of biological and emotional growth.

I will tell the story of Ms. KL's analysis that bears on the role of her female body in her dilemmas. My theoretical underpinning is a blend of drive and object relations theory; therefore, KL's communications about her body involve a study of the intrapsychic anatomy of the internalizations of her attitudes arising from both male and female influences—from *both* father and mother at different developmental phases.

As the case unfolds, I will keep the reader abreast of my thoughts about applying the "old" formulations and the "newer" ones that use female-qua-female in a basic way. I will use interpolations [in square brackets] within the text of the case to show such choices in my thinking. Along the way, I will discuss the implications of a particular comparison between the older and newer vantage points, or any useful overlap between them.

I want to dramatize how an analyst thinks along as the material is presented, while also listening. Some readers may dislike this method. Admittedly, it appears to exaggerate the "old" ideas as if straw men. Many will believe that this is an obsolete exercise. Nevertheless, I don't, alas. Despite our acknowledgement of the problems and far better intentions, an untroubled use of language can still be employed about women that includes and perpetuates male-derived theoretical terms (Goldberger, 1999). Or worse, we can deal with these discrepancies not by resolving them, but by ignoring them.

Presentation and history

Ms. KL, a 30-year-old female graduate student, knew what she wanted, which was an analysis that lasted about 4 years. This was her urgent complaint: "I don't want to be 35, married with a bunch of kids, and wake up one morning hating my husband and wondering, 'What am I doing?'" Her divorced parents had had yet another vicious fight over the children.

Later, from the couch, I heard the following tale of events that occurred when KL was 16 and attending a boarding school in the South. She was with her aunt, who had taken her to the Kentucky Derby for the first time. "We were up in the stands. I had her binoculars trained on the starting gate. They were off! Suddenly there was this pack of speeding horses, all in unison, rhythmically thundering toward the bend. They were fast. They were intense, all in time, seemingly all together. I was transported. The jockeys were whipping them on—they rocketed past our stand. I felt giddy with ecstasy. It was perfection! It was their unison that got to me. They were so effortless, all of them together—so controlled—so powerful. God, what a high! It was love at first sight!"

[I noted to myself that her fascination here, as she described it, was not with who had won, or how her aunt's bet had gone, or even the performance of her aunt's horse, all of which might have suggested a displacement of perhaps positive or negative oedipal themes of competition with the aunt as stand-in for either male or female parent. Curiously, it was "all together," "speed," and "unison" that caught her imagination. That sounded like a yearning for harmony, power, and closeness, with herself as one horse of many. Denial of the competition in the race was present, but her yearning for the power of harmony had a life of its own in her narrative. I thought it might be an image of siblings. Did it also encode a pre-oedipal love and yearning for her mother, a variety of symbiotic fantasy about blending with an all-powerful maternal figure?]

KL was an equestrian. [The topic of girls and women riding horses is related to the old single-minded phallic view of horses (Schowalter, 1983), which overlooked female-referenced meanings of horses to children. Stuart (2009), for example, in revising and adding the vision of Little Hans's crazed mother to Freud's 1905 second version of the falling horse stomping its feet as the mother in childbirth, evokes also Hans's desire for mastery in caretaking control of the mother. This interpretation would be more apt to KL.]

Riding was not KL's only sport or even her major one. In her twenties, she had became a dedicated and successful athlete in a team sport that echoed her response to the horse race, that required the intense cooperation of equals, all playing fast and in synchrony with one another. [Her constitutional athletic endowment profoundly affected the cast of KL's character and psychodynamics. In her associations, she might say casually en route to some other topic: "John and I started off the day with a nice 20-mile run. It was great. It's so great to run around here because there's all these gentle hills." I, of course, was in awe! This level of physical prowess in a woman was once assumed almost automatically to be borrowed from the male and to express male phallic aspiration. Today, however, the athletic body ideal for women has challenged this stereotype. On analysis, there can be as many female body fantasies or androgynous fantasies in the creation of this ideal as there are male body fantasies.]

KL was a shapely, tall woman with sculptured shoulders and long, powerful, elegant limbs; a pretty, expressive face; sparkling eyes; and gleaming, long, dark hair that she tied in a tight bun. She was passionate and vivacious. In a single session, her face could be miserable and tear-stained or wreathed with smiles. Nothing was done or experienced by her in a halfhearted way.

KL had experienced the following family chaos. Her father, from a wealthy Texan family, was an airline pilot on Far East runs. He was never home in her early years. Her mother was a now-voluptuous, black-haired Italian ex-supermodel. Her husband swept her off her feet in marriage and brought her to live in Bel Air, California. My patient was the oldest of five children, of both sexes, born 18 months or less apart. Her mother had been a devout Catholic. As soon as the patient's mother became pregnant with KL shortly after marriage, a sweet but elderly Italian nanny was engaged to help. She grew ancient within the family. Gradually, the mother became severely alcoholic; although we unearthed evidence later of her playfulness and better caretaking of KL up to about the age of six. Her maternal capacity seemed to deteriorate with each successive child. The father separated from this unhappy mother when my patient was nine and went off with a young female flight attendant. KL's parents divorced when she was eleven. The mother often behaved in a loud and drunken fashion or else helplessly.

My patient, who for an exhausting 2 years after the divorce had insisted on trying to care for her mother, her siblings, and her aged nanny, finally took up her father's invitation to escape and live with him and his new girlfriend during the rest of her teens. Her father took his paternal responsibilities very seriously after the divorce. In fact, I think he saved KL's capacity for pleasure and self-esteem and, by his increased involvement with her, helped her bear her anger and despair in growing up. She despised her father's girlfriend as shallow, giggly, and too girly. He never remarried. For high school, KL elected to leave them and go to the Southern boarding school mentioned earlier, and it was while out one afternoon with her father's sister that the horseracing scene took place.

In the analysis: male influences

When we started the analysis, KL revealed that one of her persistent complaints was that she failed to perform up to her ability; this happened, she said, "no matter how I break my ass." [This could be an open invitation to think "castration anxiety" and broken phalluses. However, what about the anal reference? Or a broken hymen? Or a reverberation from a traumatic memory about the effort and disappointment at the experience of loss of her virginity?]

She talked a great deal about her athletics. She hoped I could help her improve. She bench-pressed and ran stairs for hours. Her male coach urged her to more and more feats of endurance, and she thrived on the regimen. She was outstandingly active, both mentally and physically, and readily aggressive, and on the surface was quite easy with it. She was also very ambitious, and after her athletic prime and completed doctorate was headed for a top job in industrial research. She was apparently uninhibited, always striving to be number one, yet concerned and annoyed but not devastated if it did not happen. [These competitive qualities in athletics, academics, and the world of work have often been associated mainly with penis envy and male identification in a woman. Deutsch (1945), for example, shows evidence of this kind of thinking in case reports. Since libido and activity were described by Freud as masculine, any activity on a female's part needed to be designated masculine in order to fit the theory. If the contemporary analyst considers contemporary ways to characterize the female/active/aggressive/dominant axis, then further inquiry can be conducted into the nature of, say, female exhibitionism (see Chapter 2). Schafer (1974) and others have argued that Freud's vision of women was limited by his difficulty in appreciating the maternal transference. This "old" lens thus tends to dull the view of female maternal aggression by co-opting aggression and warding it off by designating it male. These issues are particularly interesting, because women notably have had a reputation for inhibition in these arenas. However, how much of this "inhibition" turns out to be embedded in our own ways of thinking as analysts?]

For about a year, KL related to me as a helpful, reliable, and admiring grownup. The transference was positive—to "good" teachers, the middle-aged male coach, the father of her teen years and after. I was mainly a male figure to her. In this stage of analysis, her father was seen as the opposite of her denigrated mother. [This could be heard as fierce oedipal rivalry, as a standard oedipal formulation. KL's repudiation of her mother was also connected to the terrible disappointment in the mother and thus a loss of maternal ideal due to the mother's addiction and abdication of her responsibilities. Blum (1981) pointed to the importance of this ideal specifically to women. Repudiation of the mother might also speak to an underlying dangerous love for her mother. This moment is a good example of the useful over-lap between newer and older thinking.]

On the couch, KL revealed an ease and attunement to her body and its sensations. These she included in her associations. [I have found that this is more usual in female athletes than with other women. Older thinking tends to assume greater secretiveness in a female's associations. This can indeed happen in individual cases (see Chapter 1) and can be understood in the borders between the old and the new, but there is marked variability among analysands. Secretiveness is actually not a gender-specific quality but rather related to body shame in either sex (Lichtenberg, 2008).]

She rearranged pillows and space to suit her needs. If she were agitated, my couch could end up looking like a whirlwind had hit it. Curiously, at this stage, she omitted any mention of her genitals. [Her overall ease with body reference highlighted this interesting omission. I would have had to force a priori assumptions from the old formulations to suppose that, in unconscious fantasy, she either had a penis or had lost one, and to suppose that it was these unacceptable ideas and affects that accounted for the omission in consciousness. Such fantasy is, of course, quite possible. Nevertheless, there were odd features here that did not seem readily explicable. For one thing, she did not act castrated, or downcast and depressed, when she failed to excel, as the old formulas suggest she would. Trying to stay in tune with her, and not to foreclose my thinking by taking up these masculinized genital connections, I thought to myself that the picture was of a young woman who admired and was fascinated with certain attributes of the male body and also of her father's mental life. She wanted to emulate these and did not show much conflict about this. Was she avoiding her genitals and her wish to have the penis, and avoiding display of her anxiety, because it would expose fully to me the fantasized inadequate vulva and clitoris? However, where was the expected phallic castration anxiety here? Was it all hidden in this oblation from her verbal associations? In sum, I thought it possible that she had blotted out the genitals altogether, as they might well be an area of danger.]

Yet, in her associations, there were many references to acquiring for herself male-like bodily strength and endurance. She wanted strong and powerful muscles "with a big hard bulge" and enjoyed watching her biceps flex in the session. She would freely ask me to look at how big she was getting. She would giggle and talk of how I would think she was showing off. I would agree that she was showing off her muscles to me. "What all do you want me to see?" I'd ask her. "I want you to see I'm strong. I'm getting results from the gym. Dad, you know is terrifically strong. He works out in his hotel rooms. He has to sit a long time in planes, and he needs to work out to absorb his pent-up energy—just like me." At a later time, she dwelled on the swelling sensation of the rising muscle. "Just like an erection—I guess you think I'm full of penis envy." "What about it, then?" I said, after we had dealt with the projective element and the oedipal desire to please me by parroting Freud. She said, "Yes. I guess it is penis envy. I think it would be great to have a penis. In athletics, it would be far easier than having periods, though now I'm on birth control and it's totally manageable. I *am* very competitive, you know. I love it that I'm stronger than many men. I'm actually more powerful than a lot of guys (laughs). Having a dick—well, it would depend on the dick, wouldn't it?" She expressed these wishes and frustrations directly and rather unconflictedly, I thought. One reason for her lack of frustration in her comparisons with men was the very fact of her muscular gifts. As she said, she could achieve realistically a body strength superior to that of most of her male peers. "It is such *fun* to compete with them. You don't have to hold yourself back, like with women. What a kick!" She wished she had been born a boy to be like her father. "Life would just have been easier for me," she said. [Her penis envy was out in the open now, but I found evidence missing, until now, for accompanying and complicating female genital denigration. Phallic castration anxiety per se was missing.]

Her dreams often depicted men chasing her. In associations, she felt anxious about burglary and rape. I tried some interpretations along the phallic castrated line, about wanting to chase the men herself and "take them"—after all, she had said she'd like to have a penis of her own. She said, "Oh yeah," but it was not an idea that developed. [I felt in retrospect that this was a formulaic and mechanical interpretation on my part, an attempt to fit the theory to her case. Again, I returned simply to the material. A newer idea would allow for less in the way of mental gymnastics—like the common analytic habit of turning "fears" into "wishes." I decided to just stay with her fears about being invaded. She might have penetration anxiety, for example, or some other genital anxiety about a man approaching her sexually.] These dreams often occurred when her training did not go well. We talked of her feelings of vulnerability if she could not be as strong as she wanted. Being strong helped allay the fearful thought that a man could rape her. Her fear of the coach's, or my or her father's anger and retaliation could trigger these dreams.

She proceeded in this vein for about a year. KL was increasingly successful at her sport and "in crush" (her words) with her male coach. Dreams revealed to us the connection between the coach and her love for her father. We established that besides wanting to be a boy, she wanted to be her father's best woman. She vied with mother, nanny, and her father's girlfriend by sharing in the father's sports and garnering his admiration.

All through this phase, I was seen as the admiring and encouraging father figure. She was an active agent on her own behalf and was relatively self-contained, pleasantly independent, but well connected to me: rarely did she make direct demands.

Thus, her womanly male strivings were fueled by male identification wishes to be close to her father by sharing his body characteristics and indulging in fantasies of being his best son. I think that this is where bisexuality, in the sense of touching on the individual blending of body hormonal components in a female,[6] works with the potential for bisexual gender fantasy. Being a son in fantasy may have served the defensive purpose of not having to cope with her female eroticism with him. I did not know and still do not. In truth, I cannot say if it is even necessary here to wonder if the boy state "defended against" the girl state. In the older model, such assumptions would be automatic, and thus judgments would be very important in order to assess the level of feminine development by dint of the extent of her renunciation of the masculine line.

In a newer model, I suggest, both can be appreciated as part of KL's gender composition. Her female strivings to please a man were thus woven into her desires to be a sportswoman, in order to excite and maintain these older men's interest in her. The tomboy model was a female model these men favored in her.

So far, so good. The gender picture was both female- and male-wish dominated. To be father's best girl/boy, best boy, and best woman was her aspiration. She expended great energy in developing her muscles into the male ideal. Within the old psychosexual formulation, one might say KL was fixated in "the phallic-narcissistic" position.

Yet, thinking along gender lines leaves genuine unknowns unresolved. After all, the only specific genital reference here so far was to her fear of being raped and robbed. The meanings were more unclear than "phallic narcissism" would suggest. I understood the function of her desire to be strong, powerful, and in control was to achieve mastery over experiencing herself as weak or out of control, which was a version of both her childhood self and her repudiated mother. The position seemed to me as much a compelling representative of what she wanted to avoid—her likeness to the negative image of her mother or to her position as a child. Thus, hers was a desire to be like her father. I have often noted that the choice of which parental gender component to favor represents who was the more enduring favorite of the child—a choice that can also, but not always, be mutual.]

In the analysis: female influences

During this year-and-a-half, KL referred to her mother as *her*: "I hate her addiction and her weakness. I hate her lack of discipline and her lack of control. Dad is strong and reliable. He has everything—I feel protected in his great big arms. She's puny and always going to bed. She's always 'effing' drunk and slurred. She never does what she says she'll do. She has no energy. Ugh!" KL would pull the analytic pillows around and give them a punch ("a swipe at *her*," she would say) to fluff them up and "give them life." [If one listens exclusively in the old mode, concerned with how maleness defends against femaleness, one is not free to hear both equally. If instead one listens for two threads of gender narrative, one will frequently hear a male attribute followed or measured by a female—e.g., father's shortcomings and mother's virtues, or vice versa. This rhythm need not be regarded as an opposition but can instead be heard and analyzed as separate lines that are in conjunction with each other.]

Here are a few additional scenes from the past that will begin to coalesce into a picture of KL on the couch, now in a phase of transference to me as female. As we know, she had requested a female analyst initially, and we would expect this to have dynamic significance.

The entry to the following material was the patient's growing and undeniable dependence on me. She expressed longings to see me around weekends, and began to wonder who else was in my life. When the transference had been in the male mode, she had just assumed she was my major interest as either tomboy, or strongest female. In the female transferential mode, she now imagined competitors, grown-up men, for whom she competed with me in fantasy but rarely won.

Dreams of coming into my house revealed associations to trying unsuccessfully to vamp her mother's boyfriends when she was pubertal. This was annoying and depressing to her. Her dependence made her "less than" me, she said. I wasn't dependent on her because I had all these important people in my life. She felt small and "less than" me. She assumed that I as senior woman was loved and catered to by others. Her jealousy connected both to her mother, in her supermodel role before marriage, and to the flight attendant girlfriend. Each had won her father sexually, and each had been sought after in a world where glamour is valued. This oedipal aspect of her transference is well described by an overlap of old and new conceptions. The female oedipal situation is by definition a view of female competition, with the male as centerpiece. This is an example of an apt and perfectly valid formulation that nonetheless is part of a phallocentric view of female functioning. Phallocentricity is rightly invoked when the girl and the woman are indeed rivalrous for the man. The newer point would be that oedipal rivalry is not the sole, or necessarily the most important, emotional origin of female competitiveness (e.g., Miner and Longino, 1987; Marcus, 2004; Wurmser and Jarass, 2008).

KL's dislike of the "girly" flight attendant ushered in a discovery of admiring thoughts about her mother's style of dress: "It is elegant, authoritative, graceful, and shows off her great long legs; even now she still has beautiful breasts." She sighed. She then said she felt like a little girl with me. I was all three mother figures in the transference. The nanny came to mind as frail and unreliable—so frail my patient felt like "Mount Vesuvius" compared to her. The nanny used to scold her for not being feminine enough. KL realized that she had three mothers to contend with. I pointed out that these three women with their long legs, big breasts, big bottoms, hairy genitals, and big opinions were a lot of competition for a young girl just beginning to get her breasts and getting used to her periods and her new figure. At this juncture, she spoke about her anxiety-laden memories of changing from being small and flat in front to getting pubic hair and having a bigger "purse"; she reported memories of her vaginal penetration anxiety, her first experiences in sex, and her disappointment because sexual intercourse was painful due to the breaking of her hymen and the boy's being rough and nervous. I felt that this was an example of a "newer" intervention directed to the girl's own body experience, as opposed to an "old" general comment about the multiple oedipal competition—apt enough, but missing the female body referents. I felt that the choice of intervention here was rewarded by the patient's expanding on various genital anxieties reported after 1970, and expanded in the latest work (see, e.g., Holtzman and Kulish, 1996; Kulish and Holtzman, 2008; Hall, 2007).

She recalled through her tears her pride at age 15 at having made the effort to lose her virginity and her anxious thoughts about subsequent intercourse. She had been urgent to get on with this rite of passage. She felt pressure to grow up quickly, to depend on herself. [I felt, in looking back, that "breaking her ass" indeed had more to do with the efforts and frustrations of this specifically female experience than with any male-derived experience about the anxieties of losing a fantasy penis or confronting the loss of not being male.] Her story about coming to enjoy sex very much by the time she was 18 was convincing. She liked men, their company, and their sexuality. [The older formulation of KL's being stuck in a "phallic castration" phase might have committed one to believing that she must be hiding her rage at men in the analysis. The analyst would then have less inclination to believe in her love of men, and her pleasure in sexual intercourse, which I found convincing.]

The voice of the maternal imago within KL's superego (Dahl, 2002) was now loud and harsh. KL was more hesitant to reveal to me as transferential mother all these thoughts about her female body in relation to frankly sexual desires than she had been when she was a girl/boy to my "father" in the transference. [This kind of transferential observation is common to both old and new formulations.] She felt that I was critical. Her associations slowed; she scolded herself for her dependence. She felt "wimpy" with me. She hated to talk about her mother's body. She compared herself to me and felt uneasy with her sense of superiority. "You are kind of short, but I like the way you dress—at least you're not in frills." [This kind of female-to-female competition for a girl or woman was limited in the older formulations, because it was eclipsed both by the concentration on the female-to-male competition and by the females' status as defined by the attentions of the preeminent male in the household. The girl's oedipal rivalry with her mother has always been well described, but I want to emphasize that I have perceived that the rivalry is not just over the love of a man; there is also a female-to-female rivalry over which of the women holds preeminence and power among themselves.] Now that admiration of her mother had come to the fore, a more textured sense of KL's angers about the mother's inadequacies emerged. As KL told me tales of her mother's inadequacies at keeping order among the children, the mother became more real.

One story was of the children spending all their time in the vast attic of the family's Bel Air mansion. In this hierarchical sibling society, the biggest, loudest, and heaviest subjugated opponents by brute force. Their mother would appear intermittently, in a rage, to provide gym equipment and then run away. Her "boudoir" was far, far away from the children.

The next 6 months of the patient's analysis was an emotional roller coaster. I began to realize that, metaphorically, I had been brought into the Bel Air attic of sibling rule, and that she feared but also longed for my intrusion as a strong, calm mother. She feared that I, like her mother, would respond with a rage indistinguishable from that of the children and throw her out. She hoped I could bring order. "When I think of you as a professor [a male image] I calm down. I think you're on my side to win and get strong. It used to be like that at the beginning. But when I think of you as a European woman with an accent, and maybe kids, I get so-o-o-o anxious." In the latter image, I was perceived as intensely critical, like her Italian mother, a powerful force to be feared in an inchoate way. My collapse from metaphoric inebriation instilled further terror.

[What criticisms did she fear? That varied according to which of the three mother figures—mother, nanny, or father's girlfriend—was involved. Those she anticipated from her mother were the most painful. It emerged that her mother had called her "selfish, weak, and a woman-hater" for wanting to "desert" her to go live with her father. Such a paradox! It was "weak" to KL when viewed from the female perspective—to become a jock. Through this lens, her sporting activities were "self-indulgent." From the male perspective, it was of course good and desirable to be athletic. KL was torn between these opposing images. Was she weak, as her mother said, or strong, as her father believed? We took up the "weak" female-to-female line. [In relation to her primary sense of femaleness, the mother's opinions and attitudes took an extremely prominent, if not preeminent, place for KL, as I think they do for most women. They were a conscious and unconscious gold standard about the best kind of woman.]

Insofar as she internalized the imperative to be "the right kind of woman," she took her mother's criticisms dreadfully to heart. She wept and wept about her discovery in analysis that she cared so much about what her mother thought. She longed for her mother's love and felt guilty about having repudiated her. With interpretive help, she understood that she viewed herself as so destructive toward her mother that she had denied the mother's importance in order, unconsciously, to try to preserve it. This was the only way she could manage after her mother's attempted suicide. KL blamed herself for her mother's decline and alcoholism.

In the ancient nanny transference, my patient feared that she was too much for me, too overwhelming. She could break my bones by blowing on them. This came in association with a dream. She perceived me as pale, and she worried about my "shakiness" when I dropped a book. This followed an angry session in which she had complained that yet again she was second, and that I wasn't much of a coach. In the transferential role of her father's girlfriend, I was castigated for not being a substitute mother or a warm enough mother to her. KL one day connected her love of being like a racehorse with men, as being joyful that they would not crumble in competition, as her mother would. At another point, she connected it to being a female bonded in a band of powerful females, with the men small and depending on their power. [So, being a horse among horses turned out to be a fantasy of symbiosis with both males and females. This fantasy was both regressive, harking back to the time her mother cared for her, and progressive, relating as it did to her teenage years with her father. This shows how fluid the building blocks of the adult body gender fantasy can be. Old formulations committed to a male/female dichotomy are less illuminating here, because they restrict the range of possibilities to an unnuanced either/or.] I therefore helped her see that the mother and nanny aspects of her inner world were connected to holding herself back in athletic competition lest she destroy them. "You need us to stick together for power" or "You'll blow me away." These were the kinds of interventions I made, depending on whether she wanted to cling to me, as either male or female, to take on some outsider, or took me on and then became afraid of the consequences.

Woven into the emerging picture of her introjects and identificatory female aspects, her body began to reemerge in the following fashion. [This is particularly where I feel it helpful to have a notion of a female developmental line with a basis in female anatomy, and not resting on the male paradigm, as in the old formulas. I include in my considerations all adult female sexual characteristics and not the genitals alone.]

The maternal body

We were now in about the third year of analysis. Associations at this time led KL to an intense disparagement of the condition of female childlessness. At that moment, she was angry with me for not affirming, as a coach would, that she *must* be the best. Her father's girlfriend had no children. The nanny too was childless. "At least my mom had five kids! His new concubine can't even get pregnant. Today I think *you* don't even have kids." These connections led to thoughts of female body strength and frailty, as she conceived them. Responding to an apparently recurrent fear that she could not one day have children, I asked, "What about these women and their babies?" She started to cry. She had read somewhere that there was a "poisoned gene," passed on by alcoholic mothers to their daughters, that causes infertility. "Something is wrong with their uteruses." I heard this as her worst-case scenario of a fantasized female neutering at the hands of her wicked mother. [If "castration" is used in this female sense of the term for women, then it is unobjectionable. Mayer (1985) has employed it thus, to signify a girl's fear of losing her own genital. However, the usage can be confusing, and "neutering" conveys the point at least as well.] KL said, "I might be fundamentally damaged as a woman. I always wanted to know what it would be like to be pregnant."

Then she told me of her experiences with her mother during the latter's pregnancies with her four younger siblings. KL had especially envied her mother's bigness, the huge hard hump of her belly, and her breasts, "powerful and strong." Now the meaning of asking me in the first year to look at the swelling "humps" of her biceps took on the resonance of female potency. The little girl was intensely fascinated with the idea that her mom had a living baby inside her. "I tried to feed it oranges under her skirt. I brought my truck under the table hoping it would come out and play." She was full of questions about how it would get out, and it emerged that one of the mother's resources was an ability to relate to the little girl about bodies—"probably because it focused on her own as the center of attention," she now laughed. Her mother had told her sensitively and imaginatively about her vulva, clitoris, and vagina. [Her mother's frankness and simplicity were unusual. KL seemed to me to have had as good a sense of her female genitals as I had ever seen. Ultimately, I believed that that was why she didn't mention her genitals much in the male influence phase of the analysis. Unlike many women, she was not confused. I also think that her core gender identity as female was a durable base for KL's more mature gender identity, which incorporated aspects of her father.]

When she asked about childbirth, her mother told about how the neck of her little "purse" was so magical that it could stretch and stretch "like magical elastic" and that the baby would pop out and then her purse would contract again. However, KL was still unsure of the exact whereabouts of the unborn baby in the pelvis or abdomen. She reported a flood of memories, things she had not thought about since the terrible night her mother went crazy. Her mother apparently loved being pregnant. She had described it to my patient as the best time in life. She also had a penchant for parading nude. She had a gym in the house, and little KL did gymnastics with her mother, both of them in the nude. The large dominant woman with the big breasts was the center of the girl's envy and longing. The mother herself enjoyed the daughter's gaze of awe, admiration, and fascination. [Some of KL's longing was to *be* inside her mother, like the little unborn baby. However, I heard more about wanting very much for herself this wondrous capacity of her body to engage in childbearing. I think that an analyst who thinks about "primary femininity" or "a primary sense of femaleness" is freed from trying to explain the *meaning* of the uterus, as is the lot of the phallocentric theoretician. The uterus simply exists in the female body. As with KL, a girl or woman makes of it what she will, as it becomes the locus of conflict and the subject of analysis.]

In her childhood, KL would imagine her own stomach swelling. It never seemed adequate and was always inferior to her mother's. The fantasy of having a poisoned uterus was attributed to her mother's retaliation. KL used to put cushions under her shirt and play "pregnancy." The rivalry with her mother, as I understood it, was only in part for daddy's baby. I perceived a strong female rivalry here for the female ability to command the biological magic of giving life and being the senior fertile woman. [This is a female-to-female rivalry qua female—not just as competition for father's attentions as expressed via competition with the mother as in the positive Oedipus complex—a complexity of competition that needs to be updated in ego psychology. It should not just be downplayed, absorbed and subsumed under the term "negative oedipal complex." This linguistic twist takes the emphasis *away* from the impact of mother's importance to the female, slants it in the direction of lack of a more "mature" male conceived oedipal complex, and retrogresses in language to the phallocentric bias. There is much more potential emotional room for such deeply connected competition in the Persephonal complex (Kulish, 2006).]

There were now many linguistic connections available between KL's athletic efforts and intentions, and her vision of maternality. The fantasied power and control of this state had especially appealed to KL when she was a child. Her surround, after all, was often in disarray. It was understandable that she wanted a godlike power to command chaos and rule over it herself, creating and destroying life at her say-so. In addition, her mother was calmer when she was "bigger" and in this magical state of being "in sync" with the baby inside her. Perhaps if she could be big like mother, she could ease the agitations she experienced growing up in her household—including her reactions to the births of her four siblings. She feared she could not fully compete with this fertile goddess that was her mother.

As we worked more and more with these female-to-female body comparisons (i.e., little girl to mature woman comparisons), KL experienced rushes of fury and murderous rage against her mother. Deeply disillusioned by her alcoholism, she also experienced the full force of her conflicted wishes to eliminate the mother as a competitor, even while fearing too much success. She felt badly let down. Her sense of the growth of her body due to workouts now took on the resonance of pregnancy. She joked about our "making this baby" (i.e., the analysis) together. She competed joyfully with me, showing off her own interpretive skills. A dream led her thoughts to the death of Sharon Tate, the actress killed by Charles Manson. We analyzed "Man/son" as her male desire, which she was using at times to kill off her own internalized mother and her seemingly unattainable pregnant woman ideal—her maleness murdering her femaleness. (Here, one can appreciate that the two narrative lines at times clash in the process of attempted integration. As a way of conceptualizing defensive operations here, this is more useful than the older view, according to which overcoming masculinity means getting rid of it in order to replace it with femininity.) KL also associated the madness of Manson with her fears that her mother had destroyed her reproductive capacity by giving her a poisoned gene that would make her a "man's son" incapable of creating a baby in her body.

It was in connection with this deepening work on the female-to-female rivalry with her mother that KL began to satisfy herself by excelling at her sport. Eventually, the work of integrating the male and female developmental lines allowed for categories of self-assessment such as "strong woman," "powerful woman," "aggressive woman," "loving woman," and "sexually potent" woman.

Concluding discussion

I hope to have demonstrated here that alertness to references to the female body and female experience, in preference to working solely within the confines of the old female body/ male body formula, opens the field of female developmental and gender theory to more searching questions. In this case material, for example, gender as a monolithic conception is certainly challenged. This affirms clinically ideas developed by Tyson (1982), Chodorow (1994, 2011), and the cultural observations and studies of many contemporary academic and psychoanalytic feminists. The gender composition that emerges here, and that for me applies to women generally, shows the following four psychological components: girl-to-girl, girl-to-woman, girl-to-boy, and girl-to-man. In all females, each component of the gender story must be grounded in, and interrelated to, possession and personal interpretation of the female anatomy (core gender identity). The female-to-female lines of gender development will often predominate in the narrative, but the female-to-male lines will be interwoven in varying degrees according to the individual. The story will emerge not in linear fashion, but piecemeal.

The unfolding of KL's analysis appears more orderly here than it was. This is an artifact, due probably to my attempt to show three of the four gender lines in a clear way (the girl-to-girl sister line was omitted). There emerged, more or less first, a straightforward boy envy, driven also by a major oedipal longing manifested as pleasing the father by being his favorite woman and young boy/girl. These male and bisexual fantasy elements turned out to be relatively easy for KL to integrate, once her female-to-female body envies and her more forbidden mothering body wishes and fears began to emerge into the picture of her gender conflicts. Important sequences concerning her fright and flight vis-à-vis her female body were traced. Body and attitudinal comparisons with her excess of three mothers had proved daunting for her. It had been especially difficult to integrate the vivid contrast between the power conveyed by her mother's pregnancies and the helplessness of her abject inebriation, divorce, and repudiation by the family. The nanny too had been frail, if vociferous. The father's girlfriend was despised as childless, a negativity that allowed KL to ward off fears of her mother's rage and accusations of disloyalty.

Developmental sequences connected to becoming like her mother figures, then, were fraught with dichotomies and ambivalence. Sequences attached to the males in KL's early life were simpler—e.g., being stronger than her brother or being admired for her gamesmanship, physical grace, and strength by her father. Built on an infantile bisexual base, KL's athleticism and body power were used to express both her connection in fantasy to her father and, even more important, her competition with her mother and triumphant reveling in being her daughter. There was no question in my mind that her male fantasy strivings joined with, and in fact effectively empowered, her adult female gender patterning.

I have proposed here that a theory of *non-competing dual gender narratives* preserves more possibilities to analyze the blend that becomes a person's gender portrait than does the old notion that maleness must be "overcome" to "create" female development. Polarized aspects such as masculine/active/dominant or feminine/passive/submissive, when found fixed in an individual, represent merely defensive solutions to the problems of establishing one's gender identity. The integration of a gender narrative requires an internal, sequenced, opportunistic blending of male and female meanings, together with a clear recognition of the function of the sexed body. (I have come to believe that males, too, show dual, interweaving threads in the development of their personal gender identity. Monolithic gender is a notion that is today obsolete. Much more work needs to be done in these areas, because the accounts of development in our case histories, especially from the ego psychological perspective, have to date failed to take psychological bisexuality seriously [Notman, 2010]).

It was Mayer (1995) who first introduced the idea of gendered "paired developmental lines" that interweave in the female psyche. Unfortunately, she maintained the name and concept of the male trajectory as a phenomenon of "phallic castration," which, as I have said, I consider obfuscating. She also tried to make generalizations about the affective states of anxiety and depression in women, according to which side of the developmental line they failed to negotiate (see Elise, 1998). Mayer's formulation has not been borne out in my clinical experience. Most affective resonances seem to me to be mixed and unpredictable, and depend on many variables, including the individual underlying meanings of the particular fantasy. Psychoanalysis clearly has no blueprint for either "normal femininity" or "normal masculinity." With each patient, we begin in a state of creative uncertainty. In each treatment, we must struggle against premature closure based on clinical and theoretical certainty that ignores the rich contemporary scholarship, especially that of the last decade. We can admit fruitfully that we still need to explore plenty the expansive territory of sex and gender. Nothing is bedrock. Nothing is monolithic. Ideology of any sort is open to question.

Notes

1 The current Supreme Court too is apparently confused about sex and gender. Justice Antony Scalia, "in an attempt to clarify usage of the terms" has written (J.E.B., 1994) "The word gender has acquired the new and useful connotation of cultural or attitudinal characteristics (as opposed to physical characteristics) distinctive to the sexes. That is to say, *gender* is to *sex* as *feminine* is to *female* and *masculine* is to *male*," Thus, while he is excited over the new ideas, and promisingly divides sex and gender into differing issues, he appears then to confine gender to the usual binaries. Justice Bader Ginsberg, confused too, though dealing in an enlightened way with many cases of what she named for the first time, "gender discrimination," admits to having been advised in her opinions to use "gender" where she might have naturally have used "sex" as interchangeable, in order to prevent the distraction of male giggles! (Internet report, under 'Sex/Gender/Whatever' lecture notes by Dr. Karl L. Wuensch, E. Carolina University Department of Psychology)
2 I partially part company with Stoller on his use of "primary femininity" in general as I am persuaded that it can be problematic to ask what exactly "primary" means; and I fully part company with him about his notion of boys' originary "primary femininity" in particular.
3 Moses and Monotheism (Freud, 1939) "In this way we reach the concept of a sliding 'complemental series' as it is called, in which two factors converge in fulfilling an aetiological requirement. A less of one factor is balanced by a more of the other" (p. 73).
4 "Ze"/"zee" in some circles is used as a neutral or androgynous personal pronoun, and "zeer" is the possessive form.
5 See Dale Boesky's (2009) concerns about conflicting issues within the same theoretical approach, such as this.
6 Recalling that this female had the physical abilities to outrun most males. her physical power made it easy for her to fulfill the tomboy model of her own sense of femaleness.

Chapter 8

Sisters and brothers

This chapter explores further an aspect of the psychic impact of both female and male bodies on the developing female. The focus here is on siblings. Little has been written clinically about how siblings effect gender identity (e.g., see the history of how siblings, especially sisters, have been mentioned, but passed over in the literature, Kuba, 2011). The case examples here involve one particular group—adult women who grew up with brothers who were dependably difficult in the family. I choose this sibling constellation to examine, because it reverses the classic role of a favored brother with a denigrated sister. Sisters' effects upon each other would be very interesting to explore also, but for the moment, I am looking at a sister with a problem brother. Questions to be explored here are: how have these particular sibling rivalries affected the building blocks of these particular women's body images? What are some implications for their gender identity struggles in development? What central unconscious fantasies have informed their related sexuality, their choice of lovers, and their interest in procreation and their work?

Clinical materials

Since I started to conduct analyses in the late 1970s, I have noticed that a number of female patients did not fit the stereotype of our literature at all, which regularly presents females with low or dubious self-regard. In worldly terms, the women here were among the most ambitious and aggressively achieving people whom I have encountered as an analyst. My full sample was seven women who had brothers who were very disappointing to them and to their entire families. Some of the features that these women had in common were the following: they had outstandingly easygoing relations to their direct and indirect aggression and competition; the durability of their self-esteem was impressive, in spite of even deserved blows from the outside world that I fancied would have made an average person cringe. They were capable of restoring rapidly their own best image to themselves; they had a vigorous appetite for life and reported a thrillingly pleasurable gambling sense toward risk-taking in a number of areas. These were presenting features that were certainly different from the stereotypic woman in treatment, who is debilitated by low self-esteem, overly caring for others, subservient to men, and afraid of aggression. The most troubled pattern common to this group was in their relationships to men. I also note, though I cannot provide evidence here because of confidentiality, that out of seven cases, five were heterosexual in their object choice (three of these will be reported in a disguised fashion here) and two were lesbian. These cases seem to me interesting and modern, because the conduct of these women in the world and their worldly success is akin to the male of old. How did they become the powerful figures that they became? What can we learn about the dynamics of these women whose families were remarkably "un-phallocentric" in their gender orientation, and perhaps even "gynocentric"?

Office first presentation: patients LM, MO, OP

Ms. LM

Ms. LM was a tall, blonde woman always dressed in pencil-slim black. Her curves were subtly emphasized by the low cut of the V-neck of her shirt, peeping out from behind the formality of her Brooks Brothers pinstriped blazer. Her long fingers flashed a set of elegant diamond wedding and engagement rings. In the first consultation with me, her beeper throbbed on her trouser belt, and she checked it regularly by squinting at it by her waist beneath her jacket, while scarcely interrupting her sentence. Her leather briefcase and laptop bag lay next to her right foot. LM talked rapidly and to the point. She was 32 years old. At 26, she had taken over her father's computer business on the West coast due to his death, but had stepped down for the present, her uncle deputizing, so that she could attend law school in the East. The business regularly consulted her (as her beeper proclaimed) and this was a part of life she wanted to "keep alive," as she said, in spite of being at school. She was troubled that she could not decide whether or not to commit herself to the prestigious law journal, because she said that, for the first time in her life, she was privately afraid that she might not be "the best" writer and thinker. LM was not clinically depressed, but she felt her spirits lower than optimal. She was anxious about feeling anxious. She was not used to any disturbance in affect. And she said she wanted to sort out "the man thing." Her husband of 2 years was a successful doctor and "kept the home fires burning" in California while she was away. Frankly, she was not sure if she loved him. She thought she married him for convenience and as yet another achievement. She saw him on breaks from school. There were no children. The patient wanted to have an analysis in this unsettled period in her life. One of her reasons was that she viewed it as "the BMW of treatments." "Nothing but the best for me," she grinned. I thought she was an only child at the time of consultation.

Ms. MO

Ms. MO was 28 when I first met her. She mentioned a young brother aged 16. He was called Teddy and was "at home with mom" in northern New England. Her father was an international lawyer, living with his girlfriend in New York, divorced from the mother when the patient was 13. MO was a brilliant doctoral student in economics. She had plans for a government career and headed toward Washington on weekends and vacations from school as surely as a swallow flies south in winter. Undaunted by her student status, MO seemed to be at ease working side-by-side with senior figures on the political world stage. It was as if to her there was no question at all that she belonged in the company of those who design the planet. MO was medium-slim build, athletic, and a serious intellectual. She wore black pants and sweaters at all times but always somewhere a flash of primary color in unexpected places—on a sock, or cuff, or a lapel. While speaking about her clothes, she referred to the play "Master Class," where Maria Callas as an ex-diva insists to a dowdy pupil, "You have to have a look! Get a look! You don't have a look!" MO felt it was vital to have a unique "look" and to "show yourself" and "get ahead of the pack." Her reason for seeking analysis now was because of a 3-year troubled relation with a male fellow student that was breaking up. She had pursued him—"hunted" him was her word—winning him away from another woman, but had never felt he was suave enough or sure enough of himself to satisfy her. He was too intimidated by her, she said.

Ms. OP

Ms. OP was a stout, divorced woman in her 40s who had three teenaged children and an ex-husband who was a very wealthy businessman. Her main complaint was that she was angry and felt that she could not stop overflowing her rage about her husband onto her children. "I pour poison in their ears," she said. Her comments about him were demeaning and hating, and she regretted her statements, not because she bethought herself, but because, "My poor children—he is their father, after all." A number of years previously, she had begun a real estate business of her own in the city. With all the network contacts from her own family and her married days, she found she was doing extremely well. Even in a poor market, the patient turned large profits. She loved "letting myself go," taking a risk, "No holes barred!" she laughed. She played the stock market to advantage. OP literally used to "roar with laughter" on the couch, often in response to some wicked fantasy to outwit her ex-husband's business associates. OP was heiress to the fortune of a wealthy and influential philanthropist. She was adored by both parents and was close to them. She talked about the family "sadness"—an only brother, George, who had died, when he was 5 years old and she was 3, of complications from spina bifida and cerebral palsy. Her parents never talked about him and did not like to be reminded of him in any way. She vaguely wondered how his life and death might have had an impact on her.

Analyses

Ms. LM

LM, the law student, revealed quickly after she lay down on the couch that she had a brother who had Down syndrome. He was called Buddy and was 2 years her junior. He was in a protected living situation an hour away from her original home. He could do simple factory work, and she emphasized how pleased everyone was with his accomplishments. Her widowed mother visited him every month. He came home only for Christmas. This crisp account was the first and last that I heard of him for 6 months, and there was an air of closure to the form of its offering.

Difficult siblings are often present only by their notable *absence* in the associative stream (Balsam, 1988). There seems to be a relationship between the degree of hatred and the length of time elapsing before bringing them into the room. In LM's case, the lag was months and not years, indicating considerable repressed negativity but not extreme splitting, which could have resulted from yet increased hostility toward a sibling born so close (Balsam, 1988). In addition, LM's associative field had an obsessional caste, which influences the slow associative speed of affectively charged materials. She controlled her affects within an intellectually distancing style of communication. LM was very slow to talk about her brother.

When Buddy returned to her associations, it was after she had spent time with him during Christmas break. After I had interpreted the decrescendos of her verbal cadences that followed facts about him, the patient became aware that she actually did have some feelings about him. "It is as if I don't want *you* to think about him either," she said. We struggled with her need to protect herself and me from the material and how that had come to be.

Gradually, over 2 years, the following stories emerged which indicated her extreme shame. Ordinary rivalry over the parents' attention seemed low-key, and envy of him seemed very mild. She did not remember his birth, but when she was about 4 years old, her first memory was watching with disgust his hands as he pushed yogurt and cottage cheese into his mouth from a plastered pile in his high-chair tray. He then vomited it, probably in a projectile fashion over her and her place at the dinner table. Being a dainty and meticulous little girl to start with, she was "unspeakably utterly disgusted." To this day, she confessed that she imagined his clothing smelled of vomit, malodorous feces, and urine. She had tried to use "all-good-girlyness," she said, to manage this disgust. This defensive maneuver helped keep apart her consciously unacceptable emotional reactions to his body. Aside from his body—as it were—she overemphasized that he could be cute. How she pulled funny faces to make him laugh! She *really* did not dislike him. He loved music, and she assured me that she let him listen to tapes when she felt he was clean enough to enter her room. Sometimes, she even combed his hair. It was soft and straight and she liked to feel it, just after his bath. He liked blue, and for presents, she bought him toys or clothes in blue. My patient had mightily struggled against her unpleasant feelings toward him and treated me in the transference as if I depended on her to keep up my own good feelings about Buddy.

All through his life, he seemed to be sent to various boarding situations and private caretakers to "give the family a rest." LM believed that her parents were frantic about his having a bad effect on her, her schoolwork, her popularity with friends, her moods, her need to accommodate, or make sacrifices for him. She knew them to be bitterly disappointed about his existence. Whether or not the family conveyed it, or it was the patient's own wish, or a family wish, my patient fervently wanted to be an only child. In the interpretation to a dream, it emerged that everyone wished Buddy had never been born. My patient was the apple of the adults' eyes. She gloried in this position, and indeed I felt that her internalization of this adoration and gift of tremendous power were quite firm building blocks of unusually durable self-esteem and genuine high self-worth. LM did not seem to feel guilty about her favored position. It was as if she was the poised royalty and Buddy was a humble peasant who knew his place.

Ms. MO

The brother of MO, the economist, was 12 years younger. She did not mention that there was anything wrong with him for about a year. There were no images in dreams that reminded her of him either. I assumed that as she was 13 years old and pubertal at the time of his birth, and that the divorce had occurred the following year, that it would be reasonable for a sister so disturbed by these events perhaps also to be subject to immense jealousy and be glad to disregard him even unconsciously. I thought of James Joyce's character Stephen Dedalus, who said that a brother is as soon forgotten as an umbrella! I thought that MO's worldly sophistication and whirlwind life also related to a need to see herself as very distinct and separate from her divorced mother, who lived in a Spartan fashion in Maine. I thought a lot, as one is wont to do, and I was not quite on target!

Teddy turned out probably to be either autistic or to have a pervasive developmental disorder. The patient openly and unapologetically despised him. He remained infantile, his speech was impaired, and he was demanding, loud, and stubborn. He frequently threw temper tantrums. He and mother were totally enmeshed. At home in Maine, before MO was sent to boarding school by her father, the mother would attempt to soothe Teddy by struggling to hold him on her lap against resistance. MO held her mother responsible for Teddy's problems, an attitude echoed from her father. Mother had had a very difficult pregnancy with the boy when MO was 12 and indeed pubertal. MO's memories of the mother's pregnancy proved to be surrounded with fear and repugnance for the female body in this state. The daughter lost what little she had had of this mother, during that pregnancy and after Teddy's birth.

Boarding school and a devoted unmarried female teacher then helped. MO turned more and more also to her father, and he, who earlier had been absent, now became much more interested in her company. He was an international lawyer who began to take her on trips with him. He was charmed by her nubile youth and her intelligence. He and MO formed a loving duo where the irritable burdened mother and "her" deformed son were excluded. From the beginning, MO aggressed against Teddy at every opportunity. She told me with little shame that she had put a pillow over his head till he turned blue. "I didn't really intend to kill him. Well maybe I did want an accident … certainly, I remember wanting to make him cry." We gathered that hurting mother was nearly indistinguishable from hurting Teddy. When she was a junior in boarding school and back for a vacation, Teddy was about 4 years old he would sometimes crawl into bed with her. She told about secretly handling his penis and delighting in seeing his erection. He was enuretic till about 7, and MO now dimly wondered if her sexual stimulation of him was connected. She was gratified that father scarcely ever saw him. She endlessly seemed to toy with Teddy—as if he were not quite human. I wondered if her cruelty were enhanced also by her lack of daily contact with him. She would lie on top of him and pin him down, not actually putting his penis in her vagina, but in her crotch. I asked what he would do at these times, "He often ended up crying and when he was big enough he'd say he'd tell mom. I had him petrified … (She still laughed at the recollection, quickly covering it over by giggling nervously.) I threatened that I'd cut his silly wee-wee off if he told on me. I don't know if he ever did. He wasn't organized enough to tell. Daddy would never have believed it anyway. He couldn't stand Teddy. And he would just have told my mother, and that didn't matter. What could she do? Nothing." She would stop and sigh, changing mood for a moment. "Alas, poor Teddy. I am very bad to him," she would add with little remorse. "I probably should feel bad … but daddy says, who is to stand in judgment over anything *we* have experienced? It's up to us."

Parental attitudes

These influences are naturally important in their details. The feelings that one sibling develops about another is inextricably blended with the perceptions of how the other is treated by each parent (e.g., Solnit, 1983), the favorite parent having a different significance from the less favorite parent. Gender input regarding highly prized traits of the parents' favored perceptions of what is "masculine" and what "feminine" behavior is an important influence in mutual gender enmities between and among siblings.

Ms. LM's parents

The law student's father encouraged her from the beginning to take an interest in his Silicone Valley business. He would put her in the big swivel chair at the head of the Board Room table and say, "One day you can be boss." Mother, a teacher, took great pride in the patient's good school performance. She avidly encouraged the patient's friendships and extracurricular activities. In addition, the girl was pretty and athletic. There was nothing their little "gift from God" could not do well, and they lavished praise on her. Moreover, LM was, without doubt, a pleasing child—enough narcissistically oriented to read others as to the best ways and means of *how* to please, and enough object-related and separated to show independence laced with a capacity to think her own thoughts. It seemed to me as if LM was the recipient of twice as much love and attention to make up for the parents' hostility to their damaged Down syndrome son. Each parent came from matriarchal-dominant families, so that their worship of LM, the girl child, did not seem so forced. Both mother and father had told LM that they were disappointed from his birth that Buddy was a boy, as well as about his Down syndrome. Boys were always more trouble, they said. This patient's representations of both male and female adults, and their mature bodies in relation to her own, were positive and sharply contrasted to her intensely negative image of this male child. Being a girl in this family was greatly rewarded.

Ms. MO's parents

The mother was depressed, worn, and downtrodden, neglected by her husband and undervalued by both daughter and husband. Her solace was the disturbed Teddy, and she alternately "loved him to death" with smothering activities or screamed at his out-of-control behavior in frustration. MO had strenuously distanced herself from the mother early, and regarded her as a helpless, useless, denigrated female with whom she would not want to identify. Later, in her teenage years, she had engaged in a sadistic, sexualized torture of her brother as a way of getting even with mother for taking herself even more out of commission by giving birth to this hated and embarrassing brother. The relation with her father seemed exclusive and worshipful. She gloried in joining his denigration of mother and brother. The differences in mental representations for this patient among the extremely negative adult female and her body and its procreative products; the extremely positive adult male; and the extremely denigrated child male were canyons apart internally, but each had its own significance.

Ms. OP's parents

This patient, the divorced real estate broker, in general liked both parents and received much adoration from both of them. They themselves were animated, humorous, and aggressive—much like my patient, I imagined. They were very distant cousins, a marriage sanctioned to protect the finances. However, the patient felt it was a love match. They frequently had loud fights, but would as easily make up and be loving and tender again. OP was convincing about her own amazement that she really had no question about their love of each other and her, in spite of the fights. They both pressured little OP to see herself the heir to the family fortune. "Heir or heiress, we don't care" was the essence of the message. They were sad and disappointed about the male baby, but transferred all of their intense expectations onto their daughter. She was plump, dark, curly-haired, and red-lipped—good enough to eat, they said, and they ate joyously. There had been powerful pioneering women in the family in previous generations, and they seemed to feel easily that a daughter/heir was entirely adequate. They cared deeply only that they had a smart and interested heir for money management, and they were gratified that OP was good at math at school, for example, and that she was a class leader. The mother was a close advisor of the father, and they were "a team" with little OP as the junior partner. The image of the boy-child, though a fearful and negative one to the girl, was tinged with some tender pathos of these parents' regrets.

Transferential dynamics in the analyses

Ms. LM

LM, the law student/businesswoman, was often ferociously and joyfully competitive. She was freely aggressive, knew clearly when she was angry, and had few inhibitions about showing it. She commanded a large and sarcastic vocabulary though also capable of being witty and charming. She was argumentative and challenged the acceptance of others' ideas—in my case interpretation—with careful examination. I used to think I'd like her to be my lawyer! She prided herself rightfully on being "nobody's fool." LM talked gleefully and appetitively of "murdering" her opponents. Law school, she said, was full of men and women just as competitive as she was. So was business. She thrived on the combative atmosphere. "I am queen of my domain," she said. "I am the king of my castle." "And nobody will knock me down!" she added, remembering the child's game.

I was portrayed in the transference as a besotted parent with a beloved and indulged child. She had no compunction about excelling and "defeating" me—as either parent. LM also seemed very fond of me and even tender in concern at times—for example, if I had a cold. Then I was a baby brother to her. She was shocked if I raised questions about her motivations. She clearly expected me always to see her as "right" and "good." Anything she did or said, including nastiness about her competitors was supposed to be read by me as justified and admirable. Her personality was in the narcissistic spectrum, but her relatedness to me as "other" had evolved somewhat beyond an intensely dyadic or mirroring stage, although when she regressed, this was a feature. She imagined that I thought that whatever bounty she received as grades, job offers, teachers' favors, she richly deserved. LM was totally (but for me, not unpleasantly) entitled, as the quality was tempered by flashes of empathy. LM seemed amazingly free of doubt about her positive attributes.

Ms. MO

The young economist, headed for the Capitol, was fast-talking and confident to the point of being at times bordering on being obnoxiously full of herself.

There was a triumphant air about her, especially when she had received special comments of praise from anyone in power. In the transference, she eagerly sought to find my mistakes, and take me to task for "sloppy thinking," interferences with her clean lines of logic and my interest in her affects. She declared that it was useless to be angry and worse to know it, because it interfered with "performance." Tears were "revolting" to her and interfered with her "look." In essence, she unconsciously regarded me as a "wimpy" woman, a caretaker of other "whiny" patients with whom she abhorred association. Countertransferentially, she tapped into some envy, outrage, and hostility of my own, and protective urges toward my other patients! Her thoughts about my husband were positive. She imagined that he was a European brilliant philosopher and was much in awe of his scholarship. I was portrayed in a dream as a dog with a bandana around its head, sitting on a park bench. The associations were to a female dog called "Rosie." The bandana reminded her of once tying her brother's wet underpants around his forehead as a punishment for wetting the bed. And the park bench was a symbol of homelessness—a wish to kick the bitch and her incontinent son out of the house! I did understand the vigorous nature of her oedipal situation, but I also thought that MO was not the nicest person one would want to meet, and sometimes I felt stung by her criticism. She deeply despised women and their birth products, and I was mostly in the hated adult female register for her.

Ms. OP

OP, in contrast to MO, remembered much pathos surrounding her damaged brother. He was either never referred to in the family, or else he was a point in time, a marker of the evolution of their lives, "at the time of the poor baby." The parents who were consumed with the management of their wealth also referred to "the time of the Depression" with the same sad affect. When the patient was angry with them as a teenager, or with me in the treatment, she would accuse me and them of thinking of her/the children as investments. Just look at what had happened in having a boy who was a bad investment, she would say to punish them. She picked on a male, gawky, and awkward adolescent patient of a colleague in my suite, believing him to be the person who preceded her into my office, and often took me to task for failing him, because he was so skinny and socially goofy. Criticism would make her own parents miserable, and then she would cheer them up with some personal success story.

OP as a girl used to feel bad about having no tender feelings herself about the dead baby. I was able to help her see that she had never really known him in any whole way, as she was only 2. Besides that, we had evidence of her ability to be concerned for this "poor" adolescent boy in my office (besides a tad of rivalry). In her omnipotence, she thought she somehow *should* have known him as well as her parents. She felt terrible that as a child she would be impelled to laugh when the phrase was used, "at the time of the poor baby," and impelled to anxious word-game associations, for example, "at the time of the flood," "at the time of Methuselah," "time and tide wait for no man," a song "dee-dee-dee-dee it's time to go-o," or "at the time of the dinosaurs." Then she would think of dinosaurs, and dinosaurs making love and dinosaur penises, and dinosaur vaginas and big bellies and dinosaurs laying eggs and she would end up screaming with laughter. We were able in retrospect to understand these emotional riffs as fraught with anxiety and fantasies of the absurdity of her parents having sex in order to create a deformed baby. "After all," she said, "It could have been me."

In analysis, OP came in touch with a considerable amount of survivor guilt and many feelings about carrying the burden of the fate of the older dead sibling, trying to live for both of them to please and comfort her parents. OP's dreams at times would be filled with deformed lumps and tumors containing hair and teeth all attached to her own body. Sometimes, they would be joined at the hip. Sometimes, they emerged from her anus, and sometimes in her breast or abdomen. Once she dreamed of him as the Tar Baby from Brer Rabbit. These we understood as images of her brother, blended with terrors of the idea of pregnancy. Probably some of these images were heightened by her intense oedipal situation and representations of wanting her daddy's baby but being punished by having a devil baby. In a dream, she referred to herself as "Rosemary's Baby," which represented a devil baby also with mother/analyst. She recalled being fearful of giving birth to a monster with each of her own pregnancies. As a child, she also thought that for a time she had invented an imaginary older brother, who was everything that her "poor dead brother" could not be. His name was Prince and naturally he was tall and handsome and accompanied her especially when she was lonely and sad. In the analysis, her tender yearning for a brother emerged in fantasies about a male patient in the waiting room. Wanting to be both boy and girl for her parents was present, but the "boy" elements were minor. Being a fellow grown-up and a fecund mother, and worrying about the unconscious aggression entailed to achieve it, were most prominent in OP's childhood fantasies.

Body image

Ms. LM

Let me now turn to what I learned about LM's body image in the course of the analysis. Every picture of the brother's body seemed fraught with ugly smells and uncontrollable mess. The following dream brought associations about his penis. Interestingly, the patient's word for the genitals of either sex was "so-and-so's sex." She referred to her own "sex" when referring to the mons, the clitoris, labiae, and vagina. The brother's penis was his "sex" too. I think this is an interesting way of simultaneously equalizing the organs and blotting out their details. These were the ways her mother had referred to genitals. The parents wanted not to be "hung up" about sex. The household was open to either child masturbating. Brother did it frequently and the parents tried to insist—with little success—that he confine the activity to his room. One night when brother was absent, the patient remembered shouting downstairs from her bedroom late at night to a dinner gathering, "Mommy, is it alright to masturbate now?" She heard the party laughing at her antics. She later laughed about her ploy for attention and her loneliness at being excluded from the grown-ups' dinner. The unbridled freedom of their household and the parents' lack of setting limits on vacations when Buddy was home, resulted in an inner range of joyous freedom and approval to an anxiety at the borders of being out of control. A dream of a Jackson Pollack-like painting provoked an extended fantasy of an anally derived, orgiastic free-for-all. Imagining mixing up all Buddy's phlegm and feces and semen with her menstrual blood and vaginal mucus resulted in her physically becoming agitated on the couch, laughing and crying simultaneously. When it was time to leave, she leapt off the couch in a rage saying, "I could tear the brass door-handle off with my teeth." I felt I had a picture of her overstimulation (the torrent of archaic imagery and unstable affects, topped off with an oral sadistic attack on my breast/penis in her greedy, omnipotent, and confused desires to calm herself by having access to everything) which had emerged historically in unmediated "play" between the two children. I thought that these scenes connected to LM's shame in talking about Buddy. LM was the perpetrator in whipping up a deal of frantic excitement. Their house was apparently big enough that it was unclear where the parents were. In this atmosphere, LM freely displayed her body to Buddy and inspected his. She was intensely curious. She remembered always having genital sensation and liking it (see Chapter 11 about our field's early denial of a girl child's vaginal sensation). She was intrigued with his little penis. Nevertheless, beyond curiosity, as if it were a minor toy to be controlled by her, she did not seem particularly covetous. "Why can I find no envy? Shouldn't I be envious of his penis? Isn't everybody, according to you Freudians?" Confrontation was one of her pleasures!

Her own body was regarded highly when she was most in control. Thus, she trained athletically. She pursued a modern slender aerobic ideal of body image, which was intimately related to helping her master, these flooding experiences of lack of control and fusion with Buddy. Her choice of a good-looking husband was a visual search for a complementary image of a man who fit with a woman in an intercourse of perfect neatness, "a yin and yang," a sculpture where each wove in elegant motion in the curves of the other, interlocked on the surfaces but without penetration. LM sought a state of being closed up and neat—in a female way with neatly closed vagina-like "pursed lips," she fantasized. I thought it an idealized virgin with intact hymen.

LM's fights with her husband concerned his weakness, as she saw it. She did not enjoy adult sex, because it "mussed me up," reminded her of loosening boundaries and out-of-control times with Buddy. When she did allow sexual intercourse, she liked to be on top and got some pleasure in the power of being in charge of his erection. She became angry at her husband's wish for sex, unconsciously considering this a male weakness. LM tolerated intercourse more in order to procreate children as a route to power. This was so prominent that any thought of personal pleasure in the sex act was entirely secondary, and repudiated, because she also felt in no way ready to have a baby. She enjoyed being on the pill, because her periods were under her own control. Living a continent apart from her husband suited her well. She possessed an ideal image of being married without having to share his bed. He actually seemed not to mind either. The image of the pregnant woman, however, was filled with horror as well as desire. LM was unconsciously terrified of bearing a monstrous child like Buddy. All fat had therefore to be trimmed off her body. There were to be no reminders of female pregnancy and "sloppy" emotions. Her spirited professional creativity and risk-taking seemed sublimated into an adult iteration of the bond with her father, a more exciting and gratifying "baby" with him than she could ever accomplish in a biological way with an ordinary male.

Ms. MO

Intrigued from the start with MO's "logo" of black with a flash of bright color, I kept relating this picture to the images of her body that were unfolding. The black symbolized sophistication for her, the very opposite of being a baby like her hated little brother. She too, as with LM, was deeply concerned with control, especially of her aggression and sadism. She had a fantasy of being a dominatrix. She had never acted it out, but the idea of long black leather boots excited her. Black seemed the right color to signal control over her environment. The flashes of color represented excitement of one sort or another—"Just a hint of the primitive!" she would laugh. "People should beware" when she wore red. "I'm cool, don't touch" was blue. "Keep off the grass" was green. Only yellow was a little vulnerable—a secret sign meaning "I'm scared shitless." I thought that Wilhelm Reich would have had many comments about this patient. Character amour seemed about right for her attitude. I tried especially to pick "yellow" days to ask about her vulnerable aspects. This was a 2-year interrupted analysis, so that we were far from termination. I did not see much of her vulnerability. In response to harsh criticism from men for her sharp tongue, she would more or less toss her head and deal by projecting all the badness to the outside. MO expected them to be her victims. When I said this she agreed. "Aren't men born to be victims?" "Even my poor father, married to that hapless bitch." MO almost had a delusion about her physical beauty. She thought her beauty made her irresistible to men. Her power over her father and his friends in social circles served to feed the fires of this omnipotence.

Internally, it was unclear to me that MO had defined any gender for herself. She was so much "everything" on the inside and so certain that she could conquer all challenges that it was hard to see any conflict at all. We did sort out why the boyfriends did not last long. They were too ordinary, in the sense of expecting to be treated as human with feelings and flesh and blood! MO did begin to understand that she treated the world in an identical fashion to her concept of home—a place where her father worshipped her power over others; where there was no rein on the ability to hurt others; and it was an advantage to hate a traditional female role, citing its passivity and masochism. I wondered in retrospect if her own unconsciously "monstrous" position in the emotional world was an enacted version of the inhuman "beast" that she found in her own brother (see the following section). Perhaps my role was to "tame" her by force as she had "tamed" him?

Ms. OP

OP was plump but pretty and elegant in her costume. She enjoyed her female habitus in more traditional heterosexual ways than the two younger women mentioned earlier. Her bitter and abiding fury at her ex-husband was connected to the fact that he had betrayed her with a young, slim woman and wanted to start another family. She felt "like a wreck on the sand, washed up, devastated, and broken to bits and pieces." The affair had taken her by surprise and, in retrospect, we thought that she had always been so much the good, adored daughter that it was inconceivable to her that someone close could turn away from her. OP was wildly jealous of the younger woman. In analysis, the idea of her own fierce oedipal jealousy was new. She had suppressed the jealousy of mother, because she was so caught up in mirroring and reverberating to the sadness of mother, and being a "good girl" companion to ease mother's loss of the "poor baby." She somehow unconsciously expected to be able to be fully both pre-oedipal and oedipal without conflict. OP's contribution of three grandchildren to her old parents was another way of making up to them for their loss. Thus, in her female way, she played her part in fertilizing the seeds of coming generations, and fulfilling their wishes. It was as if the husband was incidental in the grand plan for the family millions. It became clear to OP that she was so caught up emotionally with her parents that there was not much room for a husband, beyond the suitability of his "seed money" or genes for the fulfillment of her encompassing family destiny.

The baby and the beast

The chasm between boy-child and man was vast in these women's minds. "Boy" was an object of ridicule, unconsciously a malformed creature of horror and disgust. To defend against these unpleasant affects and attitudes, some developed a veneer of pity. The upshot was to treat the boy as a despised "baby." Thus, some could retain a modicum of humor, or sympathy, as they contemplated the damaged boy as messy and incompetent. Those who retained tenderness, a voice that also represented their own family attitude, expressed "He can't help it."

Some of the attitudes that consolidated this denigrated boy image were: "We women are in control of men. Let them think they have a brain. We—those who relate to mother in their "sameness"—have the *real* power over the man. He is at the mercy of his dick. It is up to the woman to keep the man's sex under control, and we can do that."

Beyond the clinical samples here, I would like to delineate two scenarios, which have been internalized by some in girlhood and that emerge later as adults in interaction with contemporary men. The first is a response to an unconscious fantasy expectation that the man is an all-beastly sex, and therefore cannot wait to bed the woman, will take her by force if she's not wily, and thus needs to be warded off and palliated. Such a woman can be consciously afraid of men. Her certainty that he is only interested in being a sexual predator is projected onto him. She believes that he is interested only in her body as a sexually desirable object and an outlet for his ungovernable and marauding sexually aggressive appetite. Giant beasts are insatiable. Beasts of the jungle are undiscriminating and will stop at nothing to have their way. He only wants to push his penis into her genital and rub against her flesh till he has an orgasm. This is his main and only interest in a woman in his "Beast" role. The woman tells herself that if she wants any emotional connection at all with this man, she must exhibit her body as the main interest. Thus, some adolescent female patients will don tight dresses, miniskirts, and, in front of the mirror, practice sexy lounging poses with displays of teasing curves. To accomplish this power over "the beast," Ms. MO, as a quintessential example of this genre of unconscious fantasy, looked through the imagined eyes of a sexually drooling male so that she could play both the seducer and the seduced. As soon as a real man was aroused, this would provide all the evidence she needed to "know" the truth about her formulaic script for all men. With the signs of his sexual arousal, however, her fear of him would begin. Her more elaborate fantasy now included his need to penetrate her. She imagined her vagina as a very small vulnerable soft hole. Fear, horror, and excitement attended the fantasies of pain of his gross and giant hard erect organ pressing into her small opening, and pressing for relief in action. Relief to her came mainly through access to a sense of goodness in allowing him to perform the painful act, because some day she would need a child. The pleasure for the woman with this dynamic is in joining the mother internally. She too had once submitted to this ritual of enticement and painful submission for a higher and nonbeastly cause—that of procreation. Joining the female's power in producing a child is the main pleasurable goal. Thus, LM's attitudes to me became comprehensible—"I got a live one of my own" (referring to her conquest of a male)—a prideful attitude of "Take-that, mother!" and "You never thought I had it in me!" (an unconscious reference to pregnancy). The man is both tantalized and held emotionally at arm's length by LM.

The second set of internalized female fantasies with which a man may become entangled are compelling thoughts that the sexual man is really a baby. She thus prepares to indulge him and to derive much pleasure from this side of her dual fantasy system. The main function of this fantasy is to detoxify his adult sexuality. In her mind, she not only tames the beast but can also control him much better in baby mode. Her maternal protectiveness emerges often in caricature. She thinks of him as her prized possession. As baby, he becomes not only a possibly restored fantasy phallus, but also an extension of her—that is, a birthed baby. In order for a man solely to be her prized "phallus," a little girl would have to show evidence of sustained admiration or envy about the desirability of a penis. These women—LM, MO, and OP—are at the end of a spectrum where it was hard to detect any positive attribute of the organ, except in its cooperative role in making a baby for her. The man as "baby" is a shared fantasy role in which some men collude—as in Freud's reference "His Majesty the baby" or as noted in Schafer's 1980 paper on Freud's attitude to femininity. At the first hint of a man's enjoyment at being passive and being looked after, some women find their formula affirmed. She feels she has thus mastered and tamed him. The raging beast is better off slumbering tenderly in her arms! Her fearful and uneasy subservience in sexual matters is now projected back onto him. She talks with other women (and her therapist) about his shortcomings and flaws—but with an indulgent air. In this mode, she can mobilize fondness for her man-child. However, it is laced with condescension at his small, weak, and needy status. If he is deemed too dependent, he may be the object of her rage, because he is draining her energies, setting her up as ur-Mother, and is not assuming a caretaking father role and allowing *her* to be the baby herself.

The "baby" conception of a man tends to alternate with the "beast" conception. Each defends against the other, and one version is designed to help such a woman tolerate the other version. I find aspects of this constellation in the heterosexual connections of many females, and I think of this polarity as akin to Freud's Madonna—whore split in men's view of women.

Omnipotence

These women had in common a set of features that were associated with a strong proclivity for unchallenged omnipotence. They saw themselves as powerful, and met the world in this way. They expected others to fit into their strategies and their plans for life. "Nothing but the best," said LM as she strategized plans for her software company. "It's entirely to be expected," said MO at her latest invitation to speak at a world trade conference. "Of course my investment paid off—in the hundreds of thousands," said OP. What were the unconscious worlds that gave these women such high expectations for their efforts?

The most fundamental contribution to this inner world was the dealings with the internalized parents. LM's parents seemed to pour into her all of their own high hopes. In addition, I think their communicated sense of exasperation with and negativity toward Buddy blended with the girl child's desire to annihilate her sibling competitor. The lack of much conflict about this hostility, I believe, exaggerated and reified the girl's sense of her own sadism and power.

The elements of a gender identity are in *one* sense, psychologically simple. The construction must be composed of mental representations of an adult of the same sex, plus an adult and child of the opposite sex. Complexity and unpredictability are psychological—the ego work of individuality, or the complexity of the individual's "wiring," for example, in conjunction with the variability of the experiential emphases and their meanings to the person. A child's core gender identity is established by 18 months, whether from the outside and parental naming of genitals, or in response to a constitutional unfolding—this child will psychologically have to bump into a child of the opposite sex, a child of the same sex, and a grown-up of each sex. Each of these representations of "the other" will be encoded in ways consonant with the level of psychosexual development that the child has reached.

Girls' "genital anxieties" are best referred to as such, a point I have made in Chapter 3. There are two major threads in vulval anxieties for girls, one being in relation to other little girls and adult women; and the other in relation to boys and grown men. I keep stressing in this book that the procreative aspects of the *mother's adult body* for a young girl are just as important a source of anxiety as *the genitals of* either sex alone.[1]

The subterranean world of omnipotence is an enchanted place where anything can and does happen by way of fantasy. I think that especially the first two women, LM and MO, were quite archaic in their corporeal morphological thinking and sex-defining characteristics—"*This* is female," or "*That* is male." LM regarded boys as embodied by the emanation of uncontrollable stinks from their bodies. Their anality and orality for her were more important than their genitals. One could hear her similar expectations projected into the adult-male-gendered world. The sexed male was to her incomprehensible and ridiculous in his adult sexual activity. How could he not be self-conscious and civilized like a woman? This "animal" was nothing she aspired to be herself. The degree of her early exposure to the negative aspects of messing was so overwhelming for her that she seemed to split this off as negative and male, where in contrast she fantasized the female body as neat, clean, and acceptable. As with many young women these days, her menstrual periods since adolescence had been controlled by contraceptive pills. As with other such young patients long on "the pill," I found it hard to access more than a hint of a very early pubertal sense of alarm with the blood of the first menses. Thus, registrations for her of "menstrual mess," which one might have expected to produce even more gender confusion, were much paler than one might have imagined because of her actual body experience. This too fastened a belief in her own magical powers over her body. If she thought "no mess," so be it. This was evidence to her of her own brand of what it meant to be female. Being "female and feminine" to her was having body parts all totally under the control of one's will. Any hint of fat was associated with a messy, oral, Down syndrome brother. Or else, fat represented a dread of pregnancy. This was the female-to-female aspect of her aerobic, lithe, slender body.

LM credited her father as having the real power to create babies. He thus could make poor models such as boys, or superior models such as girls. LM was more desirous of such a male power. She fantasized herself as the "yin" to his "yang," being one without needing to be penetrated. Side-by-side matching was enough. In this form of symbiotic fantasy, she became part male, part female, and ever fluidly pluripotential. The battery for this bisexual fantasy is the early battery of the belief in body morphological omnipotence (see also the medieval medical beliefs about body functioning in Chapter 3).

MO, in her fantasy of being dominatrix, also showed a belief in her powers to create herself simultaneously as both male and female. The main attraction of the boy-child was to dominate him and even believe that he was so contemptuous that he did not possess human feeling—"castration" was too specific for MO's radical fantasy of what he meant to her. Her inner world functioned as an eye for an eye and a tooth for a tooth. She felt he had stripped her of any possibilities of having a mother, and he and mother would pay the deserved price. Her power was enhanced because of the joined denigration of the father. Heady with triumph from these battlefields, MO believed in the omnipotence of women who could also fluidly take the place of men. It was a world that had transcended gender and was unconflictedly powerful. The relative lack of active rage, and the steady cold cruelty that MO possessed toward her brother and those weaker than her, I thought had been enhanced by her early environment and also school because she rarely seemed to be thwarted in her aims and allowed no experience of disappointment. By this time in her life, she also had the capacity not to notice the shaming sounds of others in the environment. She only intellectually knew shame, and when I brought it up as a possibility, she was only slightly intrigued in a polite and tolerant way. I could detect no unconscious trace in her body language or her dreams.

OP lived in a world of unreal wealth with her parents where she remembered being surprised that everyone did not travel on a Lear Jet for the Christmas vacation in the Caribbean. After the death of the "poor baby," being the only child, there was nothing material her parents would not bestow on her. When Scott Fitzgerald said that the "rich are different from you and me," I think that he saw that a world without frustration fosters an internally omnipotent expectation. Because little OP's parents were also loving and inclusive of her, she was not a "poor little rich girl" at all. She absorbed the adoration of her personality and her body, and was especially identified with and competitive with the grown-up male and female. She was overtly dyadic with each parent, but had secretly, as it were, reached an oedipal level of development which was guilt-laden due to its implications for further separation from parents, especially the mother, whom she felt was wounded by her brother's death. OP had some phallic aspirations, as observed in her imaginary brother. But her main thrust was the assumption of the omnipotence of female procreation in which she wished to give a new baby to mother and also a new baby to father. Her creativity with money was both a joining and a gift to them to continue their heritage.

I believe that all these patternings alluded to earlier are grounded in the internalizations of family-gendered attitudes and relationships, in the meanings and family myths and interpretations of sexuality, and in no way are in themselves biologically "essential." However, what *is* essential and also fascinating is how individuals' bodies and body parts and their anatomical and physiological functions become interpreted and mentalized by the growing child, and are given fluid meanings that reflect their family relationships, as they understand the animal biological life cycle of sex and procreation.

Note

1 However, as a colleague and friend said to me, "Yes, that makes a lot of sense—but you just have taken on 100 years of group repression to struggle with that—good luck!" Girls experiencing themselves as "too small", for example, encodes genital comparison with the mother. Or "expulsive anxiety" may relate to ucs, fantasy about childbirth, rather than an anal fantasy.

Chapter 9

Daughters and sons

This chapter will test further my hypothesis that the sexually procreative body (as opposed to *either* the sexual body *or* the procreative body treated as separate entities) is a centrally motivating element in the special interaction of mother to daughter and mother to son. Earlier, in Chapter 4, I showed how intensely a daughter will incorporate and internalize sensory, proprioceptive, and visual elements of her mother's pregnancies as building blocks for the future that become shaping to the internal concept of her own mature womanly body. Because of my focus on pregnancy, procreation, and sex there, a reader might argue that they were inevitably encoded together, and that my argument is hence tautological. The mother and daughter pairs discussed in the following text, however, are chosen to show that even when the topic is more general and more generally affectively charged—on whether love or hate is in the air, for example—there still are strong physical components present consciously and unconsciously, still relating to sex and procreation, in this bond between them as females.[1] Paying close attention to the physical elements of their stories helps shed light on how their emotional situations developed in the first place, and how they may evolve.

Posing the question

These daughters are manifestly *too* opposite to their mothers for us not to contemplate that this oppositional pattern in and of itself must have deep resonance that connects this particular mother with this particular child. Mirroring representations between a same-sex family couple, as being "the spit and image" of one another, are easier to follow (Mahon, 2011). Nevertheless, let us consider a different arrangement. *How can a hating mother produce a child who not only loves her, but also is even capable of love for others outside the original duo? In addition, how can a loving mother produce a child who hates her consistently and pours dislike on others outside their duo?* I want to highlight the corporeal relationships here between mother and daughter by way of these vivid contrasts, and offer them to the reader as a special key to understanding how a girl child's historically comparative same-sexed body mental representations of the adult female body may enlighten fantasies held to account for certain chronic mother–daughter battles encoded within these patients' internalizations.

Some female patients had mothers who beat and physically tortured them—the ultimate physical expressions of bodily hatred—and yet these patients seem puzzlingly bound with such loyalty and love to these mothers that a therapist or analyst can sometimes conduct treatment for many months before even the first horror will be whispered. Ultimately, one thinks that the body does not seem to remember, even as it has refused connection with the mind. When the experience is newly described to the analyst in the picture frozen in time, the beating mother alone contains the empowered body hatred. The child in the scene is helpless, overwhelmed, and often detaches herself from her body. Leonard Shengold has written extensively about the psychological vicissitudes of this kind of trauma in his 1989 *Soul Murder* and 2006 Haunted by Parents. Most clinicians, including trainees who find themselves in attendance when some of these patients are in extremis, know what it is like to feel heart-sick for these patients, exasperated in attempts to help them access even some anger at the attacker of old, and to feel frustrated in attempts to help their guilt, dissociation, and self-criticism.

In this chapter, I will use this category of daughter victim of maternal hatred to contrast with its manifest opposite, i.e., daughters who are emotionally abusive toward their hated mothers, whom *they* victimize.[2] When these latter angry daughters become patients in psychotherapy or psychoanalysis, they freely report unrelenting hatred about their mothers during many years of treatment. Yet, a number of their vociferously blamed mothers, while maddening in their habits or character traits, are not described as having gone to anything like the extremes of the first set of mothers who beat, tortured, or sexually abused their daughters as children.

I want to confine myself to trying to unravel some aspects primarily within the physicality of their relationships. In the contemporary plurality of relevant analytic theories, many ideas could help enlighten such duos: for example, the import of their object relations within such sadomasochistic bonds; or the role of dissociation in trauma; or the functioning of self-esteem and undoubted empathic failures from a self-psychological framework; or the manifestations of avoidant attachment. I will locate myself here with Hans Loewald (1961), a core image of whose theory is a mother and infant matrix, where for the infant, the instinctual drives develop simultaneously and in conjunction with the earliest object ties. "The whole complex dynamic constellation is one of mutual responsiveness where nothing is introjected by the infant that is not brought to it by the mother, although brought by her often unconsciously. … As the mediating environment conveys structure and direction to the unfolding psychophysical entity … the environment begins to take shape in the experience of the infant" (p. 237–238). I locate myself theoretically close to Nancy Chodorow (1978, 1999, 2011) who, as early as the 1970s, spoke about mutual identifications between mother and daughter within the female culture of childbearing and child-rearing in her well-known (1978) *The Reproduction of Mothering: Psychoanalysis and the*

Sociology of Gender. In current work 2011, adding her appreciation of Loewald, and in *The Power of Feelings* (1999), she explores intrapsychically the subjective sense of gender. Chodorow "consider[s] personal meaning in terms of unconscious projective and introjective fantasy" (p. 3). While against psychoanalytic universalism, she argues that "gender is individual but also that there are prevalent ingredients, including culture, anatomy and internal object relations, that most people draw on to animate gender" (p. 4). While each character in my sexed and gendered mother–daughter pair, and later in this chapter, the mother–son plots, is highly individualized, at the same time, I would like to emphasize how abidingly *reciprocal is* the interactive entwinement that builds these psychological scenarios of maternal internalization for daughters and also sons from the earliest years.

Ms. PQ: a girl's loyalty to her hating mother

PQ was a case whose analysis I supervised mostly by telephone. A woman of Greek heritage in her thirties who got married in the seventh year of analysis, she was a kind, articulate, and responsible young working woman who eventually told her analyst stories that put his hair on end about punishments visited upon her by her mother for say, losing a button off her coat, or leaving a speck of mildew on the shower curtain while doing her cleaning chores. Once, as a teenager, when under interrogation about coming home a few minutes late after curfew, she confessed to her mother that she had thought of kissing a boy. The mother shrieked at her about "sin" and her "vileness," stopped speaking to her and made her sleep at night on the floor on a mat "like the animal you are" for a month. Brutal beatings with a belt, fists, slaps, and canings were her daily lot. Yet, so much love emerged in her adult associative material about this mother that it was amazing to both analyst and supervisor.

PQ, an only child of separated parents, longed to be accepted by this hating mother who prayed daily to a pale statue of the Virgin that she kept in the basement. The quantitative force of PQ's ability to cling to some better fantasy version of this vicious mother who starved, confined, and beat her, allowed for a yearning bond to be nurtured in fantasy. No matter what the mother said or did, the daughter assumed the insults to be her own fault, and roundly deserved. The little girl was very religious. Longing to be purged of sin and forgiven by this mother, the representative of the mother of God on earth, was an endless quest for my patient.

Gradually, it may emerge with such a patient that a persistent emotional reserve conceals an unconscious refusal to become involved fully with the analyst. An unconscious fear of being beaten or emotionally abused again can manifest itself tenaciously in this fashion and can be, with difficulty, analyzed in the transference. As we know, such patients are frightened of their own aggression, lest they themselves turn into the monster mother. In the limitations she thus imposes also on regression, the patient unconsciously refuses to accept any dependency substitute for the mother, thus remaining abidingly loyal. In the paternal transference, some fears became workable also as inchoate fears of involvement with a man for fear of retaliatory maternal jealousy. Devotion to her mother was the only tolerable position for PQ. She was often unable to reflect. Any shift in this state would mean to the analyst that the analysand may be able to begin to perceive her mother's behaviors more objectively and develop a mind of her own. This separate state of mind was too dangerous. PQ preferred to stay as "innocent" as a little child even as she had managed to inhabit a split state, half as a child, and half going through the motions of adult life, such as holding a job, and having acquaintances outside her home. PQ articulated to herself over many years the unconscious fantasy addressed to her mother: "Finally, when I will look after you on your death-bed, when I give my whole life over to look after you, when I show you how I can repudiate my husband, my career—and of course, my analyst—you will finally tell me, "I've loved you best all along." This fantasy was so sweet to the patient; it was the song of the siren.[3]

The following physical manifestations came alive in the analysis: In a general way, interpretations offered by the analyst were directed in many ways at how profoundly "unsafe" was any element that introduced the possibility that he could see PQ as an adult woman. Most importantly (and for the focus of this paper), the transference involved him as her mother. There were many dreams or slips of the tongue or direct associations about how this or that would have led to a beating or a "time-out" which was more like solitary confinement, or going without meals. She dressed in large baggy shifts, and her hair was plain and tied back from her face. She never wore makeup. Her nails were bitten to the quick. She looked at the ground with eyes downcast. If the analyst smiled at her, she looked distressed and anxious. This meant that she would be tempted to "tell all" to him, like at times she had felt with schoolteachers, thus betraying mother. Gradually, it emerged that mother used to have the girl sit on a stool and watch her brush her long black wavy hair. Sometimes the daughter combed her hair for her. She would have the girl paint her nails, and during these beautifying sessions, she would tell the girl what a violent and perverted man her father was. This was the explanation given why they had separated. As soon as PQ had her menses, the mother told her she was sick on "those days" and kept her home from school. If the patient got out of bed, she would be beaten. The girl lay in bed, mostly, we thought, dissociated from her body, her feelings, or her inquisitiveness about what frightening (or exciting) changes were happening to her own body. She claimed to have lost any feeling of pain in the beatings, though she remembered the look of the welts. Her daydreams were of floating in a warm sea in Paradise. Her mother posed before her in underwear, and requested admiration for her curves, her skin, and her glorious hair. Suffice to say that the analyst helped fill out with PQ the vivid contrasts between her vision of mother as being the perfect, iconic adult female beauty, the Madonna, and herself as the "innocent child." As such a creature, she would enter God's kingdom without sin. Anger and, of course, sexual feelings were sinful. So was "knowledge" of any kind—from self-reflection to school learning, to fantasies of the meaning of carnal knowledge. It was in the last years of her analysis that she could take in and bear the painful knowledge that her mother had actually likely been psychotic from time to time during her upbringing.

By interpretations over many years, the analyst helped her feel that she had choice in the matter of giving her life over to her mother. However, PQ would often be filled with remorse and say that, at the bottom of her heart, she was still not sure that she felt she did the right thing to have a life of her own in the end. Mother for all eternity knew best. PQ was a woman who was amazingly capable of genuine empathy for this mother and for her mother's traumata of growing up in old Europe. This patient was able to sustain friendships and inspired loving tributes from her coworkers at times. I will not extend the case to provide examples, or more details of the transference, and I thus ask the reader's indulgence to believe my observation that PQ was capable of inspiring respectful and loving ties with others. I found the manifestations of her forgiveness toward her mother to be part of a characteristic pattern of giving people the benefit of the doubt, and being stalwart and supportive of others.

Ms. QR and Ms. RS: loathing daughters

These vignettes are examples of adult daughters who can be relentlessly critical of their mothers over many years of therapy.

The following is a thumbnail sketch of what analytic or therapy work is like: the story is usually told to the therapist conspiratorially as a like-minded sympathizer, with mother as an evil outsider. Therapist and patient join as "we." Mother is the "she," "the other." All the badness is placed outside the intimate therapy dyad, and is locked away within the mother.

The analyst or therapist believes the patient's story of her bad mother-care. Yet, if this were the whole story, how could this patient have any grounds for trusting another woman in her life, the female therapist, for example? The clinician may suspect that the patient's attempt is a pseudo-intimacy, and may serve to cover up rage, and mistrust, right in the room. The good analyst, the good patient, and the bad mother can become frozen together in time in an impasse. The therapist can tell that this is happening, because the stories of the evil mother maintain their frequency but lose their freshness. They have been rehearsed over and over with friends. Up until the exploratory treatment, these patients usually have not reflected on the *meanings* of their vituperative statements. Perhaps their social acceptance with friends echoes a universal interest in stories about the "Bad Mother" or fairy tales about the wicked stepmother (Almond, 2010; Tartar, 2009; Bettelheim, 1989). Chodorow (1989), with Contratto writing on *The All Powerful Mother: Blame and Idealization*, says "Feminist writing on motherhood assumes an all-powerful mother who, because she is totally responsible for how her children turn out, is blamed for everything from her daughter's limitations to the crisis of human existence" (p. 80). People love either to idolize or demonize "the mother." The response of the culture, therefore, often reflects and compounds the fixity of the patient's tale. In addition, a competitive woman listener, retreating to the safety of high ground, may sigh with relief, "I'm glad she's not *my* mother."

QR, a health-care graduate student of 25, says over and over again: "I hate her. I've always hated her. She moans and groans all the time. She's sick this way and that, nothing but pains and aches. Why can't she be like other people's mothers?" RS, a busy, elegantly dressed suburban mother, says repeatedly: "I have to do everything for her. She's useless—totally useless. She can't even balance her checkbook. She can't even cook spaghetti for my son and she dresses like a bag-lady. When I was 2, I knew she was no good. She was a bad cook."

The complaint about Mother QR was, "How dare she moan!"; about Mother RS, it was, "She's useless." These patients/daughters were so frequently in a live and constant rage with their mothers that reporting her bad behavior to make an impact on the analyst took precedence over any textured narrative detail about the mother's character. QR explained that she disliked me to comment on what she found peripheral parts of her story, because it meant that I did not believe how badly she had suffered. RS said she feared that I might exhibit an interest in her mother—some people actually did—and that undermined her own credibility.

The following are ways that the analyst may pick up extra details for a potentially fuller picture beyond what the patient actually consciously wishes the analyst to focus upon. QR tells how Mother QR, the moaner, had a recent fall: "She goddamn called up wanting to know if her ankle should be x-rayed." How should QR know what to do for her? "She devotes her whole day to scolding that I'm not right there. She fell in the Ladies Garden Club meeting." The fixity of QR's complaint shows in her selectivity of the repetition of her mantra: "she needs me right there: she's moaning again." Yet, the analyst also hears, "she fell at the Garden Club." So apparently the mother went separately to a Garden Club? The daughter/patient resists registering the meaning of this detail about mother's capacity to take outings with people other than her, and instead she wants me to join in with her observation about the mother's neediness and physical moaning. It may be even more painful for QR to view her mother as more separate from her than she thinks, but genuinely physically frail. After all, if her mother is only "moaning" and "needy," perhaps she is secretly strong and will live forever?

RS tells how useless is her mother who allowed the pasta to burn downstairs with her hungry grandchild. RS was furious that she had to interrupt totting up the family checkbook in her study to descend the stairs yelling that the house would burn down for all mother cared. She was useless, so neglectful of the poor child. Could Mother RS find no better time to phone her stockbroker than when the pasta was cooking? Oh yes, the market was collapsing, but the house could have burned down. A neutral listener might raise a question, "Useless, in whose terms?" And how may a woman suave enough to engage a stockbroker to converse about a market crash, present herself dressed like a bag-lady? Mother RS may not, after all, be an open-and-shut case of helpless uselessness. Interesting eccentricities about the mother's mental life get lost in the daughter's selection of focused complaint.

These patient/daughters reduce their mothers into unidimensional flat figures. It is as if the rage is so fresh that the urge is to destroy her mother's individual features. The daughter does battle over and over again with the particularly hated feature—the whining and moaning of Mother RS, the uselessness of Mother RS. She sees it everywhere. She reads every innuendo for the same conclusion. There is nothing new to be learned about this woman. Everyone should agree and rally against her. The transference feelings toward the analyst are often composed of the opposite.

The female analyst, in contrast, is held as an ideal model, including her choice of clothes, cars, and waiting room magazines. Her imagined family, career, background, etc., are held to be well nigh perfect. Unlike the patient, the "perfect" analyst would be incapable of hate, envy, or malice. As one such patient said to me, "I suppose you *could* envy me my Radcliffe education. But then, since you went to a British university, the likelihood is that you never even thought twice about Harvard." Even her most prized accomplishment did not count.

There is one area that is often markedly different. So different, in fact, that it is remarkable. Physically, these patients often reveal that they feel superior in their looks to other women, including the female analyst, in spite of how "wonderful" they find her. They usually consider themselves much more beautiful than her. "Your hair is thin—mine has always been thick and glossy," or "My legs are long and lean—well, I hate to say it, but yours are kind of short and fat," etc., followed by a conciliatory don't-feel-bad moment, "but you're smart—in fact, my mother used to say I'd be a good hair model/or my family thought I was a long-stemmed rose and looked like a Vogue model." In this way, they establish themselves once again in the transferential daughter–mother bond as "opposite" from the female analyst.

Comparative bodies

The mothers of these women, QR and RS—unlike Mother PQ, the child beater—had managed to evoke and nurture their daughter's highly positive physical self-assessments. Many times, each had praised the daughter's physical attributes to the skies, repeatedly telling her how beautiful she was—more beautiful than any of her friend's children, more exquisite than any film star. These superlatives, however, were regularly accompanied by self-denigrating comparisons. "You are beautiful, my child, but look at me, your mother—I am ugly" was the message, It seems as if there may be no hatred more clinically vituperative than the person who desperately desires a favorable reflection, but who looks into a cracked mirror. These mothers' sins, if you will, were that they had badly disappointed their daughters in their physical looks and being, and given a dark caste by their own subjectivity. Let us look for a moment at the mother's reaction to her own body, and appreciate how that reverberated with the daughter's hatred.

The daughters' vivid rejections of mothers QR and RS were accompanied by a strong rejection of their bodies. In turn, this reflected the mother's own denigrating self-image as a woman. The mothers worshipped their daughters' bodies. Her daughter perceived Mother QR, the moaner, as "gross, fat, and shapeless." This mother had said about herself: "Since I married your dad and had you, I went to seed. Nothing fits. Look at how huge I am—I disgust myself. *Never* get like me! My joints are thick and sore, my skin is rough—do you think I have a hormone problem? Have I a goiter? Feel my throat! You're as good as a doctor!"

My mental picture in the analysis was that this woman was size 20–24 at least. Perhaps she did have a thyroid problem, I imagined (entering fully into the patient's enactment). No. She turned out to be a tall, 70-year-old woman, size 12–14. However, it became clear how the ugly image had evolved for the daughter. Mother QR had pressed her daughter as a little girl and teen, to massage her joints, inspect her lumps and bumps, and examine her scalp for dandruff. Horrifying to her now-adult nurse identity, QR disliked my idea that touching her mother in this way had evoked her fixed revulsion—in fact she was "revolted" all over again by my suggesting this. QR initially could not bear to put into words this memory of a body contact that was accompanied by strongly disturbing feelings. Instead, she railed about mother's affective tone of voice, and, fleeing body detail, had condensed these complaints into the short-cut phrase "she's a moaner." There are additional implications here about the child's attempt to manually soothe the mother, who was all the time speaking of her own ugliness. QR's horrified reaction was also a coping mechanism evoked by the memory of homoerotic arousal invited by Mother QR and responded to by her daughter with guilt and shame. QR thus vowed to be healthy, well, fit, and a caretaker. She would be the opposite, and mother greatly admired her accent on a healthy appearance.

Her daughter perceived Mother RS, the useless, as "manly." The creak of her heavy footsteps evoked rage and contempt in the patient. (Though I could always tell when RS herself arrived for appointments, because of the sound of her heavy stride in high heels along the corridor by my office!) The bag-lady costume included tweed trousers "like an old man." Mother RS had said at one point, highlighting her constantly negative view of her own aging body: "All these women and their meeenopauses—hot fucking flashes here, and hot flashes there—they're so fucking pampered—never had one me'self—should throw all their clothes off and air themselves!" The mother sometimes walked around at home naked in the living room while the daughter visited, her sagging breasts flopping, apparently aggressively unaware of RS's unconcealed facial disgust and horror. Perhaps she was counter-phobically confronting RS's disgust. She regularly told RS she, her daughter, was "a magnificent specimen of homo sapiens." And RS believed this to be the case.

In the case vignette itself, I indicated how different RS was physically from her mother. The identifications holding the body ego ideals of PQ, QR, and RS took the form of *being the opposite of mother*. Yet, there were many traces of how the original internalization had been negotiated. Being the "opposite" of the mothers encoded a quantum of the mothers' frequent messages, "You are *not* like me. You are the *opposite* of me." For QR and RS, it was, "I, the mother, am ugly, and you, the child, are beautiful." For PQ, it was "I, the mother, am beautiful, and you, the child, are ugly." Thus, there was a paradoxical obedience to the mothers in their more conscious aspirations and strivings about themselves. QR saw herself as hyper-healthy, and berated her mother about her frailty; RS saw herself as hyper-feminine and berated her mother about her "masculinity." PQ, of course, did not berate her mother, but was berated by the mother for any sign of having a grown-up female body. This literal obedience in all the daughters, including obeying mother's self-admonishment, or in the case of PQ, her frank admonishment, was unconsciously encoded as being "good girls" for mother and doing her bidding.

The unconscious aspects of the echoing *similarities* to their mothers were brought to light in all these women in their analyses. Thus, the hyper-feminine RS walked in 3-inch heels but as if striding over the moors in a storm in *Wuthering Heights*. QR, the caretaking nurse by profession, in analysis displayed her own style of "moaning" that was a psychological variant of the mother's bodily anxious "what-can-I-do? doctor-feel-that" litany. PQ, the "innocent" child, revealed that her initially dissociated daydreams of being in Paradise were quite sexy dreams of having a gorgeous female body like her mother. As she grew less anxious in analysis, when she became angry, she would frequently thump the couch and have quite violent fantasies or give the analyst a "time-out" by not appearing for her sessions. The similarities to mother could thus be perceived.

Conclusion

Margarete Hilferding's (1911) legacy from long ago (Chapter 5) connects with these contemporary thoughts on these loving and hating mothers and daughters. She anticipated later work of that century concerning the powerful sexual and aggressive reciprocally emotional bonds that reverberate between mother and child even from the era of pregnancy (e.g., Winnicott, Klein, Greenacre). I offer as a bridge Hans Loewald's understanding of the origins of the building blocks of the developing and sustaining ego: "The child, by internalizing aspects of the parent, also internalizes the parent's image of the child—an image that is mediated to the child in the thousand different ways of being handled, bodily and emotionally ... part of what is introjected is the image of the child as seen, felt, smelled, heard and touched by the mother ... the way it is looked at, talked to, called by name, recognized, and re-recognized" (1960: p. 229–30). My case materials add clinically detailed information about the mother–daughter bond, especially in the era beyond birth and the earliest development. These mutually responsive exchanges between mother and daughter, even in cases which manifestly appear to have produced markedly opposed behaviors and attitudes in an adult daughter, on analytic deconstruction can exemplify some of the very same elements of later sophisticated variants of the early powerful incorporation of her mother's attitudes to her own sexed and gendered body, and her model motherly comportment in the world. Loewald (1979) viewed "the preoedipal identificatory bonds within the family as direct derivatives of narcissistic unity ... [and are] felt to be sacred." I think that these cases capture the dread, fear, and awe that also encode the sacred. Jessica Benjamin (1995) has named these same mutually reflexive attachment phenomenon between caretaker and child as "identificatory love"—a love that also knows even deeper hatred in some cases.

The focus of this material is on the female physical form that is the basis for expressions of comparison and hostility between women—mothers and daughters, in particular: how general complaints in the arena of positive or negative attitudes about conducting life can often, on closer scrutiny, develop into textured memories that are telling about the mutual reaction of each to the other's body. The surprisingly abiding attachment that a daughter may express toward a violent mother contains the crucial physical component of shared anatomical likeness. A daughter seems to do everything in her power to cling to a violent mother, whereas she will more readily reject a violent father. My ongoing thesis thus concerns the resultant adult conflicts about "sameness" vs. "otherness" that is vividly registered and built in through the medium of archaic and more mature reactions to the original bodies in the family. Even the manifest hostility of a daughter to her apparently good-enough mother also seems to me to find a cogent referent in her associations to the special meanings of sharing femaleness with her senior "partner"—till death do them part—her mother.

Sons of passionate mothering

When I was younger, I did not realize how deeply some women feel that the love of their lives and the love of their own bodies is over when their young fly the nest, because their children alone—and not their husbands, friends, work, or other lovers—were their *raison d'etre*, the apparent fountain of all their desires. When menopause enters their lives and their children have begun to disperse, this kind of mother loses her fleeting season of warmth in the sun. Unlike the earth, an individual human maternal season is sadly over. It is done. Young sons, in particular, for some mothers, were their one perceived chance to live with vigor, if vicariously. Their self-esteem as females was so negatively challenged by their cultural familial history, that a life-long imagined existence as a boy-child was their acme of perfection, and their escape from the sorrow of being born destined to be an individual and a woman. These contemporary mother–son duos are like Freud's *fin de siècle* Viennese female subjects, who proved in another era the accuracy of Juliet Mitchell's (1974) important idea that Freud's women's own phallocentrisim was a part of the patriarchal culture that he originally reflected in his theory. It was not through analyzing such mothers that I gained more insight, even though I grew far more empathic as I became older, but from analyzing the maternal reflections in the psyches of their sons.

"The great question that has never been answered, and which I have not yet been able to answer, despite my thirty years of research into the feminine soul, is 'What does a woman want?'," Freud disclosed to Marie Bonaparte in 1925 (according to her), about 10 weeks after she began analysis with him (Elms, 2001: p. 84). The timing is interesting. In this 1924–26 period,[4] Freud was feeling particularly needled by Karen Horney who so sensibly was challenging his boy-like view of adult females. This infamous cry from the depths of hurt puzzlement amid the maze of the "dark continent" was doomed for him by stumbling into echo chambers that repeated the same underlying sentiment as Professor Higgins in *My Fair Lady*: "Why can't a woman be more like a man?" Freud and his all-male Wednesday Society in October 1910 had had a session on the emotional dangers of being the favorite or the only child that included mention of a mother's favorite boy-child. Isidore Sadger reported that such sons were exposed by the overheated relationship to many developmental lags and preconditions for "psychic ... impotence ... homosexuality ... and dementia praecox" (Minutes p. 5, p. 122). It is well known that Freud's mother doted on him and referred to him as "Mein goldener Sigi," and that he was vastly privileged over his female siblings. And, in 1917, in "A Childhood Recollection from Dichtung und Wahrheit," he wrote glowingly: "If a man has been his mother's undisputed darling he retains throughout life the triumphant feeling, the confidence in success, which not seldom brings actual success along with it" (p. 156). My further elaboration here is on these themes of either benefit or damage that may accrue to such sons, that, depending on given previous authors, seem to emerge remarkably slanted in one direction or the other. I will trace a dynamic path revealed in some of these sons' adult psychoanalyses—and thus in their psychic development *continued into adult life*—that can, I believe, accommodate both the advantages and problems of this style of mother–son relationship.

The mother's body ego and boy-adoration

Only a biological female has the actual experience of housing another person right inside her body. A girl who is very envious of boys, not having grown up with the physical experience of erections, for example, with the *shame* encountered as well as the *pride*, has only a thrilled imagination of owning a penis that never includes its vicissitudes! A mother whose prehistory has disposed her to marked fantasies of penis envy has a new opportunity in pregnancy to merge psychically with a joyful possession of maleness that is actually created from right inside her own womb. I believe that this concrete bodily experience lends a more reified caste to a previously wishful fantasy penis that she now treats as her rightful possession. The baby son that was literally attached to the mother's uterine wall, after delivery continues into the cradle of their joint interactive psychic register as her object for mirrored self-glorification and idealization. His individuality therefore becomes a special problem for both this mother and this son.

Originally, when I read Freud's view about how a woman's greatest desire was to give birth to a son, I thought him a bit off the mark. Coming from the main-stream British psychiatric culture, I read this for the first time in my early 30s in the United States as a psychoanalytic candidate in New Haven. Immediately, though, it was crystal clear to me that one's family culture must be fundamental in whatever "truisms" one pronounced, such as this. My own family was more oriented toward valuing girls. My grandmother actually used to be disappointed when a boy was born, as she thought it sad that the mother would have no one to look after her in her old age! Adding to my sense of the limits of our understand-ings of each other being due to our own respective cultures, I later combined this in analysis with a theoretical and clinical fascination with the details about proc-esses of internalization. I believe these to be individualized by cultural influences.

Particular mothers of particular sons

In my early career, biased by my own cultural reasons then, I viewed the mothers who were so besotted with their young sons as a rather pathological lot. Reading the separation/individuation literature also, I was sure that their male offspring could not thrive emotionally coming from such a nest. As I grew more seasoned, I noticed that these overpoweringly strong mother–son bonds need *not* necessarily yield a powerless damaged sort of man, who is merely the passive tool of his mother's desires. My focus here will be on the quality of transference to me as a woman analyst that allowed me to build a more complex portrait of the inner lives of these men. I was surprised that these analyses often revealed (as Freud had noted) many men with robust, healthy, durable self-regard, and exceptional accomplishments, whose main worldly characteristic surprisingly could be described as being both effective and independent minded. However, I found that often in intimacy with women partners (or, if gay, with male dominant partners),[5] though looking "big" superficially in their homes, they often behaved in overly compliant ways, unconsciously allowing themselves to be haplessly diminished in domestic life. They created their heterosexual intimacies out of the stuff of maternal fantasy. This state reflected their controlling possessive and devoted mothers who worshipped them, now displaced onto their wives or male partners. Mother herself could never be talked to directly. Palliation, seduction, and sooth-ing were the son's specialty in his dealings with her. In turn, and in gratitude from the mothers, the sons would elicit worshipful apparently blind love and endless indulgence. This special goddess in their inner pantheon had conveyed to them with great clarity what she wanted. It was not mysterious to them. She frequently wanted them to succeed in every arena in which she felt second-class. For exam-ple, each time one of these men reported yet another business success to his mother—"my 'dearest'" as he called her, like the mother of Frances Hodgson Burnett's *Little Lord Fauntleroy*—she'd say seductively softly, "And what comes next up the ladder after this, Cedric?" My patient knew very well that she meant him to be the CEO of a Fortune 500 company before he turned 40. "Of course she'd deny it, were you to ask her. She'd say (imitating a falsetto saccharin tone) 'It's only what my Cedric wants for himself—and what Cedric wants Cedric gets—*you'll* see'." I have often wondered if Freud's despair, disappointment, and puzzlement about the inner life of women—*other* than his mother—came perhaps from imagining that *all* women wanted from him only his "goldener" aspect? My patients' judgments about women were certainly flawed by their assumptions of maternal expectations.

Clinical instance

Mr. (Cedric) ST, the CEO of a successful advertising company, an only child, was 40 when I first saw him. His complaint, briefly, was that he was unable to get married, as he had troubles committing himself to his girlfriend of many years. His problem was immediately obvious in our first interchange. He replied to my phone call return with, "I hope you're having a nice day doc!" to which I said sharply, being in-between patients, "Sorry, I really don't want to buy anything. This is not a good time!" "No, no," he protested, "You're very astute. I actually *am* in sales—but I wanted to arrange an appointment to talk about my troubles!"

The first level that we worked on in analysis was how *indirectly* he expressed himself to females who were emotionally involved with him. He believed firmly that he had an accurate read on all their psyches. I gradually helped him see, through interpreting his maternal transference to me, that his tunnel vision about women was actually one very particular familiar psychic pattern that was repeated over and over. One of its features was that any woman was too delicate to bear the truth. He spent much effort feeding her imagined narcissism. She in turn was supposed to be amused by the banter and patter of toying with his elaborate evasions, and reject any dealings with unpleasant facts. This interchange was an art form of baroque manners between him and women, constructed "lovingly" by him to protect the imagined pained psyche of his mother from itself. In return, the bargain was that she or they glowed approval.

Later, in speaking directly to me man-to-man in a contrasting father transference, it turned out that his girlfriend was a woman whom he despised. He was ashamed of her. Their sex life was minimal and he felt trapped. He would go off to a conference, usually look for a younger woman to have a brief sexual fling, and come home to find his ever-loyal girlfriend in a pool of tears. "Didn't she suspect your infidelity?" I asked. "Oh no, not at all. She just weeps at me when I go away and says, "Why don't you marry me yet? What have I done wrong? We've been together 5 years and we're not getting younger." She was, according to the patient, "a doormat." This densely wrought sadomasochistic bond served their mutual needs to remain static. ST became aware that he was misreading his mother's blind worship into this girlfriend, and simultaneously he acknowledged that he was punishing her for not being a replica of mother. "Perhaps mother is the only woman I really want?", he'd say in nervous jest.

In the maternal transference, there were similar echoes of going along pleas-antly with something I suggested. Later, however, he'd reveal that he'd think or act confidently on a secret contrary opinion, but not tell me about it. Anything but confront me with a direct contradiction! Delaying interpretation when I suspected this defense allowed me some insight into the mutual pleasantness of this dance of seduction. In my younger days, I might have been eager to interpret quickly the opposition and flattery as a clear defense against, say, a fear of being swallowed up by me as the possessive mother. The latter technicality, however, would have covered over the degree to which this interpersonal maneuver was conscious. I eventually became aware that he himself was quite aware of his motives in this "Prince Charming" role. The new analytic question then became, what element of this communication was *unconscious*? I noted that he talked to me "directly" in the margins of sessions as he rose or lay down on the couch. This represented unconsciously a space for talking to me as a marginalized father, as it turned out.

In his professional work, ST showed straightforwardness, wisdom, discrimina-tion, and caring both toward himself and others in running his business, features hidden from view in our interaction. He joked that he felt he could get away with anything, because when all was said and done—echoing Freud's confidence—he knew that at least his "dearest mother" loved him! I suspected that this was only a part of the story. Where did his capacity for emotional straightforwardness and directness fit in?

Then he launched into the internet for dates, usually for one-night stands. He said that having such a wonderful, clever analyst like me allowed him to have an adolescence his parents had never allowed. He was setting me up not to be critical in any way! Here is some live interaction from the analysis at this point 2 years into the four times/week work:

ST was arguing with me about my matter-of-fact statement that he seemed to be inviting STDs or AIDS by asking most of these one-night-stand women in coy tones if they would "do it" without a condom. His behavior seemed very rash to me, and I felt annoyed at him, and over-protective of both of them. He hated my pointing this out. He was furious for the first time with me, and called me an "interfering bitch." He felt I'd offended his intelligence. "It's not life and death these days—they've all kinds of treatments." His anger escalated: "Why would I risk this anyway? Tell me even one single time that I've EVER risked getting STDs or AIDS? Absolutely not. This is so unfair that you would think that of me. Give me one good reason why I'd do that kind of damage to myself!" he taunted.

Not my finest hour. ... I rose further to the bait, creating an interpretation based on a mother–son analogy with my own feeling about what was aroused in me: "Because then you'd be back in adolescence, justify "confessing" to your mother all about your sex life, getting rid of your guilt and the hard struggle to be separate, and getting her to be alarmed and taking care of you again like a kid." He was silenced. He was not expecting this. I felt I'd given him a low blow, because I was *angrily* attempting to "take care" of him. Next day, he came in blazing that I'd *always* been against his sexual pleasures, his Internet dating for one-night stands with no strings attached, and that I thought everyone who went on that web site was nothing but a dangerous john or whore, whereas his latest would-be lover was shy and gentle and might prove a perfect partner. "You'll see" he argued, "I know I CAN find nice women on this site."

I was calmer by that time, having thought more about my over-protection, and I was more able to listen to what he wanted me to say. To show me how I'd made far too much of his dangerous sex life, he offered disarmingly the following: "To help you understand … it would be as if *you* were naked in bed with *your* lover, and he had his penis just teasing your clitoris and he was just playing it in and out of our introitus and around your labia … and you said (imitating me in the identical saccharin falsetto tone he used for his mother,) 'UMM. *Without* a condom?' … you can see now very well that it would be just you testing your lover to *see* if he'd do it without a condom. It would be your way of saying, '*Not* without a condom.' That's what I conveyed to her—and you just jumped all over me that I was stupid enough to take risks or expose her to risks."

Quite confounded by all the layers of self-deceit, I said, "A kind of confusing message though, don't you think when you say it out loud?"

He shot back instantly, "I guess she didn't say, 'Hey dude, what the hell are you doing!'… if that's what you mean."

That was exactly what I meant. I didn't need to say anything more. I was grateful for his new demonstration of conscious awareness, and for this moment I felt he was in charge again—in charge of his own body. He was importantly able to imagine the mind of the other person—how she'd had a choice, and how she had rejected that choice as a fellow adult—and I felt released into a more comfortable separateness from an enmeshed sadomasochistic tussle of enactment of the mother of a "bad" adolescent. He was right. I was enacting an overreached sense of responsibility for him. In spite of our diversion into the possessive mother–son transference, his less conscious, but far more mature ego functioning was hidden away in the ability to imagine his sexual partner's possible outrage at his sexual behavior and thus her choice. This side of him was the one that was capable of emotional directness and linked to his CEO capabilities. I felt that this was a bridge to the integration of the two sides of his functioning.

ST showed here that he was *not* so easily swayed by what he imagined was my "maternal" objection to him having sex with random women. Also, in a thinly disguised way, he had imagined making love to me in this session. Once an oedipal pattern began to emerge, his father had at last entered the previously dyadic mother–son stage, and we became a triad.

Unconscious internalization of the repudiated father

Father had been a worldly successful but blustery, angry presence, whom the boy and his mother often ganged up against at home with fierce denigration. In loud contrast to father's "grossness," as she called it, mother adored the preadolescent, innocent, more *asexual*, apparently compliant charming "good" boy in Cedric SF. They loved the book *Little Lord Fauntleroy*. At bedtime, they lingered admiringly over little fictional Cedric's looks: "a graceful, childish figure in a black velvet suit, with a lace collar, and with lovelocks waving about the handsome, manly little face, whose eyes met ... [others] with a look of innocent good-fellowship." It was this version of him that reflected in the apple of his mother's eye. However, almost in secret, this boy grew in a repudiated identification of the father. ST's vigor, his ability to stand up for himself, his ultimate leadership positions in business were all not just to please his mother "dearest," but in association with his unconscious admiration for father. At one level, he thought himself mother's better lover. As he sexually matured and grew into late adolescence, however, he became stalled in life. Looking for a woman of his own, he'd over-share his youthful sexual escapades with this titillated mother both to elicit her admiration but also to defy her preference for the little Cedric image. He pursued unsuitable women. For ST to develop autonomously sexually, he ran a danger of spoiling this gratifying latency merger with mother and own being more like his father.

Conclusion

Such a physically and mentally maturing young male's identity, therefore, can become split off and repudiated in favor of the loyalty to a mother who is wildly devoted to her "one and only," her last hope of staying in a maternal summer. She loves best the beautiful young latency boy with his whole future before him. Both mother and son need never grow old.

Notes

1 In her rich and compelling work on female perversion, Welldon (1988) has also drawn attention strongly to the inevitable intertwinment for females between sex and their whole bodies, which carry babies, as opposed to their genitals alone. This emphases as normative for women, however, tends to get lost in Welldon, because of her stress on immature preoedipal dynamics (Klein) to understand perversion. She seems to emphasize women's failure to reach a "genital" stage—as if, were they fully "genital," they would not need to use their bodies so much.
2 I have not had experience in analysis actually with any daughters who have regularly struck their mothers, for example, behavior that would qualify as "elder abuse" when a mother becomes physically frailer than a violent, strong, young powerful daughter/caretaker.
3 Shengold (2006) speaks to this state of clinging to a malevolent parent in *Haunted by Parents*, where he shows that any change, even for the better, means only pained further loss to these traumatized patients.
4 See Chapter 5, according to Zinnia Fliegel's 1973 paper.
5 I am aware that I confine myself in talking here only about heterosexuality.

Chapter 10

Infant daughters and fathers as primary caretakers

This chapter will add further to information on the internal complexity of gender portraits that crucially include emphasis on the biological body's contributions, as well as adding a psychoanalytic subjective aspect to the small literature on hands-on infant caretaking by fathers.

The material in this section provides evidence for countering essentialist biologically gendered notions that birthing females alone can accomplish the early nurturing of infants. I wholeheartedly join with our first foremother Margarete Hilferding, who, about 100 years ago, told Freud and his colleagues (and was shot down) in the Vienna Psychoanalytic Society that there was no such thing as "the maternal instinct" (see Chapter 5). Our modern position would be that maternality is a compromise formation—just like heterosexuality and homosexuality. Analysts and therapists know, from listening to their patients, that men in certain instances are better child caretakers than women are. Such psychic elements are entirely individual. In my study, evidence that these infants' needs called forth elements of the men's capacity for symbiotic fantasy as bodily providers called forth associative links with their own internalized infant caretakers—women, in these cases—but their children's internalization will grant this tender care not as *feminine*, but a masculine quality. Contemporary writers are offering thinking that opens paths beyond old-fashioned static polarities as in "men are this way only." Corbett (2009) explores differing forms of masculinity that include behaviors that stereotypically were supposed to be only "feminine." Fogel (1998, 2005) has been tackling anew psychoanalytic views of men, and exploring ideas of interior space. He says in thinking about the "riddle" of masculinity, "By reexamining basic assumptions about heterosexual men, as has been done with ideas concerning women and homosexual men, complexity and nuance come to the fore to aid the clinician in treating the complex characterological pictures seen in men today" (p. 1139). Diamond (2004) reassesses the old notion that it was necessary and normative for a boy to "disidentify" (Greenson, 1968) with the mother in the early years to preserve his masculinity. He offers instead that attachment/individuation patterns and their outcome depend on the security of the boy's attachment to his mother, and her reflective capacity to consider father's and her son's maleness as well as her own subjectivity. These processes will undergird the boy's masculine sense of himself and the individuation process. This richness certainly resonates with the inner pictures of the men I describe next.

I offer evidence here that the storied male playful push toward a child's ability to "separate" may be connected to the sublimated uses of a father's sexual arousal in proximity to the child's body. The latter point I find extremely interesting. It involves adding a sexual dimension to the "exactly how" of the generally established notion that an aspect of the father's role is to help the child separate from the mother and modulate its aggression (e.g., Herzog, 2001); or a more received legendary notion that the Father (capital F, the way that Lacan uses the notion as in the Law of the Father) is the natural boundary setter, to save the infant from engulfment with the mother (Chasseguet-Smirgel, 2005). What is it about possessing a *sexed* male body that provokes this mutual (and often beneficial) separating behavior? The impact of the primary male caretaker with the female child in her female body provides a vivid cross-sexed corporeal template upon which to examine these issues. In addition, these examples can show the possibilities of the use of a fluid gender role identity for family life and the blended family lives that many are living presently. I am regretful that, at this point, I have had no experience in primary nurturance with children of gay men. I suspect that much is similar in the process, as the bodies of gay and straight men are the same, if not the details of how they physically respond to a child of either sex. A father who is the primary hands-on caretaker of his baby daughter can have very similar problems and rewards in the struggle to separate from her as she grows, in much the same way that traditional mothers have been regularly described. In an earlier paper (Balsam, 1989), I described from an adolescent daughter's inner point of view, a father's revitalizing crucial contribution to her development in seeking out a new closeness to his adolescent daughter, whose mother was psychiatrically disabled. That material also, but from the female child recipient's inner view, showed the impact of a male's later caretaking and involvement.

My accounts here are based on the inner landscape of three young fathers. Two men were in four times/week psychoanalyses (one case treated by a colleague from another city in telephone supervision with me); and one man was in a twice-weekly psychoanalytically oriented psychotherapy. My material is thus subjectively father-based, and adds to the still rare intrapsychic data on the topic of primary nurturing fathers. The clinical fabric here differs in texture from fathers reporting reflectively in research interviews—from family observational data; from conclusions drawn from primarily child treatments where parents also have been involved, or from joint parent child treatments—otherwise, I will cite the work of most of our few colleagues who to date have been fascinated with this topic, and from whose extremely valuable contributions to the literature about "the role of the primary nurturing father."

Pine's (2004) contemporary revisions to his and Mahler's earlier claims to a specific "symbiotic" stage of an infant's development (1975) show a shift toward the opinion that this developmental staging turned out to be somewhat overstated.

However, there remains a place in mentation for "symbiotic fantasy." We may think of "symbiosis" as a fantasy system perhaps especially adaptive and protective in a parent during this early era of infant physical helplessness. Necessarily unproven within the mind of any infant of course, the desire to fuse with another body or person remains in adults a clinically describable fantasy often heard in couch work, and frequently described within a mother in relation to her child. We are less used to describing adult men as adaptationally prone to such interactional fantasies, except as an ingredient of mature lovemaking (Freud, 1905; Kernberg, 1998). Because "symbiotic fantasy" is more mentioned in association with female dynamics or in severe male psychopathology, I wonder about an unconscious misogynist bias in our field in using this term pejoratively, as in reference to over-the-top, out-of-control women or madmen and certainly a feature that is not desirable in a regular male!

Complexity is added to this early arena of male caretaking by the predominance of these men's own memories and encoded experiences with their own early caretakers—mostly their mothers. Some paternal elements were also discernible, but the predominant relevant internalizations slanted toward the mother. Each came from an intact heterosexually organized nuclear family where the sexed and gender roles were conventional. A special activity of these bisexual fantasies appeared to play a major role in guiding these particular men's capacity to be the primary nurturer of their girls. This inner range and plasticity of gender role made these men as good (in the case of the widower) and better caretakers of children than their particular wives. I will elaborate on these themes after the clinical accounts.

Case TU

A 34-year-old male analysand, Mr. TU, lay on the couch softly stroking and twirling his thick blondish red curly sideburns. His baritone voice was low and soothing. "How I love that little girl," he said in low, musical tones. "I never dreamed I'd be so involved with a kid—maybe with an older boy who could toss a football with me—but not a girl! She's two-and-a-half now—SO cute ... well 'cute' is too mundane a word, but it's funny how you only have clichés when you're most moved. I tucked her up in bed last night and I read 'Good-night Moon'. We did the whole bit about the bunny and the cow that jumped over the moon ... her eyes were closing and she was trying to keep them open not to miss anything ... she said, 'Night, Dada ... sooo sleepy now'. I bent down and kissed her ... (sighs with intense pleasure) ... She was already asleep and I was flooded with love, pleasure, and possession all at once. My own little bird in her nest. My Robin redbreast. How much do I love you? My breast swells like a mother bird. I'll catch worms for you all my life. I'll feed you, my little Robin, see you chirp every morning, needing me, wanting me. I can't wait till she wakes up again. ... I'm in love. ... God, I'm getting soft!" He laughs delightedly and (unselfconsciously) pats his chest, that no doubt would be stout and hairy were I to actually see it, but in his mind's eye I think soft and cuddly. No doubt, I imagine that his little daughter does find it cuddly, offered as it is with such warmth as she snuggles up to him.

As the daughter grew up, this father chose her clothes for her. He would take from her closet and put by her bed every night. The little girl was reportedly angry if her mother did this. It had to be father. He was expert in all the pinks and stripes and dots of pants and tops, the dresses, the kind of "jewelry" she wore to nursery school. He was thrilled to be the parent who bathed her every night. Feelings of embarrassment emerged in front of me (as a maternal transferee) as he realized how sexual an experience this was for him. He was anxious when his associations would turn from playing with her toys with her in the bathtub to feeling sexually aroused by her white smooth skin, her round little bottom, her tiny vulva, and her own elaborate flirtations in showing off to him her "tush" and her "bagina" with gales of delighted giggles. Briefly, TU toyed with the idea of distancing himself from this bedtime ritual, and off and on tried to encourage her mother to be in the bathroom too, as we agreed "a safe chaperone." However, this mother just wanted to hurry up, get the bath over, and get the girl to bed and asleep. For TU and his daughter who wept, this uneasy maternal intrusion was an unsatisfactory solution. He was intrigued to linger with his daughter, but he became worried that he was a "pedophile." I will say more about this and his fantasies in this regard in the discussion. I believe that a father's physical and biologically marked sexual arousal by visible and noticeable and inescapable erection is a special difference from the mother of a 3-year-old at bath time with her naked flirty child, because her erotic arousal seems to draw less disruptive attention to either her or her child, because it is more discreet biologically. Few women worry about being "pedophiles."

Her blonde-red hair grew long and curly like his in her third year. It was he who washed her hair. His description of combing her hair was exceptionally sensual (To his analyst as well! His abilities to make sensual overtures to girls and women, I took from this, were quite successful!). He'd describe how he carefully brushed it, and how much his daughter loved this routine, closed her eyes and said, "Go on for ever and ever daddy." She'd cry when mother did her hair, because there were tangles to be pulled out, whereas he would use a spray he'd got at his hairdresser to loosen tangles. He was gentle. I was reminded of the word "cherishment" that Elizabeth Young-Bruehl has written about that is a quality of child-rearing in Japan (Young-Bruehl and Bethelard, 2000). He said his wife was rough with her. It seemed clear to me that these kinds of tender physical interchanges were one reason the little girl adored him, that he was the preferred parent. TU had fantasies that her long shiny red-blond hair was an extension of his own. He fused with her at these moments of bliss. The little girl would be still and soothed. He would participate in her soothed feeling, being himself on the borders of sleep in a transporting relaxation. Together, they were "one" in space. Sometimes he recalled these moments and fantasized his belly as a sphere surrounding Robin. "My balloon fantasy" he called it—fully savoring his desire for a womb. He joked, playing on the title of Virginia Woolf's feminist essay, "I need a womb of my own!" and he'd give a musical deep resonant chuckle. This wish was active from Robin's conception and during the pregnancy, which he confessed, "was wasted "on his wife. TU's wife worked at a high-stepping level in the corporate culture of big business. She was the main breadwinner, and she liked very much this caretaking arrangement that had been mutually worked out before the baby's birth.

TU was in analysis because he felt that he had never really established himself securely in the work-world. He underachieved chronically, and had a 9 am–2 pm job as a minor librarian, though at times he fantasized about becoming a high school teacher. In the analysis, he decided that this would be his future "after she gets well into school and needs me less." He terminated analysis after 5 years, while Robin was still in grade school. It was very difficult for them to separate when nursery school came along. He found himself in tears many times, as he dragged himself away from the unhappy child that he left with her teacher. He complained of having "an empty nest." I could go on, but I think the reader will have taken the point about how difficult (but not impossible) it was for him to let Robin grow separate from his tender incorporative tendencies.

I heard 10 years later (when she was in high school) that he had indeed begun to study to become a teacher. During the discussion, I will reveal some more of his physical fantasies that were related to his baby care taking, and which he disclosed during the treatment.

Case UV

In another case, a 45-year-old father, Mr. UV, was in psychotherapy while retooling in a second career by going to graduate school. He revealed a past life of being "a house-husband" for nearly 20 years, with still an ongoing closeness to his twin girls with whom he had had very intense baby-care experiences. They now were undergraduates in the same university in which he was attending graduate school. He was having a hard time getting on with his Ph.D. thesis. He said matter-of-factly that, as far as he and his wife were concerned, it had been merely a matter of "practicality—you know what twins are like—all hands aboard!" She wanted more than he did to go out to work. Later, as he became more psychologically minded, he began to examine more closely the meanings of his behavior and life choices.

This father had taken a great interest in all of his twins' activities, especially gymnastics, dance, and ice-skating—activities where he could see them use their bodies in space, and where he would watch the lessons for hours on end. He described sitting on the benches or in the wings, being "transported with delight" at the sight of the two lithe, androgynous bodies swirling gracefully on the ice. He felt "uplifted" as they vaulted over the horse in gymnastics. He "blissed out" in "mindless stare" at the sight of the elegance of their delicate slender limbs as they seemed to reach forward to "embrace the air." He himself said "I was at one with them ... now the one, now the other." If any of the teachers were critical, UV reacted as if he himself were being attacked. He would talk intensely to them, allegedly to help them with hurt feelings, but it was uncertain to an outsider if in fact he were the most hurt one himself. His girls seemed to be doing well both socially and academically. UV became quite low when they began to accept rides from peers to their activities, and it was hard to remember that there was any other worthwhile life than where they related to him. He seemed to be distant from his wife and certainly to prefer the company of the twins. Part of his anhedonia concerned a habitual suppression of forbidden sexual thoughts about the proximity of his daughters. He initially reported a lack of interest in his wife's rotund, middle-aged body.

There were dynamically connected reasons to his attachment to these two girls. When he was 2 years old, his mother had given birth to premature twins who had died within a month. They had been identical girls. Unconscious fantasies about them had been a pervasive ghostly presence (Volkan, 1997). His emphasis on the beauty of the nubile androgyny of his prepubertal daughters tapped into his own bisexual fantasies and arenas of uncertain gender role differentiation. Much more might be said, but suffice to attend here just to the proclivity for merger fantasy that I describe. This particular case narrative may add depth to the notion that this kind of father-care launched for "practical reasons—financial, or the need for both of us to work, the stress of two babies, etc.," while helpful and much more feasible in this post-second-wave feminist era, will naturally also serve the needs of the subject's internal agendas. The successful and apparently happy progeny will also have private lives that can be internally very complex while still sustaining high functioning in their worlds.

Case VW

A 36-year-old male analytic patient and widower, Mr. VW tells his analyst (a graduate colleague from another city whom I supervised for a time by phone): "You remember I told you how I didn't want Joy to get pregnant … but she wanted it so badly, and I was terrified…" When the baby was 7 months, his wife, treated for a small malignancy 6 years earlier, died of a breast cancer that had been in remission till late in her pregnancy. The ferocity of the malignancy probably had indeed been exacerbated by the hormonal shifts of the pregnancy. This father was riven with guilt that he had been instrumental in both his wife's death and his daughter's loss. Their daughter was now 10 months old, and VW was in analysis and grief stricken. He had opted to take a 4-month leave of absence from his job, and his company was supportive. He would be going back to work in a about a month, and the analyst, Dr. D, sought supervision, because he felt himself to be nearly overwhelmed with the combination of pathos for the man's grief at the loss of his young wife, plus admiration for the patient's brave determination to be the stay-at-home sole caretaker of his infant daughter.

VW was painfully aware that his baby had also experienced a very sick and weakened mother during the 7 months since her birth, because the mother had to undergo aggressive chemotherapy. There had been many moments when VW had held Mrs. W in his arms, to give her enough strength to hold the baby for feeding. In analysis, he recalled such a moment as "me and her as one, and at one with Janie. It was like we were all feeding off the bottle—the three of us together. Afterwards, when Janie smiled up at us, her mouth all milky still, I felt utterly content. It would last only for a little while, but those were dear, dear moments" … and he broke into tears.

(This scene and memory I will take up later as a readiness on his part for symbiotic fantasy, and for its potential for relief, fullness, and comfort in reassurance against loss.)

Other like moments had occurred after the baby first came home with his wife from the hospital. VW had slept closely in the same bed as both of them. "I lay spooning Joy, and she spooned Janie."

"I had a dream one of those nights that I had a woman's breasts. It felt weird and I was saying, 'what the hell?' when I looked down with great relief and saw my penis. It looked big and the foreskin was pointing forward like a nipple, and I had these two big full breasts."

"The best nights were when we put the baby between us. I'd lie right up next to her—the baby was way up on the pillow and I liked to have her toes touch my chest." His wife, in those memories, was usually portrayed as out of bed, unable to sleep, restless on the far side of the bed, or lying off by herself at her edge of the bed.

"I might have fought much more with her if she hadn't been sick," he confessed the following year as a widower when the child was 18 months old. By then, he was intensely and proudly possessive of Jamie. VW had tried several babysitters after returning to work. None of them seemed to be satisfactory with the baby. They didn't feed her correctly, dress her properly, or regulate her naps exactly, so that she would be perky when VW got home from work. He was often angry and reflected (accurately) that he was impossible to please. His analyst entered the discussion fruitfully at this point. Dr. D was able to show VW that his possessiveness was connected to trying to re-create a fantasy of having the baby inside, as he'd also experienced earlier right after the baby was born. In this imaginative reprise, he could both restore his wife to life but also impotence due to her illness, and simultaneously ward off the terrible guilt about the forbidden pleasure of being the sole parent left with Janie—taking as he said, "a mother's rightful place." His continuous anger with the babysitters expressed a displaced anger from the abandonment he felt through Joy's illness and death. He was overidentified with the vision of a dissatisfied and inconsolable infant, reading Janie's minor discomforts as major displeasure with these mother-substitutes. No one else would do for Jamie, he thought, but her own biological mother whose "place" he in fantasy had taken over. VW reactively wanted to "do it all" and "be all" to Janie himself. Much later, he dared face the possibility that his marriage to a woman who had been told that a pregnancy could be dangerous to her life afforded the fulfillment of a longed-for unconscious wish that he could "have" a baby by and for himself. In a nutshell, there were developmental antecedents that had catalyzed this readiness for baby caretaking in VW. Growing up extremely close to his mother, he had viewed himself as her "little helper" trying to make up for the loss of twin girl babies who had died when he was 4 years of age.

VW stayed in therapy through Jamie's transition to kindergarten. It was very painful for him to "share" her with teachers and her little friends. He pouted, being clipped and unfriendly when other parents, usually mothers who, naturally very pained by his story, wanted to help him. He spurned their offers to baby-sit or share afternoon care for Jamie. One woman, a single mother who seemed to the analyst to show a sexual interest in him, went unnoticed by VW. In treatment, it emerged that he felt too guilty and too disloyal to the deceased Joy to respond to the erotic overtures.

As Dr. X and I discussed the case, it seemed to us that VW usually eventually revealed several related layers of concern about allowing outsiders into this intense dyad that he had established with his daughter. The first narrative was always (naturally) about how this intensity developed to help/nurture and to compensate his daughter for her lack of a mother. All was influenced by his grief and loss of his wife. At times, however, it appeared that his grief could become a rationalization and a resistance to his more self-generated motives and the bisexual meanings of keeping so close bodily to his daughter.

Discussion

These three young heterosexual fathers, going against the social grain, took part regularly and intimately in the bodily care of their female infants in a way similar to a traditional role of a child's mother. In general, I consider each a good and successful father, judged by the apparent progress of their children and their own pleasure in the task. One could argue that the different situations of each of the men here complicates the usefulness of any attempt at generalization about their psyches—Father VW was a widower, while fathers TU and UV were elective primary caretakers by arrangement with their wives who had opted for markedly less hands-on roles. Be that as it may, I am interested in observing the common proclivities to symbiotic merger fantasies with their children, and the vicissitudes of that aspect of their attachment that were discerned in each.

Since Stan Cath, Alan Gurwitt, and John Munder Ross drew attention to fathers as emerging from a phase of being "the forgotten parent" (p. xvii) in 1982, and Kyle Pruett first focused especially on "primary nurturing fathers" in 1983, the social stereotyping of gender and sex roles has loosened, permitting more fathers to pursue this option. Numerous recent articles and research, however, also have brought to light the family role of "super-mom," where it is claimed that outer or inner gender expectations for women demand that they themselves "do it all."[1] It is therefore not surprising that it is still relatively rare to come across a father who sees himself almost solely responsible for the care of a child as women continue to fulfill this role. The earlier work (Cath, Gurwitt, and Ross, 1982; Pruett, 1983,

1985; Chused, 1986) puts to rest any notion that necessarily "mothers do it better." My sample supports this notion too. Both females and males seem to have both their own successes and problems in early caretaking. The confidence about the sturdiness and ability of male primary nurturers on the part of therapists, however, is still not reflected in culture at large.

Take the stereotype that truly "manly" males are too emotionally challenged to be able to tend to infants. This notion exemplifies the rigidly gendered culture surrounding Western males that may negatively affect how a man may think of his masculinity when he is the infant caretaker in the home. One can hear this sentiment expressed, however pseudo-playfully, by the obviously capable and warm father who castigated himself for "getting soft," and hence denigratingly feminized. A wide sociological gender perspective is provided by Galasinski (2005), a Polish-born professor of Discourse and Cultural Studies in England. He writes a scholarly overview of what the current sociological and socio-gender academic literature is contributing on the topic of men's emotions: "... however much one may disagree with the theoretical stances and methodological proce- dures of social psychological research ... the conclusion of men's alleged lack of emotionality is drawn from the research data the scholars collect in their laboratories" (p. 13). He goes on to point out the puzzle that "men's emotional incompetence" is presented "at the level of assumption, as something that does not need to be argued; it is simply there" (p. 13). "Men cannot be emotional: *men don't cry* is a saying that has different languages across Europe" (p. 12). He also says that he believes it is "fair to say ... that to-day's Western outlook on emotions is more negative than positive" (p. 12). He goes on to challenge this false axiom with meticulously proven research that favorably compares the strength of men's emotions to those of women in such situation as being out of work. Denigrating men's capacity for expressing emotion is familiar to psycho- therapists too, in terms of peoples' misinterpretation as "strength" a stereotypic "masculine" ego ideal of emotional suppression. In the gender literature of our field, we find much evidence for men's cultural internalization about what this scholar claims. By contrast with men, women supposedly hold all the keys to emotional life—especially when it comes to nurturing the young. For many reasons, because the opportunity for a father to be his baby's primary caretaker does not present itself often, men's responses are less and may therefore be assumed to be deficient. In the same vein of gender stereotyping, the phenomenon of symbiotic fantasy-systems may be under-reported in males because of their association with female childbearing. In turn, that has been naturally associated with the jealously guarded female sexual and gender role function of bonding to and caretaking of an infant.

Apart from the literature casting him in the Laius castrating patriarchal father- ing role with oedipal boys (Munder Ross, 1982), or in his activities laying down for the family and society the Law of the Father, or as the oedipal seducee of the Jocasta female, the father in the child literature in pre-oedipal arena is commonly described as functionally encouraging a child's separateness. However, fathers

TU, UV, and VW spontaneously did not seem to tell about this kind of interaction in their individual treatments. There may be several reasons: the described style of father functioning that catalyzes autonomy is often derived from the assumption of a traditional heterosexual nuclear family where the father helps a child to pull away from a dyadic intensity with a primary caretaking mother. Many of the papers about fathering in families with traditional mothers were written a few decades ago, prior to the acute awareness of and even existence of differing sorts of contemporary family arrangements. Other descriptions that most commonly emphasize the fathers' role (whether primary or secondary nurturers) as enhancing the child's separateness, activity, and explorative curiosity are drawn from a perspective in which the child's organization and welfare is more in focus than concentrating on the private, individual inner world of the father alone. One set of observations need not counter the other—they enhance each other by adding shades of subtlety and the recognition of emotional range. However, traditional descriptions of "fathering" as an entity distinct and different from "mothering" contributed a solid sense of how and in what way a father's functions may aid the emotional development of the autonomy of his children, especially when the mother is the primary caretaker. (This observational clarity about real-life men from the 1980s on was certainly a step forward to an earlier rather self-serving phallocratic psychoanalytic adage taught to me as a candidate in the 1970s, i.e., that the child's mental representation of a father was totally dependent upon the *mother's* way of talking to the child about the—usually absent—father!) The work of Fogel, Corbett, and Diamond cited earlier is yet another step forward, as it moves away from any hint of stereotypic views, and instead tries to listen closely to what contemporary real-life men are saying in their associations.

Beyond the family observations of father-function, some close behavioral observations have pointed to the differences attributed to biological and psychosocial gender influences between adult males and females observed in child caretaking (e.g., Yogman, 1984; Pruett, 2000). During observation of their play with children, men apparently show a heightened activity level compared to women. Yogman (1984) says that "the primary caretaker fathers ... while bathing, diapering, and feeding ... carry out their tasks with great skill ... but with the same vigorous, exciting quality seen in face-to-face play with secondary caretaker fathers" (p. 115). Fathers commonly "activate their children prior to interacting with them" (Pruett, 2004: p. 57). My analytic subjective clinical material can neither exactly support nor refute this. I do, however, have some detail about these fathers' free associations about their feelings and sexual bodies in close proximity to and contrasted with their daughters. Perhaps through subtle reactive anxiety about highly charged and very private sexual inevitable fantasies, in certain circumstances, fathers act motorically more vigorously than mothers do to reassure themselves that the child will not be a passive victim of their sexual fantasy or erections? Mothers' sexual arousals are more physically discreet and hence perhaps less provocative of anxiety or need for motion as a discharge phenomenon. Father TU gave the most graphic description of being sexually aroused during the little girl's bath time. He seemed to want his wife to enter as the diluting third party—not because of the meshing fantasies, but because of his fear of sexual arousal and the excitement and fantasy excitement/fear of "assaulting" his daughter by the sight of his erect penis. His wife was to be present to act as a projection of a stern controlling superego. Nevertheless, after some analytic interventions to ease the conflict of his superego restraint, he did play a great deal with his daughter. Because of his personal ego strengths, f/Father TU managed to tolerate his arousals and even occasional erotic fantasies while carrying on some "watering" game where he would spray her with the hose and she would laugh and splash back. When the bathroom floor was soaked, together they would mop it up. Father and daughter together became excited. The daughter and he would also play that a wicked witch might discover them! This enacted fantasy bears resemblance to the traditional mother role of needing to "calm down" the overexcited child *and* her "Kamikaze" action father, by becoming annoyed (Herzog, 2001). I wondered if this quality of sexually, and mildly aggressively, teasing (but ultimately "safe") interaction could well be the locus of Father TU's traditional role of helping his daughter to metabolize excitement (Tessman, 1984; Herzog, 2001). Fantasies from differing levels of ego integration may therefore be experienced by a father and reported in analysis, according to what a given caretaking task brings forth in him. The presence of the more archaic merger fantasies can be flexibly interchangeable with these more separated, individuated fantasies of sexual arousal. At times, one level may be used to defend against another. I would now like to focus further on the merger level.

To what extent do internal fantasies of corporeal fusion arise, become nurtured, and have a trajectory within *any* adult's experience—regardless of sex and gender—and vividly emerge in response to infant bodily caretaking? Limiting essentialist notions of biology, it is still possible to acknowledge that the body's sexed morphology and important biological functions are different but also do overlap in men and women. The role of the mind is to contemplate and integrate the many evoked meanings and fantasies of a body of psychic reality, or the "psychoanalytic body."[2] Following Freud's idea that "the body is first and foremost a bodily ego" (1923)—the need for the biological body as a trigger to primitive and/or sophisticated textured, differentiated fantasy can be accepted. So, how can an adult man fuse corporeally with a tiny girl child? First of all, he can deny that his body is that of an adult male. The physicality of his imagination can assume the forms of the bodies around him. Each aspect of the fusion is constructed with a dynamic purpose that expresses some wish or fear, or helps to establish a strength of some sort, or ward off a greater danger.

What of the intimate mutual physicality of fathers TU, UV, and VW with their girls?

In the context of how much he loves his toddler daughter, Father TU, condensing her name with his own physical fantasy, and thereby absorbing her in some fashion, speaks a metaphor of becoming "Robin Redbreast." He will "catch worms" for his hungry baby bird and feed her when she wakes in the morning.

Hidden in this nurturing and feeding oral fantasy (appropriate to caretaking an infant) are images of a red breast (probably female-derived) and feeding with a beak (probably a male-derived body mode tapping into his sexual experience and fantasy of delivering substance into a cavity, the open mouth of the little bird, also a vaginal reference showing awareness of the child as female). The actions of the parent bird and baby bird, mutually satisfying each other's desires and needs, creates a perfect synchrony of oral attunement. Father TU's pride swells his breast in this fantasy. This could be an unconscious reference to a pregnant state, or to the bounteous bosom of pregnancy (Balsam, 1996). The unconscious phenomenon of blending or symbiotic element of this fantasy image is featured in the amalgam of "Robin."

The whole context of this fantasy is stimulated by his tenderness in putting her to bed, activating pregnant, orally responsive, and also sexually progressive levels of integration within the experience of the mutual pleasures of the bedroom scene. One can detect the possibility here of mentalized bisexual meanings in gender-related activity. As far as drive/conflict theory is concerned, we have mainly believed that humans develop to sexual and gender maturity by actually turning away from one sex or the other and relinquishing a whole set of aspirations they once experienced less conflictedly in childhood. Overlooked in this too neat and linear developmental theory is the vitality of Freud's offered but underdeveloped idea of psychic bisexuality. If we are consistent about clinically tracing the internal patterns of these female and male trends (Chapter 7), we find each sexed and gendered thread alive and well—according to the life context that brings it forth. Rather than deciding by value-laden social categorizations what is "masculine" or what is "feminine," I think that it is only important what the persons' associations are either to a male (father, father-substitute, or brother) or to a female (mother, mother-substitute, or sister) of the past, in order to decide. In this way, one can keep the attention trained on the meanings to the individual. This thinking and technique therefore can avoid temptation to stereotypic, global, or cultural so-called "normative" external value judgments about an individual's "masculine" and "feminine" behaviors. In TU's case, the associations that I propose as "feminine" were those associated with his own mother. His mother, for example, was lovingly recalled in a red dress, with her ample bosom on display. His associations to "Robin Redbreast" were thus informed by his internalized mother. A favorite photo of his mother in this pose decorated a wall in his current home. TU had always been fascinated by pregnancy and delivery. He was the first of three siblings, and he studied his mother intently and enviously (Balsam, 1996).

Father UV described his fusion fantasies with the androgynous nubile prepubertal twin girls. In other aspects, his sexuality with his wife was suppressed in favor of his involvement with his twins—a safe involvement, because it was externally socially acceptable while his fantasies of physical fusions were privately pleasing. He imagined himself possessing an omnipotently pluripotential body. He thus could stay forever young and undefined but powerfully physically strong and fleet. These proclivities did not seem to interfere with his overall parenting and certainly made him a devoted and attentive father. It was in the conduct of his own life in completing his Ph.D. thesis that he was troubled, thus facing the threat of a more defined adult male role in the future. Associations to these fantasies were limited due to the treatment being a once/ weekly therapy. I am not sure of the early connections to his life with his family of origin, but these merger fantasies were part of the "glue" that held him to his twins, and led to great sorrow at working them through due to the girls growing apart from him.

Father VW adored his little infant girl. His possessiveness toward her, increased by the responsibility of being her sole parent and his guilt for forbidden wishes to "steal" the mother's role, expressed his fusion with her. VW's oral language stressed the "neediness" of Janie, as also a sense of his own neediness of his dead wife. Father VW "needed" to hold Janie so close mentally that she was not supposed to form other attachments to babysitters. Through the severe illness of his wife, VW's capacity for fantasies of bodily fusion helped garner his own strength and emanate it toward the others. By "spooning", he emotionally "fed" his sick wife, enfolded in his bodily warmth and closeness, while he felt fed by the bottle that also fed baby Janie. Later in his life, his preference for fusion with Janie was supposed to help ward off the threat of adult women who might want him to be sexual, thereby activating his survival guilt about replacing the dead wife. In addition, he feared a relationship with a new adult woman who might die and involve him in further painful loss. Life was safer clinging on to Janie's childhood.

Father VW's background fitted in with this scenario. He had been a depressed mother's "little helper" with all of the overheated oedipal implications. Safety had been achieved by an over-identification with her, especially in her role as a nurturer of little children.

Bergman (2004), in her discussion of a new father in analysis, also describes evidence for a man's merger fantasies with a woman's pregnancy and calls for a greater need to "understand the development of the new father." She suspects that the pre-oedipal relationship, especially to his own nurturing mother, has not been sufficiently considered. All three of my cases called strongly on their experiences and fantasies of their internalized mothers to respond to their infants' needs. (Their fathers rarely emerged in these associations. Father TU, who laughingly spoke of "getting soft," did emerge with associations to what his father would think of him if still alive, and reckoned that he would be "ribbed" for letting his wife "wear the pants." Hence, it was more in working on the reassessment of TU's own sense of masculinity that his own father played a part in the analysis. None of my patient's fathers had involved themselves with infant care, so that it made sense to me that they were not an inner pre-oedipal resource for this task.) Bergman's case involved her patient's early history of heart surgery and intensity with his mother. My fathers did not experience such childhood traumata and yet experienced quite an intense immersion in their infants.

Conclusion

Writers in the contemporary scene (e.g., Parens, 2004) have noted the more open possibility that "fathering" in fact may well turn out to be a cocreated plastic and adaptive state in males, according to the specific needs of the child and guided by the father's internal and external social structural environment. The fathers I am describing seemed best conceptualized along these lines, and not only within a consistently vigorous "pro-separation" typology that has been frequently noted as the father's special role. Fathers TU, UV, and VW seemed to me more similar in their intimate descriptions of themselves to home-based mothers. Perhaps the mothers in these families, when available, became more like the active male triadic instigators of traditional families to these children? Unfortunately, I do not know this. Pruett (1983), while supporting the typology of the vigorous father tendencies, also allows for a range of characteristics in individuals and the richness of mutual attunements: "It is generally agreed ... that fathering as a process serves most importantly through fostering autonomy and the enhancement of individuation and independent functioning. Yet, it is also clear that such "unattachment" theory per se is of limited use in assessing father–infant relationships as it fails to acknowledge the very mutual regulation by both infant and parent of the dyadic process" (p. 259).

These men's symbiotic fantasy lives were stimulated within the care giving of the children. Each man took his responsibility very seriously. The men were fully in touch with the pleasures of exclusiveness with their daughters, and each resented the perceived intrusion of others—Father TU from the mother, Father UV from the coaches, and Father VW from babysitters and the helping mothers in nursery school. It was a pained process for each to relinquish control over these children and to metabolize their growing attachment to others in their worlds.

"Symbiosis" is one of those terms that has taken on a weighty mantle in development that has gone awry and the adult pathology of narcissistic and borderline states or in regressive and fixated character pathologies. In a developmentally more adaptive tenor, it has classically been associated with mothering and female development. We may alternatively consider that this fantasy system could well be a vitally constructive aspect of early child-rearing, no matter the sex and gender of the caretaker. Such capacity for enmeshment certainly enhances a protectiveness of the young from the outside harsh world. The detail of the inner world that informs a mutual regulation or "attunement" between caretaker and child involves such corporeal fantasies. They signify devoted involvement with a child and an effort to connect sensitively and emotionally to a nonverbal infant. Their vitality serves as a conduit into inner contact with the emotional atmospherics of the caretaker's own past, making such resources (or lacks) available to the present task of baby minding. Based on the work of others cited here, the interactional style of each parent may support a notion of certain gender differences, presumably either on constitutional or acculturated grounds or internal grounds, or some combinations of all these factors. My own position on the categorization of this kind of difference is mixed. On the one hand, I am very interested in what kinds of external observations we can glean to help us understand differences in men and women. On the other hand, my work with the internal lives of individuals has made me leery of making many gender generalizations along the lines of "men do this" and "women do this," due to the complexity of how sex is processed and how gender representations are built up. I suggest that we recognize that archaic body fusion fantasy may play a recognized, perhaps ubiquitous, and certainly adaptive role in both men's and women's caretaking of their children.

Notes

1 A 2005 study, from the University of Michigan Institute for Studies in Women and Gender, confirms that working women from two-job families took on the same childcare workload as stay-at-home women who raised their children full-time (Studer, 2005). In addition, the large number of single parents with children at home is usually headed by women.
2 I intend to try to develop this concept in future papers, as a coming into being in "the third", a co-creation of analyst, his theory, inner life, and reactions to the patient, and the latter's biological body in consort with his inner world and dilemmas as told to the analyst.

Chapter 11

Some implications for theory

In my reading of the psychoanalytic literature on female psychology, a field ever more pluralistic and complex, I detect six important trends. I know well that many complex ideas and theories have been put forward and are presently in use in the clinical office and in the academy regarding the vast topics of gender, sex, and sexuality. In all of these topics, the body needs to have a place, but it is handled differently within each, and there is no way that I can absorb, encompass, or do justice to all of them. In my preoccupation with my own central thesis, I am bound to underplay, or even pass over, inspired writings of others that I may well appreciate later as having had an important bearing on my present claim. Nevertheless, I will go ahead with my project in any case, because I retain a conviction about its importance, and because I have received much encouragement from others in our field.

I imagine that all psychoanalytic authors would say that they think about the body often and agree with me that it is extremely important. However, I am focusing on how psychoanalytic authors *write* about the body, and on the articles that editors endorse for publication and which therefore have ongoing influence in the field. Clinicians and theoreticians talk about their approaches in conferences, and there too they communicate how they do or do not think about the body. I assume that their thinking influences what they are listening for when they are working with patients, and what they interpret. I offer here, therefore, my own thoughts and impressions on what "listening for the female body" means in the literature and in conferences.

The following six trends, and their historical development, have each been, in their own ways, crucial to the story of women in psychoanalysis. Indeed, I propose that these six agendas have guided psychoanalytic discourse about women for the last 110 plus years. Yet, for complicated reasons, the female biological body has not readily fitted into any of them. A partial emphasis that enlightens one therapist about females looks like obfuscation to another. The conversation is often propelled by political and personal pressures. I do not want to disparage in any way the need to press both politically and socially for women's emancipation.

However, to quote Freud's cautionary note, much "joins the conversation" when many political issues in our theories that need to be voiced overlap at once. Even a vital central issue may be lost in the noise. The same may be said for personal issues, though "personal" reactions and countertransferences are bound into and welcomed into the nature of psychoanalysis itself. The female body is often the loser. We members of the psychoanalytic discipline also seem passionately to favor and follow the theories of charismatic single leaders from loosely related schools. They mostly claim a foundational relationship to Freud, have established their own concepts and terminologies, and may have become associated with idiosyncratic theoretical and technical recommendations (Reed, 2009). Psychoanalysis can enjoy reliance neither on consensus building within the field, nor on the more sober progress that a search for evidence-based criteria and rigorous research might have afforded (Boesky, 2008). In this sense, psychoanalysis is a hybrid discipline somewhere between science and the humanities. Chodorow (2003) reflects, for example, "... it must be said that psychoanalysis is initially and fundamentally a theory and practice involving people whose thoughts, feelings, motives, passions, fantasies, and desires are at stake and who interact with and affect each other in a clinical situation. Its subject matter is individual subjectivity, its method directed to discovering the patient's subjectivity" (p. 466). Psychoanalysis has been called a science of intersubjectivity by Stolorow and Atwood (1992,1998), or a subjective science, or, for example, topic of critical realism and epistemological subjectivism has been examined in light of the analyst's subjectivity by the Hanlys (2001).

Let us say that, as far as psychoanalysis is concerned, the subject matter of the biological body (as talked about by a patient) is situated perhaps over half in the "science" aspect (observationally lending itself to objectivity), and under half in the "subjective arena" (lending itself to experiential mentalization). Psychoanalysis can create a *virtual* body—a special "psychoanalytic body" which is a hybrid of the objective and subjective. It can neither be solely subjective nor solely objective. The contemporary emphasis on "psychological" as the true focus of psychoanalysis—meaning mentalization *without* any blending concept of the original instinct theory (where instinct is a demand on the psyche made by the body)—treats the contribution to mental life of the biological or "concrete" body with hostility. Alas, the very Cartesian split, which dwelling in a pure psychological mind was supposed to heal, is recreated, due to the impossibility and impracticality of contemplating a psychological mind without giving due weight to the body that houses it. The six trends that I delineate in the following section, spanning the 110+ years of analysis, could be thought of as representing a chronologically gradually *decreasing* emphasis on the bodily detail that delineates a female from a male. As we move away from Freud and his anatomically incorrect female, we have thus more and more lost the possibility of constructing, as one of the major pillars of a durable and viable developmental theory of mind, an anatomically correct female body that takes its place alongside an anatomically correct male.

A focus on external genitalia

Laqueur (1990) has pointed out that Freud's idea that the girl starts out as a little boy (Freud, 1925) belongs in the tradition of a one-sex theory of humans. For Freud, Laqueur says that the female genitals were famously "an anatomical marker of woman's lack of what man has" (p. 233). Laqueur notes that, for 2,000 years before about the eighteenth century, "Woman was understood as man inverted" (p. 236). Freud reinforced an atavistic element in the sex and gender debate by ignoring evidence for early vaginal sensation and by separating the clitoris from the rest of the female genitalia and denoting it as "male." Yet, he also elaborated a two-sex model, positing at one time male libido, and at another a universal one and insisting that vaginal orgasm must achieve dominance over clitoral orgasm if a female is to develop into a mature adult. In this model, Laqueur agues, men and women were intensely closely compared and contrasted (even if Freud's reasoning was fantastical). Moreover, adult females were seen as sexually capable but different from men in "every physical and moral aspect" (p. 5). Freud's main focus remained upon the external genitals, and eventually his two models collapsed into one, in what Laqueur calls an incomplete struggle toward a form of a two-sex model. Young-Bruehl (1990) contends, and I concur, that Freud's undeveloped contribution of universal bisexuality still stands. It is this concept that allows for the modern notion of a complex adult gender identity, derived and psychologically established from traits of one or other gender in patterned form within an individual's psyche.

Jones (1927) and Horney (1926) were early dissenters to the one-sex model. Gyler (2010) considers Klein (1928) also to be a dissenter, but I believe that she did not view herself this way. However, Jones was influenced by her conviction of infants' very strong early attachment to the mother. As I read Klein, boy and girl infants are indeed distinguished from the beginning in their very early oedipal conflict. Nevertheless, like Freud, she too imagines the boy favored developmentally due to his penis. The poor Kleinian girl, although anatomically correct, once more is seen as in such pain compared to a boy! Klein, far more tuned in than Freud to the girl's dim awareness and wish to have a baby herself some day, believes, however, that she is mainly handicapped by this futuristic situation. Klein's girl also then suffers severely from being so envious of the mother's insides and desire to rob her womb, both of babies and of the father's penis. The girl worries about retaliation constantly. The only role of a good mother to this girl is seemingly to modify some of her phantastical natural inner hatred. Loving connections between mother and daughter seem far-fetched in this scheme. Jones's ability to distinguish girls from boys was likely positively influenced by Klein. Both Freud and Klein left quite a gap between their concepts of the struggles of little children, and how they grew up to be the anatomically correct adult men and women parental objects that also appear in their theories. In the 1930s, the controversy within Freud's ranks was great about whether or not girls were girls from the beginning, These early sex and gender discussions then went by the wayside (see Chapter 5). While Freud was alive, however, most writers continued to follow him in interpreting the woman's sexual organs as originally "male." As Gyler (2010) says, "Had Freud recognized the existence of the vagina and its meaning, his theory, especially the female Oedipus complex, would have been overturned" (p. 34). It took a second wave of feminism before later analysts (from the 1970s onwards) began to describe the female in relation to her own body rather than the male's. These papers pointed to early awareness of the vagina and introitus, infantile masturbation in girls, a female sense of inner space, reactions to sphincter control, and so on (e.g., see Erikson, 1968; Kestenberg, 1982; or Richards, 1992).

The adolescent girl's reactions to the onset of menses and her rapidly changing body have been noted (Ritvo, 1976; Shopper, 1979). However, here too, the focus has been on the genitals and on formulaic abstractions about the girl's *need* to integrate these perceptions into a hopefully maturing body image, lest she become stalled in a so-called "phallic-narcissistic" stage of development as an over-compensating castrated "boy"[1]—a bleak prospect. Little is mentioned, for example, about the girl's experience of the budding breasts. The female body in these texts remains the site of struggle for or against being a male body, and in this too we can see the fear that girls will not develop as "feminine" women.[2] Some of the texts (for instance, de Beauvoir [1947] and Lax [1997]) that emphasize "becoming a woman" seem to me to be based on the peculiar premise that to be housed in an adult female body is automatically hard-earned and against the grain. "Becoming a woman" implies to me a metamorphosis from something other than female—as if it is overly amazing that sexual maturity could happen to those born with intact female gonads and the usual, average-expectable hormone and brain signals! Sexual maturity is going to happen to all but a miniscule few, regardless of the mind's conscious or unconscious cooperation. The mind is powerful ... but not *that* powerful. I know that by using "becoming" instead of "being," the authors mean to stress that there may well be a gap between body and mind, and that we can neither imply from the look of the outside of the body, nor its scientifically tested anatomy and physiology, that the mind's own stance will match this sexually mature body. My point is that the body will take its own path to physiological maturity regardless, even while the psyche is intimately reacting to these shifts, constantly creating its own meanings, and creating social behaviors that may be psychologically near or far away from that individual body's biologically stable patterning. A person at any place on this near/far spectrum, unless born with ambiguous genitalia, is still "female." I reject the words "feminine" or "femininity" as having any necessary links to female biology. These words take us into the realm of gender that is a mental and social achievement. I prefer the less ambiguous terms "female" and "male" to describe the biological body. Joining the concept of "feminine" with that of "female" in this subjective science has confused biologically and socially derived criteria that, in my opinion, need to be treated as separate, if related, issues (see also Elise, 1997).

In this psychoanalytic theory that is derived from the main spotlight being on genitalia, after her initial misery about humans being unisex males, *the girl develops painfully, by the uphill efforts of her own psyche alone, more or less into a female. What body pleasures she has are viewed as compensatory for not being male.*

Woman as separate from man

Some theorists did accept that the sexes are different from birth, and, accepting this difference, explored it more fully than Freud did. Helene Deutsch (1944/1945), for example, with Freud's blessing, pioneered a view of women through the life cycle. Even Deutsch, following the master, though, did not question a girl's earliest beginnings as embedded in one-sex ideas. However, she did recognize the fact and importance of menstruation, pregnancy, and menopause for the female, as opposed to the male. This literature progresses further toward a two-sex model than Freud and his original colleagues did. Some notable examples are: G. Bibring et al. (1959, 1961)'s interest in pregnancy and the early mother/ child interaction; Benedek (1970) on parenting; and in more modern times, Pines (1993) on women's unconscious fantasies about their bodies, and Raphael-Leff (1995/2001, 2000, 1991/2005) on pregnancy and the vicissitudes of pro-creation. Notman and Nadelson (1991) wrote on women and men, talking of the biological bases of difference. There have been many significant papers and books on gender issues, especially since the 1970s, that tell and retell in their own ways the tale of the what, where, why, and when of "femininity" and women. However, here I am trying to confine myself to those who have specialized in thinking about specifically female *physical* attributions to the psychology of women. It was recognized, too, that women therapists as well as women patients dealt with sex- and gender-specific situations that never confronted male thera-pists or patients. Papers on the pregnant therapist belong here—e.g., Lax (1969), Nadelson (1974), Balsam (1974), Uyehara et al. (1995). After the 1970s, increas-ing reports became available. Goldberger and Evans (1985) explored confusions about whether a female analyst could elicit the homoerotic transference of the male patient, or a paternal transference, and provided supporting data to affirm the possibilities. It seemed to be assumed that male analysts found it unproblem-atic to elicit maternal transferences—or at least I can find no papers asking these questions! Received wisdom till the 1980s was that the choice of the sex of the therapist was unimportant, because the mechanisms of transference would super-sede the actual sex of the analyst or therapist. To an extent, this can be the case, but nowadays we also admit to awareness that therapists will likely elicit a pre-ponderance of one or other sort of transference based on their characteristics as people—including sex, and how they present their gender portraits in the office. I wonder if the earlier iron clad certainty about the transference-blind sexuality of the patient in fact was one of those hidden denials about female difference.

Feminist critics pushed for social debate that encompassed the equality of women, and an analytic theory that recognized women as separate beings distinct from men. They decried Freud's original one-sex model of female development as a social construct that he derived from his own family and cultural experiences. In most of the feminist writing, however, the biological body itself was and is little to be seen. This is a purposeful strategy. Female biology was held responsible via social expectations to become pregnant and be a mother for female subjugation (see the feminist and psychoanalytic arguments against its equation with "biological essentialism" in Chapter 2, and my defense of liberating "biological" from its old evil partner, "essentialism"). Chodorow (1978) importantly discussed the mother's pregnancy and childbearing as part of the psychological and identificatory heritage of girls, but also as an unfortunate social oppression imposed on females. The latter opinion was in tune with the social upheavals of the times. *The fate of the adult female herself acknowledged as different from male (as well as a debate about cultural and workplace oppression connected to her pregnant potential and becoming a mother) is the focus in these writings.*

Children and mothers

The richest source of material on children and mothers together, naturally, is the child analytic archive. *The Psychoanalytic Study of the Child*[3] was launched as a new journal in 1945 right after the Freud-Klein controversies in London. It was originally edited by Anna Freud, Heinz Hartmann, and Ernst Kris, and it carried a strong ego psychological conviction. It widened the influence of Anna Freud into the United States. It kept North American analyses close to a Freudian ground base, and encouraged and documented an era of analytic blossoming and creativity in the 1950s and 1960s. This was the journal of record of child analysis in the United States. Klein and Bowlby were roundly repudiated in the very first volume, which marked a turn away from London, and the strengthening of an independent North American analysis. When Winnicott in 1968 presented his "The Use of an Object and Relating through Identifications" (1968) at the New York Institute, American analysts claimed that they did not understand him at all (Khar 1996, Baudry 2009). Samuel Ritvo, from the Yale Child Study Center (where Anna Freud was greatly appreciated and visited often), and who was a young analyst present at that event, even in his eighties, pronounced Winnicott a "poet"[4] (which was not a compliment from him, and would have to be considered a put-down given the then-ambitious American aspiration of the time for psychoanalysis to be accepted as a general psychology with a systematic theory, which was hopefully going to be backed up by hard science).

Whatever the theoretical differences between the Americans and the British, however, the effects of mothers as nurturers of their children as seen through the lens of the child's psychosexual development and need is explored extensively in the child psychoanalytic literature. So far, I have found few references, though, to young girls' specific reactions to the mother's pregnant body per se. In a case study of Winnicott's (1975), there is a specific reference to a little girl's questions and fantasies about her own body in relation to her mother giving birth.

Winnicott (1960) also penned the most beautiful awareness of many aspects of the maternal body as seen through the eyes of a child that has ever graced in our literature: "For the mother who is right there in it, there is no past and no future. For her there is only the present experience of having no unexplored area, no North or South Pole but some intrepid explorer finds it and warms it up; no Everest but a climber reaches to the summit and eats it. The bottom of her ocean is bathyscoped, and should she have one mystery, the back of the moon, then even this is reached, photographed, and reduced from mystery to scientifically proven fact. Nothing of her is sacred. Who would be a mother?" (p. 74).

There surely may be material hidden in a single case study that I have missed. Nevertheless, it is fair to say that the young girl's comparative bodily excitement or anxiety to her procreative mother's body was *not* singled out for any detailed attention by Anna Freud or Melanie Klein. Nor has it been examined by more recent writers (as I read them). Jessica Benjamin, for instance, the feminist intersubjective psychoanalyst (1988, 1995) who writes voluminously, employing many abstract conceptions about the inner fantasy life of a girl child and the input of her mother (and father), does not include in her case materials many observations on this very basic corporeal piece of observable data.

Freud himself developed late an awareness that the mother is important to the girl child's first desire to produce a baby, and in conjunction with Mack-Brunswick (1940), he detected a wish for a baby in the pre-oedipal girl that antedated her awareness of her genital difference from boys. Klein knew well the desire in children of both sexes to acquire the power of the mother, but she dealt with this generically and only intrapsychically as part of her monolithic theory of object relations. These theories deal purely with the child's *wishes* or "*phantasies*" and not with the details of their thoughts about and interactions with the pregnant adult. Children's conception theories were known to Freud (1908) and are familiar to all. Anal and phallic male-derived and oedipal fantasies about children's wished-for "pregnancy" are recorded.[5] The mother's own reactions to genital difference are cited as a contribution to the girl's internalized reactions to her own genitals by Lerner (1977). Much of the attention paid to mothers and babies in the psychoanalytic literature has to do with the threat that the older child feels from the newborn rival. Also very important is the quality of attachment that the mother and child pair evoke in each other, and the quality of caring attention that the mother is able to pay to her children and how it affects them subsequently. Aggression or depression in the mother has also been dealt with often, and how this reverberates with her child's inner life (e.g., Hoffman, 1999; A. Green's description of the "Dead Mother" (in Kohon 1999/2005), and elaborations by, e.g., Parsons [1999] or Bollas [1999] in Kohon, (1999). Fonagy (2008) has shown how attachment theory (known for its detailed observations of mother and infant together, and deductions from these about the later adult's mind), can be extended to a child's or adolescent's psychosexual development. To build a picture of the child's internal sexual attitudes, Fonagy focuses on how negative or positive affective messages are conveyed by the mother to the child over time.

One would think, with so much attention to maternal caretaking and its impact, that the child's reaction to the maternal body itself would not get lost. It does. However, surely, this body information must be imaginatively crucial to any girl's early identifications with her mother. *The child's reaction to the pregnant and corporeal maternal body remains slighted, in spite of the emphasis on the impact of maternal caretaking.*

Ego psychological female gender studies

The concept of "core gender identity" (Stoller, 1968) is controversial in the contemporary literature, which questions anything that suggests a primary or defined beginning state. Still, formulation of this concept represented a major step forward in the psychological recognition of sex and gender differences. Kleeman (1971), Tyson (1982), and the Tysons (1990), for example, use it. Gender role identity and sexual partner orientation are developmental additions to this basic building block. An unusual and highly original 1971 paper by Kleeman attends specifically to the way a 2–3-year-old girl compares herself to her pregnant mother—in addition to the male body—to help her sort out anatomical differences. This is the only such paper I have found in my search for details about females comparing bodies with females, and it enriches the concepts of body image development that would later be fitted into the guidelines suggested by the Tysons in the trajectory of gender role identity formation.

The literature before Kleeman's benchmark advance in the 1970s, and some of the literature after it, reflected more phallocentric confusions. For example, the concept of a "phallic-narcissistic phase" in normative female development puts linguistic emphasis on the male body, not the female, and betrays the underlying one-sex orientation to gender theory. A more accurate term might have been "female genital avoidance phase." Mayer (1985), looking for a way out of this dilemma, provided an arresting, fresh, and sensible perspective in her case of a little girl who thinks that her own genitals are the same as everyone else's. However, she did not go quite far enough. She also became tangled in some of the semantic confusions obfuscating the gender field. Mayer (1995) articulated *dual* normative developmental lines in women, one line emanating from "primary femininity" and one line involving "phallic" concerns. In her case study, she demonstrated how an impasse in an adult female's analysis occurred around the patient's phallic castration attitudes, a situation which yielded to forward movement only when the analyst began to take note of an underlying but repressed primary feminine constellation. Mayer offered that this analytic work suggested evidence of an interrupted line of development from the patient's core primary femininity, which had interwoven with her more evident phallic body concerns. Mayer's consideration stopped with genital comparison with males and the stage of anatomical distinction.

Grossman and Stewart (1976) did much to help an ego psychological shift away from phallocentric devotion in their work on the *symbolism* of penis envy as a developmental metaphor for women: in addition, they suggested that a concrete (as opposed to metaphorical) persistence of this concern in adulthood is pathological. Later literature, especially from the 1990s on, paints much freer portraits of the body's sex and gender alignments for both males and females. The questions that have been probed on behalf of females have now stimulated more questions about the male body too (Corbett, 2009; Diamond, 1991; Fogel, 2006; Moss, 2012 and others). There has been laudably close attention to recasting female genital anxieties that are anatomically accurate and whose description evolve from listening closely to women talk, e.g., importantly, Bernstein (1990) on a range of female bodily genital anxieties; Dahl (1996) on comparing early and mature body fantasies in females; Holtzman and Kulish (1996, 2000) in paying attention to the hymen, defloration, or righting the balance in their work on the feminized oedipal complex; or Breen (1993) on studying in the newly enlightened way, the "gender conundrum." Arnold Richards, as chief editor of *The Journal of the American Psychoanalytic Association*, in 1996 brought out a female development supplement of the journal that included many of the contemporary American writers on these topics. e.g., Stimmel (1996), Frenkel (1996). These, and many other clinician writers, have advanced markedly the recognition of gender identity formation in females. *Sexuality is usually emphasized in this sector of interest, or the impact of general identificatory mother—daughter relationships. These ingredients certainly help create the building blocks of gender. However, physically, they often lack recognition of a powerful procreative trajectory of development. It is as if sexuality, especially in light of post-1970 emancipation, needed to be kept away from the functions of baby making and delivery.*

The Kleinian and object relational traditions

Klein certainly viewed the mother's body as equally weighted with the father's in a child's development. She allowed girls to have a special interest in making babies. Phallus, vagina, breasts, parental intercourse, womb cavity, embryos, and pregnancy are of equal fascination. Attention to the detail of body surface, however, never drew Klein's interest, or that of any of her contemporary followers. Their theoretical focus uses drive theory and is more purely internally derived than Freud's, given their belief in a universal originary fantasy system that inevitably, in an instinctual fashion, imagines procreation. This contrasts with those analysts, such as Loewald, who think of early development as emerging from an archaic undifferentiatied ego struggling within its caretaking environment. I have often wondered how analysts' or therapists' experiences, before they are professionally trained in analysis, affect the way they see the human body. Mrs. Klein was a layperson, as it were; before she was analyzed and started her child practice, she was a daughter, a wife, and a mother who was deeply concerned about the vagaries of her own children, her troubles with her husband, and her uneasy life with her own mother (Grosskurth, 1995). How vastly different from Freud's perspective on females must hers have been—the anatomical and physiological detail of their bodies, as well as their emotional lives. Freud's background included years of chastity, of scholarly pursuit, of anatomical dissections, medical research, and work on general medical wards. He spent a year with Charcot's many presentations of female hysterics, all before becoming a husband and father and branching into the practice of his own, out of which he developed psychoanalysis. It is not surprising that Klein's experiences were intensely personal, emotional, and filled with her own fantasy. Freud's experiences were perhaps more experience-distant, more cerebral and intellectual, but more curious about the human body. Klein's followers in London, as with Anna Freud's, were not usually medically trained, although the later middle group of psychoanalysts were. Sigmund Freud's approach, despite his welcome and encouragement of lay analysts, was decidedly that of a medical doctor who had to loosen his symptomatological focus to join his patients in their imaginative flights. At first, the medical profession resisted his claims, and his followers of the first analytic generation were often from other fields. Nevertheless, as his reputation and respectability grew—especially in the United States in the years after the Second World War— his fellow physicians became fascinated with psychoanalysis and, in fact, claimed it as their own. In the United States, for many years, most psychoanalysts were medically trained.[6] Most of the important struggles to correct the original Freudian theory about females and their bodies has taken place in the United States, and involve those very schools that at one time contained mostly medical practitioners. Even as APsaA institutes and their teaching represent to some the entity to rebel against, the likelihood of seeing *the body* as a major site of struggle for a better theory for females was likely higher in a medicalized community. The chances of seeing *the mind* as *the* site of the struggle may have been more likely in institutes that were populated by psychologists, social workers, or academics. Hence, it may be easier for a psychologist or a philosopher to write and believe that gender is a way to "solve" a basic mental problem, and to minimize the body's role, whereas those with medical training may think more basically about body problems in the biology of sex and gender, hardwiring, and DNA, and be drawn secondarily to thinking about how the mind "solves" these problems. Nowadays, with the encouragement of integration of all members of the mental health professions and academics within most of our analytic institutes, I think we can afford to reflect this community integration. We can pay attention to the detail of the body's mental representations, and not just relegate it as denigrated as per Foucault with a heroic power struggle associated with "bad" medical practitioners. We can approach the body in the more enlightened nonmonolithic way that feminists have taught us, and with an additional close attention to culture that Erikson taught us.

The contemporary ego psychologists of the American independent tradition, (with whom I identify most) think of themselves as not confined to conflict theory, but as expanding object relational interests (influenced by Kernberg and Klein), and now also involving relational or intersubjective perspectives, to expanding ego concepts to accommodate these essential additions. For the female project, this can lead to highlighting the importance of the registration of emotional and individual *bodily* details, say, of mother–daughter interaction (see articles on this topic in *Psychoanalytic Inquiry*, 2004, 2006, edited by Balsam and Fisher); or of procreation (see articles on this topic in *Psychoanalytic Inquiry*, 2011, edited by Bornstein). Klein's acknowledgment of females' psychological equality to males, her theory's well-developed sense of aggression, the rich archaic unconscious phantasy systems she postulated, and her remarkable insights (and those of her contemporary followers) into the depths of the "paranoid position"[7] can be of great value in grasping the earliest possible mental interactions between a mother and her baby, especially when imagining the range of pathological possibilities. Gyler (2010), in fact, makes a case for Kleinian analysis as a superior way for a female's work on her own gender issues and socialization, just because of Klein's appreciation for aggression compared to the work of traditional feminist analysts. However, aggression, and not only the archaic kind, is actually an equally important contemporary awareness and emphasis in ego psychology (e.g., see Rizzuto, Meissner and Buie 2004; Hoffman, 1999; Gray, 1994; or Loewald, 1989). Aggression also features in many self-psychological, relational, and intersubjective writings, even if it is not the privileged organizing theme in their theoretical systems that it is in Klein's.

Postmodern influences

A new vitality of interest in gender and sexuality (in that order) in the United States can be attributed to the upsurge of postmodernism in the academy and its influence on psychoanalysis in North America in the 1980s, and also subsequently (for a scholarly overview, see Dimen and Goldner, 2005). Many complex issues of gender or sexuality have come up and have been elaborated in that context, and of course the biological body, however contestedly, has been and still is an aspect of most of them. They offer many important connections to my topic. Most of these issues, however, I will not address here. As things stand, I think we have a clearer picture of how varying identifications, etc., play a role in a gender portrait or we interest ourselves in the mind's processes to investigate gender— say the handling of aggression toward a father—than we do of how the sexually procreative body is integrated into that same gender constellation. The relational schools and practitioners of intersubjective psychology have contributed richness and variation to these case interactional and unconsciously interactional understandings. Less room is available in these schools to consider anything like a historical internal trajectory of the sexual procreative body. Thus, the portraits are patchy. In ego psychological theory also, there is little room. An overhaul of the understanding of the female body is necessary before the contemporary male understanding can be revised and accepted; and developmental issues about how female and male procreative potentials become integrated also would need to be studied. We all know that sexual partner choice is a topic of great interest to analysts, but a theory of how this is influenced and effected is not at all obvious, nor how it is or is not related to gender identity. We talk much more readily these days and with greater knowledge about an individual's capacities for "intimacy," "retreat," distance or closeness, or even capacities for "love" or "enactment" than we do (or can) about eroticism and choice of sexual partner. It was not always so. Early analysts had much more to say about these issues than we do. But then, I believe, their female psychology was exposed as so awry that the field lost its focus on these interesting sexual and procreative elements. A new cohesive and encompassing theory of sex and gender, I believe, is needed. I am not the person to tackle this. My role is to point to the overwhelming evidence that the female body qua female needs to be a focal point.

There are so very many topics I have not even touched in this book but that are intimately related to the body. I have not talked about lesbian females' pregnancies, and birthing; lesbian routes in developmental attitudes to the sexual body (such as in the case report by Marcus, 2004); queer attitudes to the sexed body (e.g., the paper by Marcus and McNamara which won the APsaA Roughton prize in 2011); pregnancy aspirations in males; attitudes of transsexual and transgendered individuals to their bodies and their procreative potentials. I have not talked as much about the contested issue of bisexuality as the topic warrants, nor spoken of bodies and assisted reproduction. I have essentially ignored menopausal bodes; bodies of color; well bodies and sick bodies; disabled bodies; disfigured bodies; anorexics and bulemics (e.g., Zerbe 1995) or barometric surgery; those who torture themselves or others; "abject." bodies (Kristeva, 1982); tattooing, body decoration, (e.g., Lemma, 2010) body artists, and compelled body manipulations such as in scarification or clitoridectomy; fashion or cosmetic surgery; and a host of other fascinating "body" topics. My interest is narrower here: I am mainly interested in listening for the body (e.g., Lieberman 2000) in its *female presence* and, importantly, listening also for its *absence*, advocating trying to understand more of the body's meaning to its individual owner. My focus has been on the clinical demonstration of a glaring across-the-board theoretical absence.

The relational and intersubjective schools of analysis have been especially (and excitedly) immersed in the tumultuous intellectual and cultural currents surrounding gender and sex. Thinking on these subjects was freed up as the traditional expectations that developed and then hardened during the postwar fifties broke down—such as the old insistence that a heterosexual family life with children (and with it, the oedipal situation) is a rigid "norm" and all other lifestyles are deviant. The European postmoderns' joy in decentering, deconstructing, and subverting was and remains infectious. It brought in, for psychoanalytic study, topics that had previously been sanitized, ordered, and controlled, such as the binaries and polarities of gender marked as either "masculine" or "feminine"; the topics relegated to the periphery such as homosexuality or race; and the way untraditional gender constructions manifest themselves in vivo. Freud founded psychoanalysis with a strong interest in science, history, mythology, anthropology, language, and literature, but postmodernism opened psychoanalysis more than he had to other epistemological systems of thought, such as feminist criticism, critical theory, linguistics, philosophy, the social sciences, and applied nonbiological sciences such as chaos theory. Challenges confronted topics in psychoanalytic practice and theory that in themselves are far from new[8]—such as the nature of change, the impact of the therapeutic interaction, authority in "doctor–patient" roles, and the special power of transference and counter-transference—but that could be explained afresh from a poststructuralist vantage point. New thinking and new voices were heard. They drew encouragement from their own new, nontraditional groups. Older thinkers previously marginalized in mainstream North American psychoanalysis were reintroduced—Bowlby, Ferenczi, Bion, Fairbairn, and Klein. Italian, French and South American analytic authors were newly read and increasingly invited to give their papers and lead study sessions in this country. By now, once-new schools—the self psychologists, relationists, intersubjectivists, and attachment/relational or complexity theorists—have developed their own traditions and expectations. Indeed, I would say they have developed their own authority bases and insistences. Psychoanalysis has been transformed into a pluralistic field, where the hegemony—if one exists—is that none *should* exist, and indeed that seems to be more the case than not.

The postmodern body

To the extent that a physical body is noted in postmodern terms, it is unrecognizable as a biological entity. This "virtual" body, seen from the postmodern, relational, or intersubjective perspective, is created this way on purpose. Part of Michel Foucault's philosophy—including doctors' claims to scientific objectivity and the establishment of norms, diagnoses, and behavioral categories—motivated to create dominance over others. To Foucault, the body of a patient seems only a site for control and coercion. For one thing then, this relational postmodern body can never assume one form for long enough to study. It is mobile, always changing, a chameleon-like form that keeps shifting according to what is wanted of it by outsiders, including the observer—who may already have preconditions established that would attempt to limit this purposefully elusive virtual body. This virtual body can assume the form of any other human therefore who is relating to it or observing it—whatever "observation" means in terms of who is looking at whom or what, and with whose purposes in mind. As Josh Cohen writes, in a *Times Literary Supplement* review[9] of *The Beast and the Sovereign Vol 1* by Jacques Derrida, "is such sonic play not merely confirmation of the frequently voiced suspicion that deconstruction is a gratuitous exercise in verbal sophistry?" (p. 9). It may be, but again it may not be. Reading the body (as well as the texts that are the main preoccupation of Derrida) means that "the stability of meaning is conditioned by a priori or "founding instability" (p. 9). What is the result, for psychoanalysis's view of sex and gender, of a commitment to a philosophy that so radically shifts the paradigms of the old positivist science? It challenges the objectivity of the observer, and forces us to examine our own biases more deeply. It creates novel openings to contemplate claims to knowledge. It liberates us by setting no limits on the imagination: in fact, it supports a soaring ambition of imagination, in which individual feats of vision can yield new insights about perceptions of the body and the body in social interaction. It encourages us to smash previous stereotypes and categories, and to look freshly at the body and find new ways to perceive it. It holds no past claims sacred—this can be helpful, but, at the same time, it sometimes implies that nothing already established can be of value. At that point, postmodernism approaches the limits of usefulness. New concepts such as "bodymind" or "embodiment" suggest earnest involvement with the physical body, and an attempt in new amalgamation to overcome a sexed polarity with which we all struggle. However, the end result can be a hodgepodge of thoughts that exceed the helpful tolerance of ambiguities at the same time that it supposedly mirrors the contents of our minds. The effort can go too far into a nihilistic virtual vision of body formlessness, and get too far out of touch with physical and physiological necessities. Especially, it can get seriously out of touch with functional anatomy.

I consider procreation and procreative fantasies emanating deeply and mean-ingfully from the individual's *sexed* body as a Darwinian element of species sur-vival, in consort with the individual's mind, and responded to by the mind's functional mode as in a "Rorschach" (Dimen, 2000: p. 10). Dimen offers an exam-ple of poststructural clinical theory, but does not in my opinion necessarily exclude the body's biological functioning. She is experientially highly appreciative of the life of the body and I can link up with her thinking in the phrases that acknowl-edge the corporeal body, for instance: "The body, if it is a fact, is also an idea" (p. 10); or "Psychic reality is as real as physical reality" (p. 10); or "Certainly physical bodies exist" (p. 2). I know that her point in the paper is to argue color-fully for a reading of the body considering psychic reality dominant (which the reader will have gathered, I certainly agree, but as especially relevant to *gender* considerations).

The postmodern influence can convey an overly abstract sense of body form-lessness toward infinity, envisioning a body that functions and exists entirely at the behest of the mind. An explicit effort has been made frequently to "unyoke body and desire from gender" (Davies, 2007).[10] I would argue that this kind of radical denial of the biological body just creates a new polarization—a revisita-tion of the old split between body and mind, where body once again is denigrated and forbidden to consciousness. That is a sinking ship, as we know, and despite the intentions of feminist postmodern literary critics to promote psychic freedom for women, the female body and its procreative capacities in the postmodern turmoil have been the first to leave it—but not for the lifeboats. They have been thrown overboard, "Women and children first!"

The late (often, but not always great) Chasseguet-Smirgel, in her last book *The Body as Mirror of the World* (2005), is bracing on this topic. She shares my sense of the modern missing body, but she is far, far more pessimistic than I am. With the full force of her European post-Holocaust sensibility, she apparently cannot believe that there has also been genuine liberation in this poststructuralist critical literary and philosophical movement—that it has helped us deconstruct the over-weening gendered power relations that have ruled theory-making, and that it has brought new light not only to the matter of transgender, but to the homosexualities and heterosexualities too (in the plural, Chodorow, 1994). Chasseguet-Smirgel takes on American deconstructionism and social constructionism with venom, forecasting a bleak outlook for a world in which generational and gendered boundaries will be destroyed in consequence of this social and academic urge to annihilate the structures. She forecasts that the freed omnipotence will assume its cruelly dominant and upper hand in a freed will to crush the submissive. Chasseguet-Smirgel is extreme, but if one agrees that the pregnant and birthing body is currently virtually erased in our literature, one needs, I guess, to consider deeply the sheer and breathtaking force of the desire that would deny its ongoing role in the psyche.

Conclusion

Perhaps now that psychoanalysis as a field has survived into the twenty-first century, and has been (at least in part) educated away from the reifying dictates of intellectual authoritarianism, the time has come when we can search the past for the body—the vanished but abiding body that endures over the years, surviving the ups and downs of culture, anxiety, and academic fashion. The body being common to all of us, I suggest that it is a good place to look for anchorage when we seem to drift too far into abstractions of the mind's work and lose touch with our animal and even libidinal and mortal selves. Valuable aspects of the past can be thrown away in the urge to go forward and create new ground (see also Stimmel, [2000], Bassin [2000], and Elise [2000] in discussion with Lynne Layton, [2000]). Judith Butler's (2004, etc., and many others by now) perceptions of the body as actually *created* by gender, rather than the other way around, delib-erately turns on its head the scientific epistemology of the body. Nevertheless, as with the body, science endures, flawed or biased as it may be. Darwin's sense of our evolution to preserve our species still rules. We all tend to acknowledge the front-burner importance of the concrete body as more than just an abstraction of the mind when we want to remold these bodies—be it in looking for a cure for illness, or a sexual transformation in transgender and sexual reassignment sur-gery. I hold that the sight of the hugely bulging belly of a pregnant woman is one of the biological wonders of our human world. It cannot be ignored, one would think. Except that it *can* apparently, as I outline, by sleight of mind. However, no matter what the mind creates, it seems evident that the body can and will still exist in all its intimate individuality and yet recognizably like other people's bodies in form, functionality, and mortality. Transcending the abstractions of contingency, paradox, and thirds, the biological body is still present. Vivona (2006) points out that "Loewald's metaphorical use of early development identifies and thus poten-tiates a central role for language in psychoanalytic treatment. By contrast, Stern and his colleagues exaggerate the abstract, orderly, and disembodied qualities of language, and consequently underestimate the degree to which lived interpersonal experience can be meaningfully verbalized" (p. 87). This surely captures an aspect of the contemporary drift we risk away from the earthy body and its evoked metaphoric language toward a virtual image—a "cyborg" (to borrow a usage from the feminist Donna Haraway's borrowed usage, 1991),[11] a creature state that becomes "disembodied" in its human affinitive propensities. Procreation and sex are "facts of life," just as we were taught when we were young. Make of them what we will, and use them or not as we choose, their potential exists nevertheless. Gender both "exists" (internally and with psychological meanings) and also does not "exist" (externally and in body morphology) as does role play. Perhaps that is where the conviction emerges that gender is a matter of performativity (Judith Butler, 1990). Body fantasy also does and does not "exist." Adrienne Harris calls gender a "necessary fiction." Perhaps the range of variable gendered expressions are docudramas in which elements of people's inner lives, including reactions to their own and others' bodies from early childhood and onward, are brought to life, appreciated, and given the chance to make an impact. Gender, Nancy Chodorow felicitously says, is "animated" (p. 2004) in the sense of coming to life. Life is not possible apart from the body. It is not possible to conceive of gender without somewhere considering the body one is born into and its encoded history. It has been my intention in this book to demonstrate the importance of the procreative components of the female body functioning as they exist and are perceived early in a girl's life, strongly informing the conscious and unconscious elements of the adult mind. Surprisingly, there has been no room for this influential and personally powerful physical narrative at the heart of our theories so far. Yet, the more we marginalize the female body itself, the farther we are from theoretically reclaiming this most powerful creatively sexed iconography of the female body.

Notes

1 This theoretical attitude being one of the vicissitudes of the "either/or" way of thinking about conflict that is so common in ego psychology, as opposed to a "both/and" way of thinking (e.g., Chodorow, 2003, 2011; Balsam, 2001; Kulish, 2006).
2 "Feminine" is one of the most confused concepts in psychoanalysis. Clarity about it is rare, as in Elise, 1997.
3 The journal was based in New Haven, Connecticut, with many associations to the Yale Child Study Center, and when formed in 1952, also The Western New England Institute for Psychoanalysis.
4 Personal communication from Samuel Ritvo, one of my senior colleagues at WNEIP and a supervisor during my candidacy. See also Baudry, 2009.
5 In 1966, Freitler and Kreitler did an Israeli study of Western and Oriental 4–6-year-old children's conception and birth theories that showed up Freud's and Piaget's inaccuracies. They reported that almost all, both males and females, noticed the connection between a baby and a bulging mother—so much for my apologia that the absence of mention of the maternal pregnancy in our psychoanalytic child analytic literature might have to do with the child not noticing! This study would point more toward the analyst discounting this information. The children mostly thought that their mother eating a lot and getting fat was the route to pregnancy. Strangely, though, while asking closely

about how babies are born—typical of my sad claim of widespread denial of the female body—these authors, when asking about how babies were made and got into the world, only gave the questioned children orifice options of "the pipi," "the bottom," the mouth, and the belly (to be cut open). The vagina or vulva were not mentioned once!

6 This history also, of course, was problematic, as in the challenge and necessity for a legal defense of lay analysts against accusations of "quackery," in the 1926 case of Theodore Reik, and later, the lawsuit for restraint of trade brought by psychologists against the American Psychoanalytic Association in the 1980s.

7 In ego psychological terms, various regressed states within a narcissistic or preoedipal register.

8 Few if any topics are "new" in psychoanalysis. That may be less because, as some claim, Freud was always, and gallingly, there first, so that we modern analysts must overcome his too powerful influence, because it is the nature of our field. What is "new" in psychoanalysis, one notices over time, is usually a different or extended slant upon familiar materials, heard in their infinite variety by individual analysts.

9 "Differences" by Josh Cohen in *The Times Literary Supplement*, 2 July 2010, No. 5596: p. 9–10.

10 The lecture for the 2007 Stephen Mitchell lecture in the Toronto Institute of Contemporary Analysis was given by Jody Davies, and the summary began: "Unyoking body and desire, this workshop emphasizes the endless complexity and infinite variability of our erotic selves. It reconceptualizes positive and negative oedipal configurations, not as specific phases of childhood sexual development, but as a life-long struggle to sustain erotic, romantic, sexual attachments. 'Self' is viewed as a kalei-doscope of ever-shifting self/other organizations."

   This is a good example of what I perceive of as a denial of the role of the body in these mature forms of gendered self.

11 Haraway D. (1991) "A cyborg is a cybernetic organism, a hybrid of machine and organ-ism, a creature of social reality as well as a creature of fiction. Social reality is lived social relations, our most important political construction, a world-changing fiction. ... This experience is a fiction and fact of the most crucial, political kind. ... *The cyborg is a matter of fiction and lived experience that changes what counts as women's experience in the late twentieth century. This is a struggle over life and death, but the boundary between science fiction and social reality is an optical illusion*" (italics mine, p. 149).

Bibliography

Abram, J. (1997) *The Language of Winnicott: A Dictionary and Guide to Understanding His Work*, Northvale, NJ: Jason Aronson.

Adelman, J. (1999) 'Making Defect Perfection: Shakespeare and the One-Sex Model', in V. Comensoli and A. Russell (eds.) *Enacting Gender on the English Renaissance Stage*, Urbana and Chicago: University of Illinois Press, pp. 23–53.

Akhtar, S. (2009) *Comprehensive Dictionary of Psychoanalysis*, London: Karnac.

Akhtar, S. and Kramer, S. (eds.) (1999) *Brothers and Sisters: Developmental, Dynamic and Technical Aspects of the Sibling Relationship*, North Bergen, NJ: Jason Aronson.

Alizade, M. (ed.) (2002) *The Embodied Female Part of the Committee on Women and Psychoanalysis (COWAP) Series of the I.P.A.*, London: Karnac.

Alizade, M. (2003) *Studies on Femininity (COWAP) Series of the I.P.A.*, London: Karnac.

Alizade, M. (2006) *Motherhood in the Twenty-first Century (COWAP) Series of the I.P.A.*, London: Karnac.

Andahazi, F. (1998/1999) *The Anatomist: A Novel*, New York, Toronto: Anchor Books: A division of Random House Inc.

Anderson, F. (ed.) (2008) *Bodies in Treatment: The Unspoken Dimension, Relational Perspectives Book Series Vol 36*, New York, London: The Analytic Press.

Appignanesi, L. and Forrester, J. (1992) *Freud's Women*, London: Weidenfeld and Nicolson.

Aron, L. and Anderson, F. (1998) *Relational Perspectives on the Body*, Hillsdale, NJ: The Analytic Press.

Arlow, J.A. (1961) 'Silence and the Theory of Technique', *J. Amer. Psychoanal. Assn.* 9:44–55.

Balsam, A. and Balsam, R. (1974/1984) 'The Pregnant Therapist', in *Becoming a Psychotherapist: A Clinical Primer*, 2nd edn, Chicago: University of Chicago Press.

Balsam, R. (1994) 'Rational and Irrational: Remarks on the Clinical Gendering of Language in Psychoanalysis', *Psychoanal. Study of the Child* 49:145–159.

Balsam, R. (1996) 'The Pregnant Mother and the Body Image of the Daughter', *J. Amer. Psychoanal. Assn.* 44(suppl):401–427.

Balsam, R. (2000) 'The Mother Within the Mother', *Psychoanal. Q.* 69(3):465–493.

Balsam, R. (2001) 'Integrating Male and Female Elements in a Woman's Gender Identity', *J. Amer. Psychoanal. Assn.* 49(4):1335–1360.

Balsam, R. (2003) 'The Vanished Pregnant Body in Psychoanalytic Developmental Theory', *J. Amer. Psychoanal. Assn.* 51(4):1153–1179.

Balsam, R. (2003) 'Women of the Wednesday Society: The Presentations of Drs. Hilferding, Spielrein, and Hug-Hellmuth', *Imago*. 60(3):303–342.

Balsam, R. (2008) 'Women Showing Off: Notes on Female Exhibitionism', *J. Am. Psychoanal. Assn.* 56:99–121.

Balsam, R. (2009) 'Sexuality and Shame', *J. Amer. Psychoanal. Assn.* 57:723–739.

Balsam, R.H. (1996) 'The Pregnant Mother and the Body Image of the Daughter', *J. Am. Psychoanal. Assn.* 44S:401–427.

Balsam, R.H. (1999) 'Sisters and their Disappointing Brothers', Chapter 4 in S. Akthar and S. Kramer (eds.) *Brothers and Sisters: Developmental, Dynamic, and Technical Aspects of the Sibling Relationship, Margaret S. Mahler Symposium on Child Development Series*, Northvale, New Jersey & London: Jason Aronson Inc.

Balsam, R.H. (2001) 'Integrating Male and Female Elements in a Woman's Gender Identity', *J Am Psychoanal Assoc* 2001 49: 1335–1360 DOI: 10.1177/00030651010 490040401 http://www.sagepublications.com

Balsam, R.H. (2003) 'The Vanished Pregnant Body in Female Developmental Theory', *J Am Psychoanal Assoc* 2003 51: 1153–1179 DOI: 10.1177/00030651030510040201 http://www.sagepublications.com

Balsam, R.H. (2005) 'Loving and Hating Mothers and Daughters: Thoughts on the Role of Their Physicality', Chapter 2 in Sheila Feig Brown (ed.) *What Do Mothers Want?* The Analytic Press.

Balsam, R.H. (2008) 'Fathers and the Bodily Care of their Infant Daughters', *Psychoanalytic Inquiry* 28:1–16.

Balsam, R.H. (2008) 'Women Showing Off: Notes on Female Exhibitionism', *J. Amer. Psychoanal. Assn.* 56: 99–121, DOI: 10.1177/0003065108315686; http://www.sage-publications.com

Basseches, H., Ellman, P., Elmdorf, S., Fritsch, E., Goodman, N., Helm, F., and Rockwell, S. (1996) 'Hearing What Cannot be Seen: A Psychoanalytic Research Group's Inquiry into Female Sexuality', *J. Amer. Psychoanal. Assn.* 44(suppl.): 511–528.

Bassin, D. (1996) 'Beyond the He and She: Toward the Reconciliation of Masculinity and Femininity in the Postoedipal Female Mind', *J. Amer. Psychoanal. Assn.* 44(suppl.): 157–190.

Baudry, F. (2009) 'Winnicott's 1968 Visit to the New York Psychoanalytic Society and Institute: A Contextual View', *Psychoanal. Q.* 78(4):1059–90.

Bell, R. (1999) *How to Do It: Guides to Good Living for Renaissance Italians*, Chicago and London: University of Chicago Press.

Bem, S. (1993) *The Lenses of Gender: Transforming the Debate on Sexual Inequality*, New Haven, London: Yale University Press.

Benedek, T. (1970) 'The Psychology of Pregnancy', in E.J. Anthony and T. Benedek (eds.) *Parenthood, Its Psychology and Psychopathology*, Boston: Little Brown.

Benjamin, J. (1988) *The Bonds of Love: Psychoanalysis, Feminism, and the Problem of Domination*, New York: Pantheon.

Benjamin, J. (1998) *Like Subjects, Love Objects: Essays on Recognition, Identification and Difference*, New Haven: Yale University Press.

Bergler, E. (1959/1969) 'Psychoprophylaxis of Postpartum Depression', in *Selected Papers of Edmund Bergler M.D. 1933–1961*, New York and London: Grune and Stratton.

Bernstein, D. (1990) 'Female Genital Anxieties, Conflicts, and Typical Mastery Modes', *Int. J. Psychoanal.* 71:151–165.

Bibring, G. et al. (1961) 'A Study of the Psychological Processes in Pregnancy and of the earliest Mother–Child Relationship', *Psychoanal. Study Child* 16:9–72.

Bibring, G. and Valenstein, A. (1976) 'Psychological Aspects of Pregnancy', *Clin. Ob. Gyn.* 19:357–371.

Birksted-Breen, D. (1986) 'The Experience of having a Baby: a Developmental View', *Free Associations* 4:22–35.

Birksted-Breen, D. (1996) 'Phallus, Penis and Mental Space', *Int. J. Psycho-Analysis* 77:649–657.

Bloom, H. (1973/1997) *The Anxiety of Influence: A Theory of Poetry*, US: Oxford University Press, 1997.

Blum, H.P. (1976) 'Masochism, the Ego Ideal, and the Psychology of Women', *J. Amer. Psychoanal. Assn.* 24S:157–191.

Blum, H.P. (1981) 'The Maternal Ego Ideal and the Regulation of Maternal Qualities', in S. Greenspan and G. Pollock (eds.) *The Course of Life: Psychoanalytic Contributions toward Understanding Personality Development, Adulthood and the Aging Process, vol. 3*, Adelphi, MD: U.S. Department of Health and Human Services, NIMH, pp. 99–114.

Boesky, D. (2008) *Psychoanalytic Disagreements in Context*, Latham Boulder, New York: Toronto Plymouth UK, Jason Aronson.

Bordo, S. (1993/1999) 'Feminism, Foucault, and the Politics of the Body', in M. Shildrick and J. Price (eds.) *Feminist Theory and the Body: A Reader*, New York: Routledge, pp. 246–258.

Bornstein, M. (2011) Epilogue. Psychoanal. Inq., 31:434.

Bouchara, C., Mazet, P., and Cohen, D. (2010) 'Jean Martin Charcot 1825–1893: Did he anticipate Freud's First Typology?', *Amer J. Psychiatry* 167:387.

Breen, D. (ed.) (1993/2002) *The Gender Conundrum: Contemporary psychoanalytic perspectives on Femininity and Masculinity, The New Library of Psychoanalysis*, East Sussex, New York: Brunner-Routledge.

Brunswick, R.M. (1940) 'The Preoedipal Phase of the Libido Development', *Psychoanal. Q.* 9:293–319.

Burnett, F. and Hodgson, F. (1886) *Little Lord Fauntleroy*, St. Nicholas Magazine.

Burton, A. (1996) 'The Meaning of Perineal Activity to Women: An Inner Sphinx', *J. Amer. Psychoanal. Assn.* 44(suppl.):241–260.

Butler, J. (1990) *Gender Trouble: Feminism and the Subversion of Identity*, New York: Routledge.

Butler, J. (1993/1999) 'Bodies that Matter', in M. Shildrick and J. Price (eds.) *Feminist Theory and the Body: A Reader*, New York: Routledge, pp. 235–246.

Caton, D. (1999) *What a Blessing She Had Chloroform: The Medical and Social Response to the Pain of Childbirth from 1800 to the Present*, New Haven, London: Yale University Press.

Carter, C.S. and Ahnert, L. (2005) *Attachment and Bonding: A New Synthesis*, Cambridge, MA: MIT Press.

Chasseguet-Smirgel, J. (2005) *The Body as Mirror of the World*, trns. S. Leighton, Free Association Books.

Chehrazi, S. (1986) 'Female Psychology: a Review', *J. Amer. Psychoanal. Assn.* 34: 141–162.

Chodorow, N. (1978) *The Reproduction of Mothering: Psychoanalysis and the Sociology of Gender*, Berkeley CA: University of California Press.

Chodorow, N. (1987) 'Feminism and Difference: Gender, Relation, and Difference in Psychoanalytic Perspective', in Mary Roth Walsh (ed.) *The Psychology of Women; Ongoing Debates*, pp. 249–264.

Chodorow, N. (1989) *Feminism and Psychoanalytic Theory*, New Haven. London: Yale University Press.

Chodorow, N. (1994) *Femininities, Masculinities, Sexualities: Freud and Beyond*, Kentucky: University Press.

Chodorow, N. (1999) *The Power of Feelings: Personal Meaning in Psychoanalysis, Gender, and Culture*, New Haven, London: Yale University Press.

Chodorow, N. (2003) 'From behind the Couch: Uncertainty and Indeterminacy in Psychoanalytic Theory and Practice', *Common Knowledge* 9(3):463–487.

Chodorow, N. (2010) 'Beyond the Dyad: Individual Psychology, Social World', *J. Amer. Psychoanal. Assn.* 58:207–230.

Chodorow, N. (2011) *Individualizing Gender and Sexuality: Theory and Practice (The Relational Book Series: 53)*, New York: Routledge.

Chused, J.F. (1986) 'Consequences of Paternal Nurturing', *Psychoanal. St. Child* 41: 419–438.

Chused, J.F. (2007) 'Little Hans "Analyzed" in the Twenty First Century', *J. Amer. Psychoanal. Assn.* 55(4):767–778.

Corbett, K. (2009) *Boyhoods: Rethinking Masculinities*, New Haven. London: Yale University Press.

Dahl, K. (1996) 'The Concept of Penis Envy Revisited: A Child Analyst Listens to Adult Women', *Psychoanal. St. Child.* 51:303–325.

Dahl, K. (2002) 'In Her Mother's Voice: Reflections on "Femininity" and the Superego', *Psychoanal. St. Child* 57:3–23.

Danto, E. (1999) 'The Berlin Poliklinik: Psychoanalytic Innovation in Weimar Germany', *J. Amer. Psychoanal. Assn.* 47(4):1269–1292.

Davis, N.Z. and Farge, A. (eds.) (1993) *A History of Women in the West v.III Renaissance and Enlightenment Paradoxes*, Cambridge, Mass: Harvard University Press.

De Beauvoir, S. (1989/1953/1949) *The Second Sex*, trans. H. M. Parshley, New York: Vintage Books, A Division of Random House.

Deutsch, H. (1944/1945) *The Psychology of Women: A Psychoanalytic Interpretation. Vols. I and II.*, New York: Grune & Stratton Inc.

Diamond, M. (1991) *Manhood in the Making: Cultural Concepts of Masculinity*, New Haven, London: Yale University Press.

Didi-Huberman, G. (1882/2003) *Invention of Hysteria: Charcot and the Photographic Iconography of the Saltpetriere*, trans. Alisa Hartz, Cambridge Mass, London: The MIT Press.

Dimen, M. (1991) 'Deconstructing Difference: Gender, Splitting, and Transitional Space', *Psychoanal. Dial.* 1(3):335–352.

Dimen, M. (1999) 'From Breakdown to Breakthrough', in D. Bassin (ed.) *Female Sexuality*, New York: Jason Aronson.

Dimen, M. (2000) 'The Body as Rorschach', *Studies in Gender and Sexuality* 1:19–41.

Dimen, M. (2003) *Sexuality, Intimacy, Power*, Hillsdale, NJ: Analytic Press.

Dimen, M. (2005) 'Sexuality and Suffering, or the Eew! Factor', *Studies in Gender and Sexuality* 6:1–18.

Dimen, M. and Goldner, V. (eds.) (2002) *Gender in Psychoanalytic Space*, New York: Other Press.

Dimen, M. and Goldner, V. (2005) 'Gender and Sexuality', Chapter 6 in E. Person, A. Cooper, G. Gabbard, (eds.) *Textbook of Psychoanalysis*, Washington DC, London: American Psychiatric Publishing Co. Inc., pp. 93–11.

Dimen, M. and Harris, A. (2001) *Storms in her Head: Freud and the Construction of Hysteria*, New York: Other Press.

Dorsey, D. (1996) 'Castration Anxiety or Feminine Genital Anxiety?', *J. Amer. Psychoanal. Assn.* 44(suppl.):283–303.

Elise, D. (1988) 'The Absence of the Paternal Penis', *J. Amer. Psychoanal. Assn.* 46: 413–442.

Elise, D. (1997) 'Primary Femininity, Bisexuality, and the Female Ego Ideal: A Re-examination of Female Developmental Theory', *Psychoanal. Q.* 66:489–517.

Elise, D. (1998) 'Gender Repertoire: Body, Mind, and Bisexuality', *Psychoanal. Dial.* 8:353–371.

Elise, D. (2000) ' "Bye-Bye" to Bisexuality?: Response to Lynne Layton', *Studies in Gender and Sexuality.* 1:61–68.

Elise, D. (2006) Personal Communication.

Elms, A. (2001) 'Aprocryphal Freud: Sigmund Freud's Most Famous "Quotations" and Their Actual Sources', *Ann. Psychoanal.* 29:83–104.

Erikson, E. (1963/1968) 'Womanhood and the Inner Space', in *Identity: Youth and Crisis*, New York: Norton.

Fast, I. (1984) *Gender Identity: A Differentiation Model, Advances in Psychoanalysis, Theory, Research and Practice, Vol 2*, Hillsdale, NJ: The Analytic Press.

Fast, I. (1999) 'Aspects of Core Gender Identity', *Psychoanal. Dial.* 9:633–661.

Flax, J. (1990) *Thinking Fragments: Psychoanalysis, Feminism, and Postmodernism in the Contemporary West*, Berkeley: University of California Press.

Fliegel, Z. (1973) 'Feminine Psychosexual Development in Freudian Theory—A Historical Reconstruction', *Psychoanal. Q.* 42:385–408.

Fogel, G. (2006) 'Riddles of Masculinity: Gender, Bisexuality and Thirdness', *J. Amer. Psychanal. Assn.* 54:1139–1163.

Fonagy, P. (2008) 'A Genuinely Developmental Theory of Sexual Enjoyment and its Implications for Psychoanalytic Technique', *J. Amer. Psychoanal. Assn.* 56:11–36.

Frankiel, R. (1992) 'Analyzed and Unanalyzed Themes in the Treatment of Little Hans', *Int. Rev. Psycho-Anal.* 19:323–333.

Frenkel, R. (1996) 'A Reconsideration of Object Choice in Women: Phallus or Fallacy', *J. Amer. Psychoanal. Assn.* 44(suppl):133–157.

Freud, S. (1905) 'Three essays on the Theory of Sexuality', *Standard Edition* 7:135–149.

Freud, S. (1909) 'Analysis of a Phobia in a Five-Year Old Boy', *Standard Edition* 10:3–149.

Freud, S. (1914) 'On Narcissism: An Introduction', *Standard Edition* 14:7–102.

Freud, S. (1915) 'On the Universal Tendency to Debasement in the Sphere of Love in Contributions to the Psychology of Love', *Standard Edition* 11:179–190.

Freud, S. (1917) 'A Childhood Recollection From *Dichtung Und Wahreit*', *Standard Edition* 17:145–157.

Freud, S. (1917/1918) 'The Taboo of Virginity (Contributions to the Psychology of Love III)', *Standard Edition* 11:192–208.

Freud, S. (1920) 'The Psychogenesis of a Case of Homosexuality in a Woman', *Standard Edition* 18:147–172.

Freud, S. (1923) 'The Ego and the Id', *Standard Edition* 19:3–66.

Freud, S. (1924) 'Remembering, Repeating and Working Through (Further Recommendations on the Technique of Psycho-Analysis II)', *Standard Edition* 12:147–156.

Freud, S. (1930) 'Civilization and its Discontents', *Standard Edition* 21:57–145.

Freud, S. (1931) 'Female Sexuality', *Standard Edition* 21:223–245.

Freud, S. (1933) 'Femininity New Introductory Lectures', *Standard Edition* 22: 112–135.

Freud, S. (1939) 'Moses and Monotheism: Three Essays Standard Edition', *Standard Edition* 23:7–137.

Galatzer-Levy, R. (2009) 'Finding Your Way Through Chaos, Fractals, and Other Exotic Mathematical Objects: a Guide for the Perplexed', *J. Amer. Psychoanal. Assn.* 57: 1227–1249.

Gay, P. (1988) *Freud: A Life for our Time*, New York, London: W. W. Norton & Co.

Gentile, K. (2007) *Eating Disorders as Self Destructive Survival*, Mahwah, NJ, London: The Analytic Press.

Gilmore, K. (1998) 'Cloacal Anxiety in Female Development', *J. Amer. Psychoanal. Assn.* 46:443–470.

Glick, R. and Meyers, D. (1993) *Masochism: Current Psychoanalytic Perspectives*, Mahwah, NJ, London: The Analytic Press.

Goldberger, M. (1999) 'Obsolete Terminology Constricts Imaginative Thinking', *Psychoanal. Q.* 68:462–469.

Goldberger, M. and Evans, D. (1985) 'On Transference Manifestations in Patients with Female Analysts', *Int. J. Psychoanal.* 66:295–309.

Greenacre, P. (1950) 'Special Problems of Early Female Development', *Psychoanal. St. Child* 5:122–138.

Grosskurth, P. (1995) *Melanie Klein: her world and her work*, Northvale, NJ: J. Aronson.

Grossman, W.I. and Stewart, W.A. (1976) 'Penis Envy: From Childhood Wish to Developmental Metaphor', *J. Amer. Psychoanal. Assn.* 24S:193–212.

Goldner, V. (2000) 'Reading and Writing, Talking and Listening', *Studies in Gender and Sexuality* 1(1):1–9.

Gray, P. (1994) *The Ego and Analysis of Defense*, Jason Aronson Inc.

Gyler, L. (2010) *The Gendered Unconscious: Can Gendered Discourses Subvert Psychoanalysis? (Women and Psychology)*, London: Routledge.

Hagglund, T.B. and Piha, H. (1980) 'The Inner Space of the Body Image', *Psychoanal. Q.* 49(2):256–283.

Hall, C. (2006, unpublished) 'First Time Mothers' Experiences of Childbirth: Perspectives on Psychological Responses to Their Bodies', Washington DC: Doctoral Dissertation, Clinical Social Work Institute.

Hall, C. (2007) 'Poster Summaries II. Human Development: Intersections with Psychoanalytic perspective: Exploration of Women's Body Experiences Surrounding First Childbirth', *J. Amer. Psychoanal. Assn.* 55:275–279.

Hanly, C. and Hanly, M.A. (2001) Critical Realism: Distinguishing the Psychological Subjectivity of the Analyst from Epistemological Subjectivism, *Amer. Psychoanal. Assn.* 49:515–532.

Haraway, D. (1991) 'A Cyborg Manifesto: Science, Technology, and Socialist-Feminism in the Late Twentieth Century', in *Simians, Cyborgs and Women: The Reinvention of Nature*, New York: Routledge, pp. 149–181.

Harris, A. (2000) 'Gender as a Soft Assembly: Tomboys' Stories', *Studies in Gender and Sexuality* 1:223–250.

Harris, A. (2005) *Gender as Soft Assembly*, Hillsdale, NJ, London: The Analytic Press.

Hoffman, A. (2009) 'Archival Bodies', *American Imago*. 66(1):5–40.

Hoffman, L. (1999) 'Passions in Girls and Women: Toward a Bridge between Critical Relational Theory of Gender and Modern Conflict Theory', *J. Amer. Psychoanal. Assn.* 47:1145–1168.

Holtzman, D. and Kulish, N. (1996) 'Nevermore: The *Hymen* and the Loss of Virginity', *J. Amer. Psychoanal. Assn.* 44S:303–332.

Holtzman, D. and Kulish, N. (2000) 'Femininization of the Female Oedipal Complex, Part I: A Reconsideration of the Significance of Separation Issues', *J. Amer. Psychoanal. Assn.* 48(4):1413–1437.

Horney, K. (1924) 'On the Genesis of the Castration Complex in Women', *Int. J. Psychoanalysis* 5:50–65.

Horney, K. (1926) 'The Flight from Womanhood: the Masculinity Complex in Women as Viewed by Men and Women', *Int. J. Psychoanalysis* 7:324–339.

Horney, K. (1933) 'The Denial of the Vagina: A Contribution to the Problem of Genital Anxieties Specific to Women', *Int. J. Psychoanalysis* 14:57–70.

Irigiray, L. (1977/1985) *This Sex Which is not One*, trans. Catherine Porter, Ithaca: Cornell University Press.

Jacobson, E. (1959) 'The "Exceptions" An Elaboration of Freud's Character Study', *Psychoanal. St. Child.* 14:135–155.

Jaffe, D. (1968) 'The Masculine Envy of the Woman's Procreative Function', *J. Amer. Psychoanal. Assn.* 16:521–548.

Jones, E. (1927) 'The Early Development of Female Sexuality', in R. Grigg, D. Hecq, and C. Smith (eds.) *Female Sexuality: The Early Psychoanalytic Controversies*, London: Rebus Press.

Jones, E. (1955) *Sigmund Freud: Life and Work Vol. 2 1901–1919: Years of Maturity*, New York: Basic Books.

Jordan, J.F. (1990) 'Inner Space and the Interior of the Maternal Body: Unfolding in the Psychoanalytic Process', *Intl. Rev. Psychoanal.* 17(4):433–444.

Khar, B. (1996) *Donald Winnicott; A Biographical Portrait*, London: Karnac Books.

Kaplan, L. (1991) *Female Perversions*, New York: Doubleday.

Kemp, M. and Wallace, M. (2000) *Spectacular Bodies: The Art and Science of the Human Body from Leonardo to Now*, London: Hayward Gallery and Berkeley, Los Angeles, London: University of California Press.

Kernberg, O. (1998) *Love Relations: Normal and Pathological*, New Haven. London: Yale University Press.

Kestenberg, J. (1982) 'The Inner Genital Phase: Prephallic and Preoedipal', in D. Mendell (ed.) *Early Female Development*, New York: S. P. Medical and Scientific Books.

King, P. and Steiner, R. (1990) *The Freud/Klein Controversies in the British Psycho-Analytical Society. 1941–1945 (Section 1–5) The New Library of Psa. no11*, London: The Institute of Psychoanalysis and Routledge.

Klapisch-Zuber, C. (ed.) (1992) *A History of Women: Silence of the Middle Ages*, Cambridge, Mass: Harvard University Press.

Kleeman, J. (1971) 'The Establishment of Core Gender Identity in Normal Girls. 2. How Meanings are Conveyed Between Parent and Child in the First Three Years', *Archives of Sexual Behavior* 1(2):117–129.

Kleeman, J. (1971) 'The Establishment of Core Gender Identity in Normal Girls', *Archives of Sexual Behavior* 1:103–129.

Klein, M. (1928) 'Early Stages of the Oedipus Conflict', in *Love, Guilt and Reparation and Other Works: The Writings of Melanie Klein, Vol. 1*, London: Hogarth Press, 1975.

Kodera, S. (2010) *Disreputable Bodies: Magic, Medicine and Gender in Renaissance natural Philosophy*, Toronto: Center for Reformation and Renaissance Studies.

Kohon, G. (ed.) (1999/2005) *The Dead Mother: The Work of Andre Green (The New Library of Psychoanalysis)*, Brunner-Routledge an imprint of the Taylor and Francis Group.

Kristeva, J. (1995) 'Woman's Time', in trans. Ross Guberman, *New Maladies of the Soul*, New York: Columbia University Press.

Kuba, S. (2011) *The Role of Sisters in Women's Development*, Oxford University Press.

Kulish, N. (1991) 'The Mental Representation of the Clitoris: The Fear of Female Sexuality', *Psychoanal. Inq.* 11:511–536.

Kulish, N. (2000) 'Primary Femininity: Clinical Advances and Theoretical Ambiguities', *J. Amer. Psychoanal. Assn.* 48:1355–1379.

Kulish, N. (2006) 'Frida Kahlo and Object Choice: A Daughter the Rest of Her Life', *Psychoanal. Inq.* 26:7–31.

Kulish, N. (2010) 'Clinical Implications of Contemporary Gender Theory', *J. Amer. Psychoanal. Assn.* 58:231–258.

Kulish, N. and Holtzman, D. (2002) 'Baubo: rediscovering woman's pleasures', in A.M. Alizade (ed.) *The Embodied Female*, London: Karnac, pp. 109–119.

Lacan, J. (1982) *Feminine Sexuality*, Juliet Mitchell and Jacqueline Rose (eds.) trans. Jacqueline Rose, New York, London: W.W. Norton and Co.; New York, Pantheon Books.

Langer, M. (1951/1992) *Motherhood and Sexuality, Translation, Introduction and Afterword by Nancy C. Hollander*, New York, London: The Guilford Press.

Laqueur, T. (1990) *Making Sex; Body and Gender from the Greeks to Freud*, Cambridge: Harvard University Press.

Lax, R. (1969) 'Some Considerations about Transference and Counter Transference Manifestations Evoked by the Analyst's Pregnancy', *Int. J. Psycho-Anal.* 50:363–371.

Lax, R. (1997) *Becoming and Being a Woman*, Northvale, NJ: Jason Aronson.

Layton, L.B. (2000) 'The Psychopolitics of Bisexuality', *Studies in Gender and Sexuality*, 1:41–60.

Lemma, A. (2010) *Under the Skin: A Psychoanalytic Study of Body Modification*, New York, London: Routledge.

Lerner, H. (1976) 'Parental Mislabeling of Female Genitals as a Determinant of Penis Envy and Learning Inhibitions in Women', *J. Amer. Psychoanal. Assn.* 24(suppl.): 269–283.

Lewes, K. (1977) *Psychoanalysis and Male Homosexuality*, *(The Masterwork)*, Jason Aronson. New York: Simon and Shuster.

Lichtenberg, J. (2008) *Sensuality and Sexuality Across the Divide of Shame, Psychoanalytic Inquiry Book Series*, New York: Routledge.

Lieberman, J. (2000) *Body Talk: Looking and being Looked at in Psychotherapy*, Northvale, NJ: Jason Aronson.

Loewald, H.W. (1951) 'Ego and Reality', *Int. J. Psycho-Anal.* 32:10–18.

Loewald, H.W. (1960) 'On the Therapeutic Action of Psycho-Analysis', *Int. J. Psychoanal.* 41:16–33.

Loewald, H.W. (1989) *Papers on Psychoanalysis*, New Haven, London: Yale University Press.

Long, K. (2005) 'The Changing Language of Female Development Panel Report', *J. Amer. Psychoanal. Assn.* 53(4):1161–1174.

Mahler, M., Pine, F., and Bergman, A. (1975) *The Psychological Birth of the Human Infant: Symbiosis and Individuation*, New York: Basic Books.

Mahony, P. (1983) 'Women's Discourse and Literature—The Question of Nature and Culture', *Contemporary Psychoanalysis* 19:444–459.

Mahony, P. (1989) 'Aspects of Nonperverse Scopophilia within Analysis', *J. Amer. Psychoanal. Assn.* 37(2):365–399.

Marcus, B. (2004) 'Female Passion and the Matrix of Mother, Daughter, and Body: Vicissitudes of the Maternal Transference in the Working Through of Sexual Inhibitions', *Psychoanalytic Inquiry* 24(5):680–712.

Marcus, B. and McNamara, S. (2011) 'Strange and Otherwise Unaccountable Actions: Category, Conundrum, and Transgender Identities', presented at Winter Meetings of American Psychoanalytic Association, New York City.

Matthews, S. and Wexler, L. (2000) *Pregnant Pictures*, New York and London: Routledge, the Taylor & Francis Group.

Mayer, E. (1985) ' 'Everybody Must be Just Like Me': Observations on Female Castration Anxiety', *Int. J. Psycho-Anal.* 66:331.

Mayer, E. (1995) 'The Phallic Castration Complex and Primary Femininity: Paired Developmental Lines Toward Female Gender Identity', *J. Amer. Psychoanal. Assn.* 43:17–38.

McDougall, J. (1989) *Theaters of the Body: A Psychoanalytic Approach to Psychosomatic Illness*, New York, London: W.W. Norton and Company.

Mijolla, A. (ed.) (2005) *International Dictionary of Psychoanalysis, Vol.1 Macmillan Reference USA Detroit*, New York, London, Munich: Thomson Gale.

Millett, K. (1969/2000) *Sexual Politics*, Urbana and Chicago: University of Illinois Press.

Miner, V. and Longino, H. (1987) *Competition: A Feminist Taboo?* City University of New York: The Feminist Press.

Mitchell, J. (1974/2000) *Psychoanalysis and Feminism: A Radical Reassessment of Freudian Psychoanalysis*, New York: Basic Books, a member of the Perseus Book groups.

Mitchell, J. (2001) *Mad Men and Medusas*, London: Basic Books.

Mitchell, J. (2003) *Siblings: Sex and Violence*, Cambridge: Polity Press.

Mitchell, S. (1996) 'Gender and sexual orientation in the age of postmodernism: The Plight of the Perplexed Clinician', *Gender and Psychoanalysis* 1:45–73.

Moi, T. (2005) *Sex, Gender, and the Body: The Student Edition of What is a Woman?* Oxford: Oxford University Press.

Moss, D. (2012) *Thirteen Ways of Looking at a Man: Psychoanalysis and Masculinity*, Routledge.

Nadelson, C. et al. (1974) 'The Pregnant Therapist', *Amer. J. Psychiat.* 131:1107–1111.

Newton, P. (1995) *Freud: From Youthful Dream to Mid-Life Crisis*, New York and London: The Guilford Press.

Notman, M. and Nadelson, C. (1991) Women and Men: New perspectives on Gender Differences, American Psychiatric Pub.

Notman, M. (1996) 'Some Observations on the Female Body Image', Presentation at the Scientific Meeting of the Western New England Society for Psa.

Notman, M. (2010) 'Personal Communication: APsaA COPE Study Group', report on The Female Body: Integration of Psychoanalysis and Biological Concepts.

Novick, J. and Novick, K. (2007) *Fearful Symmetry: The Development and Treatment of Sadomasochism (Critical Issues in Psychoanalysis)*, Jason Aronson Inc.

Nuland, S. (2000) *Leonardo da Vinci, A Penguin Life*, A Lipper/Viking Book, Penguin Group.

Nunberg, H. and Federn, E. (1963) *Minutes of the Vienna Psychoanalytical Society Vol. III 1910–1911*, New York: International Universities Press.

O'Driscoll, D. (2008) *Stepping Stones: Interviews with Seamus Heaney*, New York: Farrar, Straus and Giroux.

Olesker, W. (1998) 'Female Genital Anxieties: Views from the Nursery and the Couch', *Psychoanalytic Quarterly* 67:276–294.

Pajaczkowska, C. and Ward, I. (2008) *Shame and Sexuality: Psychoanalysis and Visual Culture*, London: Routledge.

Parens, H. (1990) 'On the Girl's Psychosexual Development: Reconsiderations Suggested from Direct Observation', *J. Amer. Psychoanal. Assn.* 38:743–772.

Parens, H. (2004) 'What is the Father to the Child? Concluding Reflections', in S. Akhtar and H. Parens (eds.) *Real and Imaginary Fathers: Development, Transference and Healing*, Lanham, Boulder, New York, Toronto, Oxford: Jason Aronson, pp. 143–167.

Person, E. (1999) *The Sexual Century*, New Haven, London: Yale University Press.

Peto, A. (1959) 'Body Image and Archaic Thinking', *Intl. J. Psycho-anal.* XL:223–231.

Pine, F. (2004) 'Mahler's concepts of "symbiosis" and separation-individuation: Revisited, reevaluated, refined', *J. Amer. Psychoanal. Assn.* 52:511–533.

Pines, D. (1993) *A Woman's Unconscious Use of Her Body*, New Haven, London: Yale University Press.

Pruett, K. (1983) 'Infants of Primary Nurturing Fathers', *Psychoanal. St. Child.* 38:257–281.

Pruett, K. (1985) 'Oedipal Configurations in Young Father-raised Children', *Psychoanal. St. Child.* 40:435–456.

Pruett, K. (2000) *Fatherneed: Why Father Care is as Essential as Mother Care for Your Child*, New York: The Free Press.

Pruett, K. (2004) 'Fathers and Young Children: Longitudinal Lessons on Autonomy, Gatekeeping, Overnights etc.', in S. Akhtar and H. Parens (eds.) *Real and Imaginary Fathers: Development, Transference and Healing*, Lanham, Boulder, New York, Toronto, Oxford: Jason Aronson, pp. 45–63.

Raphael-Leff, J. (1995/2001) *Pregnancy: The Inside Story*, London: Karnac Books.

Raphael-Leff, J. (1991/2005) *Psychological Processes of Childbearing*, London: Anna Freud Center.

Raphael-Leff, J. (2000) *Spilt Milk: Perinatal Loss and Breakdown (Psychoanalytic Ideas)*, London: Karnac Books.

Raphling, D. (1989) 'Fetishism in a Woman', *J. Amer. Psychoanal. Assn.* 37:465–491.

Reed, G. (2009) "In the same way that a poem contains the Alphabet": the significance of Translation in William I. Grossman's Freud, *J. Amer. Psychoanal. Assn.* 57:37–60.

Renik, O. (1993) 'Analytic Interaction: Conceptualizing Technique in the Light of the Analyst's Irreducible Subjectivity', *Psychoanal. Q.* 62:553–571.

Richards, A.K. (1992) 'The Influence of Sphincter Control and Genital Sensation on Body Image and Gender Identity in Women', *Psychoanal. Q.* 61:331–351.

Richards, A.K. (1996) 'Primary Femininity and Female Genital Anxiety', *J. Amer. Psychoanal. Assn.* 44(suppl.):261–281.

Richards, A.K. (1999) 'Freud and Feminism: A Critical Appraisal', *J. Amer. Psychoanal. Assn.* 47:1213–1239.

Ritvo, S. (1976) 'Adolescent to Woman', *J. Amer. Psychoanal. Assn.* 24(suppl.): 127–137.

Rizzuto, A. Meissner, W. and Buie, D. (2003) *The Dynamics of human Aggression: Theoretical Foundations, Clinical Applications*, Brunner-Routledge.

Ross, J. (2007) 'Trauma and Abuse in the Case of Little Hans: A Contemporary Perspective', *J. Amer. Psychoanal. Assn.* 55(3):779–797.

Saisto, T. (2001) *Obstetric, Psychosocial, and Pain Related Background, and Treatment of Fear of Childbirth, Academic dissertation, Department of Obstetrics and Gynecology*, Finland: University of Helsinki.

Safer, J. (2002) *The Normal One: Life with a Difficult or Damaged Sibling*, London, Toronto: The Free Press.

Sayers, J. (1989) 'Melanie Klein and Mothering: A Feminist Perspective', *Int. Rev. Psycho-Anal.* 16:363–376.

Schafer, R. (1974) 'Problems in Freud's Psychology of Women', *J. Amer. Psychoanal. Assn.* 22(3):459–85.

Schmidt-Hellerau, C. (2001) *Life Drive and Death Drive, Libido and Lethe: A Formalized Consistent Model of Psychoanalytic Drive and Structure Theory*, New York: Other Press.

Schmidt-Hellerau, C. (2006) 'Fighting with Spoons: On Caretaking Rivalry Between Mothers and Daughters', *Psychoanalytic Inquiry* 26(1):32–55.

Schowalter, J. (1983) 'Some Meanings of Being a Horsewoman', *Psychoanal. Study Child* 38:501–517.

Schuker, E. and Shwetz, M. (1991) 'Pregnancy and Motherhood', in E. Schuker and N. Levinson (eds.) *Female Psychology: An Annotated Psychoanalytic Bibliography*, Hillsdale, NJ and London: The Analytic Press, pp. 239–273.

Shaw, R. (1995) 'Female Genital Anxieties: an Integration of New and Old', *J. Clin. Psychoanal.* 57:311–313.

Shengold, L. (1989) *Soul Murder: The Effects of Childhood Abuse and Deprivation*, New York, Fawcett Columbine: Balantine Books.

Shengold, L. (2007) *Haunted by Parents*, New Haven, London Yale University Press.

Shopper, M. (1979) 'The (Re)discovery of the Vagina and the Importance of the Menstrual Tampon', in M. Sugar (ed.) *Female Adolescent Development*, New York: Brunner/ Mazel.

Silverman, D. (1996) 'Arithmetic of a One- and Two-Person Psychology: Merton M. Gill, an Essay', *Psychoanal. Psychol.* 13:267–274.

Silverman, M. (1980) 'A Fresh Look at the Case of Little Hans', in M. Kanzer and J. Glenn (eds.) *Freud and His Patients*, New York: Aronson, pp. 95–120.

Solnit, A. (1983) 'The Sibling Experience—Introduction', *Psycoanal. St. Child* 38:281–284.

Stein, R. (2007) 'Moments in Laplanche's Theory of Sexuality', *Studies in Gender and Sexuality* 8:177–200.

Stein, R. (2008) 'The Otherness of Sexuality: Excess', *J. Amer. Psychoanal. Assn.* 56(1):43–71.

Stimmel, B. (1996) 'From "Nothing" To "Something" To "Everything": Bisexuality And Metaphors Of The Mind', *J. Amer. Psychoanal. Assn.* 44S:191–214.

Stimmel, B. (2000) *The Baby with the Bath Water: Response to Lynne Layton.* Studies in Gender and Sexuality, 1:79–84.

Stoller, R. (1968) *Sex and Gender, Vol. 1*, New York: Science House.

Stoller, R. (1985) *Presentations of Gender*, New Haven and London: Yale University Press.

Stolorow, R. and Atwood, G. (1992) *Contexts of Being*, Hillsdale, NJ: Analytic Press.

Stolorow, R. Atwood, G. and Orange, D. (1998) 'On Psychoanalytic Truth'. *Int. Journal of Psychoanalysis*, 79:1221

Stuart, J. (2007) 'Work and Motherhood: Preliminary Report of a Psychoanalytic Study', *Psychoanal Q.* 76:439–485.

Stuart, J. (2007) 'Little Hans and Freud's Self-Analysis: A Biographical View of Clinical Theory in the Making', *J. Amer. Psychoanal. Assn.* 55:799–819.

Suchet, M. (2009) 'The 21st century body: Introduction', *Studies in Gender and Sexuality* 10:113–118.

Tessman L. (1989) 'Fathers and Daughters: Early Tones, Later Echoes', in S. Cath, A. Gurwitt, L. Gunsberg (eds.) *Fathers and their Families*, Hillsdale, NJ, Hove and London: The Analytic Press, pp. 197–225.

Tyson, P. (1982) 'A Developmental line of Gender Identity, Gender Role, and Choice of Love Object', *J. Amer. Psychoanal. Assn.* 30:61–86.

Tyson, P. and Tyson, R. (1990) *Psychoanalytic Theories of Development: an Integration*, New Haven and London: Yale University Press.

Uyehara, A. et al. (1995) 'Telling of the Analyst's Pregnancy', *J. Amer. Psychoanal. Assn.* 43:113–137.

Vivona, J.M. (2006) 'From Developmental Metaphor to Developmental Model: The Shrinking Role of Language in the Talking Cure', *J. Amer. Psychoanal. Assn.* 54: 877–902.

Vivona, J.M. (2007) 'Sibling Differentiation, Identity Development, and the Lateral Dimension of Psychic Life', *J. Amer. Psychoanal. Assn.* 55(4):1191–1215.

Weisner-Hanks, M. (1999) 'Introduction in Erdman, A. (1999)', *My Gracious Silence: Women in the Mirror of 16th Century Printing.* Luzern, Switzerland: Gilofer and Ranschburg GimbH, pp. vii–xxv.

Wendell, S. (1996) *The Rejected Body: Feminist Philosophical Reflections on Disability*, New York, London: Routledge.

Wexler, L. (2010) 'Personal Communication, and Response to a Paper of Mine on the Missing Body at the Western New England', Institute for Psychoanalysis.

Williams, P. (1998) "The Analyst's Subjectivity and the Analyst's Objectivity" by Owen Renik (including the response by Marcia Cavell), *Int. J. Psycho-Anal.* 79:1263–1270.

Winnicott, D.W. (1960) 'What irks?', in C. Winnicott, C. Bollas, M. Davis and R. Shepherd (eds). *Talking to Parents.* Reading, MA: Addison-Wesley,

Winnicott, D.W. (1975) *Through Paediatrics to Psycho-Analysis*, Collected Papers London: Karnac Books.

Woolf, V. (1929/1981) *A Room of One's Own*, London: Harcourt Brace & Co.

Wrye, H. (1998) 'Voice of the Analyst: The Body/Mind Dialectic Within the Psychoanalytic Subject: Finding the Analyst's Voice', *The Amer. J. Psychoanalysis* 57(4):359–369.

Wurmser, L. and Jarass, H. (2008) *Jealousy and Envy: New Views about Two Powerful Emotions*, New York: The Analytic Press.

Young, R. (1999) 'The Human Nature Review', http://www.human-nature.com/rmyoung/papers/pap/08h.html.

Young-Bruehl, E. (ed.) (1990) *Introduction to Freud on Women. A Reader*, London: The Hogarth Press, 1990, pp. 3–47.

Young-Bruehl, E. (1988/2008) *Anna Freud: a Biography*, New Haven, London: Yale University Press.

Young-Bruehl, E. and Bethelard F. (2000) *Cherishment: a Psychology of the Heart*, NY: Free Press.

Zanardi, C. (ed.) (1990) *Essential Papers on the Psychology of Women (Essential papers in psychoanalysis)*, New York: New York University Press.

Zavitzianos, G. (1971) 'Fetishism and Exhibitionism in the Female and Their Relationship to Psychopathy and Kleptomania', *Int. J. Psycho-Analysis* 52:297–306.

Index

Drawings are given in italics

Adler, Alfred 76, 79–80
adolescence 98
Alizade, Alcira 32, 34
All Powerful Mother, The: Blame and Idealization (Chodorow) 148
American Psychoanalytic Association 110, 191n.6
anal fantasy 88, 92n.5
Anzieu, Didier 75n.2
Appignanesi, L. 80
'Archival Bodies' (Hoffman) 12
attachment theory (Bowlby) 79

babies 139–40
Balsam, A. 179
Balsam, R. 179
'banal oedipal fantasy' 100
Basseches, H. 110
Bassin, D. 189
beasts 139–40
Beast and the Sovereign Vol 1 (Derrida) 187
Bell, Rudolph 36
Benedek, T. 34, 179
Benjamin, Jessica 107, 153, 181
Bergler, Edmund 99–100
Bernstein, D. 24, 183
Bibring, G. 34, 179
biological essentialism 10, 22, 46, 180
Birksted-Breen, Diana 7, 82
bisexuality 25
Blackwell, Elizabeth 21
Bloom, Harold 6, 6n.2, 85
Blum, H. P. 14
Bodies That Matter (Butler) 15
'bodymind' 188

Body as Mirror of the World, The (Chasseguet-Smirgel) 188–9
Boesky, Dale 6, 125, 176
Bonaparte, Marie 154
Bowlby, John 79, 180
Braverman, Melanie 53
Breen, D. 82, 183
brothers *see* siblings
Burnett, Frances Hodgson 155
Butler, Judith 15, 34, 189

Carter, C. Sue 78
case studies *see* patients
case vignettes *see* patients
castration anxiety 24, 33, 110, 113
Cath, Stan 167
Charcot, Jean Martin 12–13, 184
Chasseguet-Smirgel, J. 188
Chehrazi, S. 110
childbirth 76–92, 93–105
'Childhood Recollection from Dichtung und Wahrheit, A' (Freud) 154
Chodorow, Nancy 10, 123, 145–6, 148, 176, 180, 190
clitoris 82–3, 105n.3, 177
Cohen, Josh 187
core gender identity 182
COWAP 34

Dahl, K. 183
daughters/fathers 160–74
daughters/sons 144–59, 159n.2
Davies, Jody 191n.10
de Beauvoir, Simone 10
deconstructionism 189
Derrida, Jacques 187